RABINDRANATH TAGORE'S *ŚĀNTINIKETAN* ESSAYS

This book provides a critical introduction and translation of fifty *Śāntiniketan (Abode of Peace)* essays written by Rabindranath Tagore between 1908 and 1914. It provides key insights into Tagore's fundamental meditations on life, nature, religion, philosophy and the world at large.

As the first of its kind, this volume is a definitive collection of Tagore's *Śāntiniketan* essays translated into English which contains a substantial amount of scholarly material on them. The essays look at Tagore's ideas of universality, his socio-cultural location along with the development of his thought, his reflections on Buddhism, Vaiṣṇavism, Bāul philosophy, the Bhagavadgītā and to a great extent the Upanishads and their contemporary relevance. It also connects Sri Ramakrishna's concepts of *vijñāna* and *bhāvamukha* with Tagore's thought, an original contribution, through the study of these essays. A nuanced exploration into translation theory and praxis, it fills a lacuna in Tagore Studies by bringing to the fore profound religious, spiritual and philosophical knowledge in Tagore's own voice.

This volume will be useful for scholars and researchers of Translation Studies, Tagore Studies, Language and Literature, Cultural Studies and readers interested in Tagore's philosophical ideas.

Medha Bhattacharyya is Assistant Professor at the Department of Basic Science and Humanities (English), Bengal Institute of Technology, Kolkata, India. Her areas of interest include Translation Studies, Tagore Studies, Comparative Literature, World Literature, South Asian Diaspora Literature, Postcolonial Literatures Communication, English Language Teaching and Soft Skills.

RABINDRANATH TAGORE'S *ŚĀNTINIKETAN* ESSAYS

Religion, Spirituality and Philosophy

Medha Bhattacharyya

Routledge
Taylor & Francis Group
LONDON AND NEW YORK

First published 2020
by Routledge
2 Park Square, Milton Park, Abingdon, Oxon OX14 4RN

and by Routledge
52 Vanderbilt Avenue, New York, NY 10017

Routledge is an imprint of the Taylor & Francis Group, an informa business

British Library Cataloguing-in-Publication Data
A catalogue record for this book is available from the British Library

Library of Congress Cataloging-in-Publication Data
A catalog record has been requested for this book

ISBN: 978-1-138-36154-6 (hbk)
ISBN: 978-0-367-32102-4 (pbk)
ISBN: 978-0-429-31659-3 (ebk)

Typeset in Bembo
by Apex CoVantage, LLC

To my dear parents Maya and Mukur Bhattacharyya

CONTENTS

Preface ix
Acknowledgements xi
Transliteration of Sanskrit, Bengali and Pali alphabets xiii

PART I
Introduction 1

Notes 49

PART II
Translation of the fifty selected essays 53

Arise! Awake! 53
Lack 54
Sin 55
Sorrow 56
Renunciation 58
The Prayer 59
Dispersed Fair 62
End of Festival 63
Ferry Me Across 65
This Shore – the Other Shore 66
Day 68
Night 70
At Dawn 71
The Unique 72
Beauty 73

Law 75
Three 76
The Whole 78
Power 79
Prana 81
Place for Pilgrimage 82
Observer 84
The Eternal Abode 85
Three Levels 86
Philosopher's Stone 88
Prayer 89
Detachment 90
Collectedness 93
Dedication 94
The Function of Dedication 95
The Obverse 97
To See the Truth 99
Creation 100
Loaded Boat 101
Attainment of Nature 102
Commandment 103
Completeness 105
Om 106
Supreme Obtainment 109
Self-surrender 110
Self-confidence 112
The Bonds of the Mantra 113
The End of the Year 114
Mukti 116
After the Holidays 117
End 119
Awakening 121
The Day of the Initiation 123
More 124
Innermost Peace 126

Glossary *142*
Works cited *145*
Further reading *148*
Index *153*

PREFACE

My occupation with Rabindranath Tagore's *Śāntiniketan* essays began in 2006 when I contemplated pursuing my PhD degree from Ramakrishna Mission Vivekananda Educational and Research Institute, Belur Math, West Bengal, India. The idea was to select a novel area of research interest and my field of specialization was Translation Studies.

I was motivated to work on Rabindranath Tagore's *Śāntiniketan* essays because, firstly, there was a dearth of reference material in this field in English and I felt that there was a lot more one could contribute in this area as Tagore scholar and translator. Secondly, I took it up as a challenge because I understood that though it was a daunting task, these talks were perhaps the closest one could get to Tagore's spiritual writings and hence it would enable the reader to get a glimpse of the great mind of Rabindranath Tagore who is popularly known as 'Gurudev'. His Bengali religious and philosophical prose writings have not been carefully researched. I have tried to locate Tagore's *Śāntiniketan* essays within the gamut of Tagore's thought and have undertaken a novel study of Tagore's religion, spirituality and philosophy as evident in these essays. This book details several aspects of Rabindranath Tagore's *Śāntiniketan* essays – not only religious, spiritual and philosophical aspects, but also aspects relating to the translation methodology of the fifty selected essays.

While translating these essays, I read and reread them – the philosophy inherent in them appeared so very profound. In fact, there are several essays which provided me with respite in this uphill task. I have also translated the Sanskrit slokas of the Upanishads and the Bhagavadgītā which were referred to by Tagore in this text as they form an integral part of these essays. This task of translating the *Śāntiniketan* essays was a sadhana in itself.

This book in no way claims to be an exhaustive treatise relating to Tagore's thought, but illuminates the readers with two new concepts initiated by me on Tagore's thought which I have precisely dealt with, namely the concepts of Sri Ramakrishna's *vijñāna* and *bhāvamukha*, both being closely associated with Tagore's thought as reflected in his *Śāntiniketan* essays.

This book is pioneering research as it is the only book which contains a critical introduction detailing several aspects relating to Rabindranath Tagore's *Śāntiniketan* essays along with their translation.

ACKNOWLEDGEMENTS

The basis of this book is my doctoral dissertation submitted to the Department of English (Translation Studies) at the Ramakrishna Mission Vivekananda University (now Ramakrishna Mission Vivekananda Educational and Research Institute), Belur Math, West Bengal, India, in June 2013.

My humble praṇāms to Revered Srīmat Swami Suhitanandaji Maharaj, one of the present Vice Presidents of the Ramakrishna Math and Mission, who at the time of my pursuing PhD was the General Secretary of the twin organizations and the Chancellor of the Ramakrishna Mission Vivekananda University (now RKMVERI), for his blessings and encouragement.

I humbly offer my deep sense of gratitude and respects to Revered Swami Atmapriyanandaji, the honourable Vice Chancellor of Ramakrishna Mission Vivekananda University (now RKMVERI), for his blessings and inspiration.

I wish to thank my thesis supervisor, Dr Swarup Roy, Associate Professor and Head, Department of English, Ramakrishna Mission Vidyamandira and Adjunct Faculty, Department of English (Translation Studies), Ramakrishna Mission Vivekananda University (now RKMVERI), for his guidance during the course of my doctoral research. I thank my esteemed external examiners as well. I also thank the authorities of the Ramakrishna Mission Vivekananda University (now RKMVERI) for their support and blessings.

I am indebted to the renowned scholar Professor Shyama Prasad Ganguly, former Professor and Chairperson, Centre of Spanish, Portuguese, Italian and Latin American Studies at Jawaharlal Nehru University (JNU) and an eminent scholar in Hispanic and Comparative Studies for his expert advice regarding certain aspects of my PhD dissertation. I will also like to take this opportunity to express my gratitude to Professor Panchanan Mohanty, former Professor, Centre for Applied Linguistics and Translation Studies, University of

Hyderabad for his meaningful suggestion regarding my PhD dissertation. Professor Dwijadas Banerjee, a former Professor of English and a former Registrar of Visva-Bharati, carefully read the final manuscript prior to the submission of my PhD dissertation and offered suggestions. I am grateful to him.

I would like to express my grateful thanks to Revered Swami Vidyanathanandaji Maharaj (Mahan Maharaj), Professor of Mathematics at Tata Institute of Fundamental Research (TIFR), Mumbai, previously the Dean of Research and Professor of Mathematics, Ramakrishna Mission Vivekananda University, for his helpful suggestions. I am indebted to Ayon Maharaj, Assistant Professor and Head, Departments of English and Philosophy, Ramakrishna Mission Vivekananda University (now RKMVERI), for his useful classes and critical comments and general suggestions he offered after reading few of my translations at the time I was a PhD scholar.

My special thanks to the two anonymous referees for Taylor & Francis. I would also like to thank Mr Nilanjan Bandyopadhyay, Special Officer, Rabindra-Bhavana and Mr Sukumar Das, Professional Assistant, Temporary In-Charge, Rabindra-Bhavana Library, Visva-Bharati, Śāntiniketan for helping me to access the Rabindra-Bhavana Photo Archive at Visva-Bharati and for helping me to reconfirm few bibliographic information. I would also take this opportunity to extend my gratitude to Mr Santanu Chanda of National Library of India, Kolkata for his help in providing me with certain bibliographic information.

I would like to express my heartfelt gratitude to the entire team at Taylor & Francis who worked with me.

On a more personal note, I thank my parents, Maya and Mukur Bhattacharyya, for their consistent encouragement in my efforts to do this onerous task. They were the initial readers and critics of this manuscript as it went through several revisions. My mother painstakingly taught me from an early age the subtleties and nuances of the Bengali language, which, although is my mother tongue, I had to learn on my own as we lived abroad then and my regular academic curriculum did not include Bengali. My father patiently read through each of the drafts of my translated essays and critical introduction and offered numerous useful suggestions. My debt to them is immense.

The five years of hard work which saw this thesis taking shape (ultimately revised into this book), also saw the 150th birth anniversary of Rabindranath Tagore and Swami Vivekananda. I pay my humble and respectful homage to the memories of these two illustrious personalities who shaped modern India with their profound vision and have been and still remain eternal source of inspiration to millions of people in India and abroad.

TRANSLITERATION OF SANSKRIT, BENGALI AND PALI ALPHABETS

It is necessary to mention at the onset that the standard scheme of transliteration with a slight variation was employed for the Romanization of Sanskrit, Pali and Bengali alphabets throughout this translation. This was to ensure that the non-Bengali or the international readership would be able to go through the text without much constraint. Only the pronunciation of Sanskrit, Pali and Bengali transliteration incorporated throughout this translation will be provided in the following list and not the pronunciation of the entire transliteration pattern of Romanization of these languages. The translator has refrained from rendering Sanskrit, Pali or Bengali source alphabets in the following list so as not to confuse the readers unfamiliar with these three languages. The aim of providing the following list and its annexure was not to make the reading cumbersome but to facilitate a smooth reading of the translated essays and their introduction. The underlined letters yield the pronunciation of the alphabet.

Pronunciation of transliterated Sanskrit, Pali and Bengali letters:

Vowels

'a' (vowel) as 'o' in s<u>o</u>me
'ā' (vowel) as 'a' in c<u>a</u>r
'i' (vowel) as 'i' in f<u>i</u>t
'ī' (vowel) as 'ee' in f<u>ee</u>l
'u' (vowel) as 'u' in p<u>u</u>ll
'ū' (vowel) as 'ū' in p<u>oo</u>l
'ṛ' (vowel) as 'ri' in <u>ri</u>ver
'e' (vowel) as 'e' in r<u>e</u>d.
'ai' (vowel) as 'ai' in f<u>i</u>ve
'o' (vowel) as 'o' in <u>o</u>de.
'au' (vowel) as 'ow' in <u>ow</u>l

Consonants

'ka' (Guttural) as 'ka' in k̲ite
'kha' (Guttural) as 'ckha' in blac̲k̲head
'ga' (Guttural) as 'ga' in G̲od
'gha' (Guttural) as 'gha' in log̲-house
'na' (Guttural) as 'ng' in rin̲g̲
'ca' (Palatal) as 'ca' in c̲hair
'cha' (Palatal) as 'cha' in muc̲h̲ h̲ate
'ja' (Palatal) as 'ja' in j̲udge
'jha' (Palatal) as 'jha' in sledg̲e̲hammer
'ña' (Palatal) as 'ña' in en̲joy
'ṭa' (Cerebral) as 'ta' in t̲alk
'ṭha' (Cerebral) as 'tha' as in ant̲h̲em
'ḍa' (Cerebral) as 'da' in d̲one
'ḍha' (Cerebral) as 'dha' in god̲h̲ead
'ṇa' (Cerebral) as 'na' in thun̲der
'ta' (Dental) as 'ta' in French t̲arte
'tha' (Dental) as 'tha' in t̲h̲under
'da' (Dental) as 'da' in the French d̲ate
'dha' (Dental) as 'dha' in red̲h̲ead
'na' (Dental) as 'na' in n̲ot
'pa' (Labial) as 'pa' in p̲in
'pha' (Labial) as 'pha' in up̲h̲old
'ba' (Labial) as 'ba' in b̲ook
'bha' (Labial) as 'bha' in ab̲h̲orrent
'ma' (Labial) as 'ma' in m̲onth
'ya' (Semivowel) as 'ya' in y̲am
'ra' (Semivowel) as 'ra' in r̲ub
'la' (Semivowel) as 'la' in l̲imb
va' (Semivowel) as 'va' in v̲iper
'śa' (Palatal sibilant) as 'śa' in German ic̲h̲
'ṣa' (Cerebral sibilant) as 'sa' in s̲h̲ip
'sa' (Dental sibilant) as 'sa' in s̲ea
'ha' (Sonant aspirate) as 'ha' in h̲is
'ṁ' (Nasal consonant) as 'm' in French bon̲
'ḥ' (Aspirated vowel) as short 'h' in ah̲!

Notes and exceptions to the above list

In Bengali, the pronunciation of the letter (য) 'antahstha [lying within] "ja" (জ)' is pronounced as 'ja' but is written as 'ya' while (য়) 'antahstha [lying within] "a" (অ)' is pronounced as 'ya' and is written as 'ẏa' where transliteration of Bengali words are concerned. An example of the former would be 'yātrā'[1] in the last essay. It would also be interesting to note that in Bengali there are two 'ta's, one (ত) is pronounced as in the French 't' and the other, known as 'broken ta' (ৎ), is a shorter version of the French 't'. It is demarcated by underlining the 't' in the transliterated words. Bengali also has (ড়) [as the 'ra' with a dot below 'da'] transliterated as 'ṛa' in 'Baṛo' and (ঢ়) ['ra' with a dot below 'ḍha'] transliterated as 'ṛha' in 'Aṣaṛh'. Both of them are cerebrals. There is also a nasalized vowel that could be translated into English as the moon-dot (ঁ), it is transliterated as 'n̐' or 'm̐' as the case may be. The pronunciation of 'jña' in the cases of both Sanskrit and Bengali is 'gya' not as in 'gymnasium' but as in 'gynaecology'. Instead of Sanskrit and Pali 'sa', Bengali dental sibilant (স) is pronounced as 'sha' as in 'shake'.

Another important point to be noted is that in each of the transliterated Bengali words, the last 'a', pronounced as 'o', as in 'some', is silent unless otherwise specified. This is because unlike in Sanskrit, Bengali pronunciation does not include the last vowel 'a'. So, in the transliteration of Bengali words here the last 'a' of a word is dropped unless it is present in the Bengali word itself. However, in the Sanskrit words the 'a' was appropriately retained. Bengali, Sanskrit and Pali do not have upper and lower cases as in English. But upper and lower cases are employed using the rules of English in the transliterations of Bengali, Sanskrit and Pali words to facilitate reading.

Words which are included in the eleventh edition of the *Concise Oxford English Dictionary* (will be referred to as COD) and have meanings compatible with the context of this translation are not provided with diacritical marks. Apart from the aforesaid exceptions, all the other letters that require diacritics are written accordingly. In this translation, the names of Tagore's contemporaries are not given diacritical marks and are written in the way they were inscribed in *Rabijibanī* (in Bengali). The same also applies for contemporary names which are not part of the translated text. Except for Śāntiniketan to which diacritical marks have been added as it is not only a location but also the said text for translation here, common spellings of other places have been maintained. In the transliterated titles of the essays, Bengali manner of writing compound words are retained as in 'Barṣaśeṣ', 'Nababarṣa' and others.

Note

1 It is an open-air folk musical or dramatic performance or both, of rural origin devoid of any proscenium or background screen.

PART I

Introduction

General introduction to Rabindranath Tagore: Some significant texts and events in his life

Rabindranath Tagore (7 May 1861–7 August 1941) was the first Asian to receive the Nobel Prize. Awarded the Nobel Prize in 1913, he is the only Indian to have received it in the category of 'Literature'. Tagore is famous for having written in a variety of genres, such as poetry, drama, essay, novel, novella, short story, dance-drama and song. He is also well known as a critic, educator, painter and philanthropist.

Some of Tagore's famous poetry collections are *Offerings* (*Naivedya*, 1901), *The Ferry* (*Kheyā*, 1906), *Gitanjali*: *Song-offerings*[1] (1912), *The Gardener* (1913), *Wreath of Songs* (*Gitimālya*, 1914), *Small Songs* (*Gitāli*, 1915), *The Flight of Cranes* (*Balāka*, 1916) and *Fruit-Gathering* (1916). Among his well-known plays are a musical drama named *The Genius of Valmiki* (*Valmiki-pratibhā*, 1881), *Sanyasi, or The Ascetic*[2] (*Prakṛtir Pratiśodh*, 1884), *The Sacrifice* (*Visarjan*, 1890), *Chitrā: A Play in One Act*[3] (*Chitrāngadā*, 1892), *The King of the Dark Chamber*[4] (*Rājā*, 1910), *The Immovable* (*Acalāyatan*, 1912), *The Post Office* (*Dākghar*, 1912) and *Red Oleander*[5] (*Rakta-karabi*, 1924). One of his famous novels is *Gorā*[6] which was initially serialized in the Bengali journal 'Prabāsī' from August 1907 to February 1910. His other famous novels comprise *The Eyesore* (*Chokher Bāli*, 1903), *The Home and the World* (*Ghare Bāire*, 1916) and *Crosscurrents* (*Yogāyog*, 1929). Some of his popular short stories are 'The Postmaster'[7] (1891), 'The Fruitseller from Kabul' ('Kābuliwāllāh', 1892), 'The Castaway' ('Āpad', 1895), 'The Hungry Stones' ('Kṣudita pāṣāṇ', 1895), and 'Boṣtamī' ('The Devotee', 1914). His famous novellas include *The Broken Nest* (*Nastanir*, 1901).

Tagore wrote several essay collections, including *Abode of Peace* (*Śāntiniketan*, 1908–1914), *Religion* (*Dharma*, 1909), *Sādhanā*: *The Realisation of Life* (1913), *Personality* (1917), *Thought Relics* (1921), *Creative Unity* (1922), *The Religion of*

Man (1931), *Religion of Man*[8] (*Mānuser Dharma*, 1933) and *Man* (1937).[9] Tagore's essays are not too well known compared to the other genres in which he wrote, especially his philosophical essays written in Bengali – namely, *Śāntiniketan* and *Dharma*. The first is a collection of 152 lectures and the second is a collection of fifteen lectures. The Bengali titles of the two essay collections will be retained hereafter. Though *Dharma* was published after the commencement of the *Śāntiniketan* lectures, the *Dharma* essays were written much earlier except for the essay 'Sorrow' ('Duḥkha') which was written in 1908. *Sādhanā: The Realization of Life* (1913), a collection of eight essays originally written in English, reveals similar philosophical strain as *Śāntiniketan* and *Dharma*.

The period in which the *Śāntiniketan* essays were delivered, written and published made them important in the course of Tagore's career and in the understanding of Tagore's thought. Prior to these collections of essays, Tagore had written other essays which had philosophical strains, as for example a collection of essays titled 'Miscellaneous Topics' ('Vividha Prasanga', 1883). Out of several of these essays in this collection, the essay 'Nature-Man' ('Prakṛti-Puruṣa') reveals Tagore's philosophical interest even at an early stage of his writing career. Another collection of short essays titled 'Discussion' ('Ālocana', 1887) reveals more of Tagore's philosophical views. It is essential to explore significant personal and professional events in Tagore's life to understand the nature of Tagore's thought at the time he was delivering the *Śāntiniketan* talks.

There were several important personal and professional developments in Tagore's life from 1908 to 1916. Tagore started delivering the *Śāntiniketan* talks in 1908. Though these talks came to an end in 1914, the fourteenth section was published in 1915 and the next three sections of the collection were published in 1916. After Tagore returned from abroad in 1913, he got the news of being awarded the Nobel Prize for Literature. Tagore was awarded the Nobel Prize for Literature on 13 November 1913 but the news did not reach him till 15 November 1913 at Bolpur. The official telegram of the Swedish Academy was sent from London on 14 November 1913 and it reached Calcutta on 15 November 1913. But a couple of newspapers in Calcutta had already published this news on the evening of 14 November 1913. The Nobel Prize was received by the British ambassador in Stockholm on behalf of Tagore on 10 December 1913.

Preceding the *Śāntiniketan* talks, towards the beginning of the Bengali new year in 1908 (1315 BE) when Tagore arrived in Calcutta, he used to deliver regular lectures at the Adi Brahmo Samaj Hall every Wednesday, which were neither recorded nor printed. Those lectures mainly dealt with the word-for-word explanation of the Upanishadic slokas chanted during the prayers of the Brahmo Samaj. Apart from providing Saṁkara's interpretation of the slokas, Tagore also provided an alternative interpretation of his own to those mantras. In a way they bore some similarities to the *Śāntiniketan* talks. However, the *Śāntiniketan* talks were much more than just word-for-word interpretation of the Upanishadic mantras, though he did interpret portions of some of the Upanishadic mantras in those talks. But mere interpretation of mantra was not the sole essence of the *Śāntiniketan* talks.

Before Tagore started delivering the *Śāntiniketan* talks and eventually composing them into essays, there had been several happy and sad occasions for a few years preceding and during their conception. In 1901 Tagore founded the Brahmacārya Āśram, his experimental school, at Śāntiniketan. Tagore gave much thought to the school and he not only considered it a place of learning, but also a place where one could practise sadhana for the manifestation of the Atman. Initially it had five students (Mukhopadhyay 193). Among them was Rathindranath Tagore, his eldest son. He kept the *tapovana* (forest hermitage) of ancient India in mind when he established this school.

In 1901 two of Tagore's daughters got married, but his happiness was short-lived due to the death of his wife, Mrinalini Devi, in November 1902 in Calcutta. Within a year of her death, his second daughter, Renuka, died in 1903 as well. Satish Roy, a brilliant teacher at Śāntiniketan, who was also a Tagore translator and close to Tagore, died in January 1904. In January 1905, Maharṣi[10] Devendranath Tagore, Tagore's father, also died. As a result of the death of his father, Tagore had to incur great financial difficulties to maintain his school at Śāntiniketan. Tagore's youngest daughter got married in 1907 while his fifth child, Samindranath, died at a tender age in the same year. Sisirkumar Ghose in his biography of Rabindranath Tagore regards Samindranath's death as the 'crowning tragedy' of Tagore's life (Ghose 17). Ghose remarked about the impact of this tragedy on Tagore, 'Those who think Tagore's life was "untouched by the tempest" do not know him' (Ghose 17). He definitely did not let the 'tempest' linger in his mind to destroy his creative genius or his faith in the Supreme Reality. Tagore's second son-in-law, Satyendranath Bhattacharyya, caught fever while travelling, returned to Calcutta and passed away on either 25 or 26 October 1908 (9 or 10 *Kārtik*[11] 1315 BE) (Pal 6: 32). Tagore conveyed in his letter dated 15 November 1908 (30 *Kārtik* 1315 BE) to Manoranjan Bandyopadhyay that he was tired of the 'sports of death' (own translation) (Pal 6: 32). Yet again, there was another death, that of Tagore's long-time friend, Shrishchandra, who was afflicted with heart disease all of a sudden and died on 8 November 1908 (23 *Kārtik* 1315 BE). One of Tagore's well-wishers, the Maharaja of Tripura, Radhakishore Manikya, died in a car accident on 12 March 1909 (28 *Phālgun*[12] 1315 BE). This death inspired Tagore to deliver the *Śāntiniketan* lecture, 'Death and Immortality' ('Mṛtyu o Amṛta') on 17 March 1909 (4 *Caitra*[13] 1315 BE) in which he expressed his great sorrow philosophically on the loss of his friend. In 1910 Rathindranath's marriage was arranged with Pratima Devi,[14] a child-widow, daughter of Binayinee Devi, the sister of Gaganendranath Tagore. The death of Sharojchandra Mazumder, nicknamed Bhola, occurred due to massive cardiac arrest at the night of 25 June 1911 (10 *Āṣāṛh*[15] 1317 BE). Sudhirranjan Das, Mazumder's classmate, wrote about what he saw: 'Even today I have not forgotten the very image of sorrow and compassion that appeared on the absorbed countenance of *Gurudev* [Rabindranath Tagore]' (my translation) (Pal 6: 159). The last meeting between Rajanikanta Sen, a famous poet and composer of that period, and Tagore was a moving one. After the meeting, Tagore later wrote in his letter to Sen on 30 June 1911 (16 *Āṣāṛh* 1317 BE) 'I had seen a luminous manifestation of the human atman [in Sen]' (my translation) (Pal 6: 156). Sen was suffering from cancer and died three months after that meeting on 13 September 1910 (28 *Bhādra*[16] 1317 BE). The deaths of his friends and relatives and his own ailing health had moved him to the extent of intensely seeking God within. According to Tagore biographer Prasanta Kumar Pal, these unhappy incidents neither left any mark of distress nor did they interrupt Tagore's writings during that period. But all these sorrows gradually turned him inwards, made him introspective and deeply devoted to God (Pal 6: 33).

On receiving a complimentary copy of *Grandmother's Bag* (*Thākurmār Jhuli*), Tagore wrote a letter to its author, Dakshina Ranjan Mitra Majumdar, a celebrated children's writer, on 18 October 1908 (2 *Kārtik* 1315 BE) to congratulate him and to inform him that he had not fully recovered from the fever he had been suffering. This revealed Tagore's ailing physical condition at that time. On 6 November 1908 Tagore wrote to Ajit Chakraborty telling him about his physical ailment, his inability to continue with his mental work and his aspiration about the Bolpur school that he established. He wrote:

> My health has become very delicate and unfit – it gives me pain to even stand for a while. . . . I do not have a very long time left before me – it is only you all that have to run with the flag rested upon your shoulder.
>
> *(my translation; Pal 6: 33)*

This clearly reveals Tagore's failing health and his expectation from the handful of young men in whom he had great deal of faith in entrusting his school to their care.

Tagore was supposed to embark on a voyage to England on 19 March 1912 but had to move to his family estate at Shelaidah (now in Bangladesh) to take rest due to illness. This marked an important phase in Tagore's life. This was the time when Tagore decided to translate some of his Bengali poems into English, a task which he considered less laborious than working on something completely new. This exercise culminated in what we know as the English *Gitanjali*: *Song Offerings* which fetched him the Nobel Prize a year later in 1913.

Other significant publications of Rabindranath Tagore from 1908 to 1914

It is not that Tagore delivered only the *Śāntiniketan* talks during this period. He made other significant literary contributions during this period as well. Knowing about them will help the reader to understand the vast corpus of his thought. Tagore delivered a lecture titled 'Two Wishes' ('Dui Iccha') in the morning of 24 January 1909 (11 *Māgh*[17] 1315 BE) at the Adi Brahmo Samaj. Towards the end of 1909 (*Agrahāẏaṇ*[18] 1316 BE), Kshitimohan Sen made another appeal to Tagore to have some Vedic mantras translated into Bengali for the students and teachers of Śāntiniketan ashram. Tagore translated a total of eleven mantras. The first mantra to be translated was 'You are our Father' ('Pitā nohasi') on 8 December 1909 (22 *Agrahāyaṇ* 1316 BE). This mantra has also been included in few of the *Śāntiniketan* essays as in 'The Bonds of the Mantra'. Christmas was observed for the first time in the temple at Śāntiniketan on 25 December 1910 (10 *Pauṣ*[19] 1317 BE). On this occasion Tagore delivered a talk explaining the significance of Christ's sadhana and message. The summary of this talk was published as 'The Life of Jesus' ('Jiśu Carit').

Rabindranath Tagore wrote his famous play, *The Immovable* (*Acalaẏatan*) in 1912. He published the story 'Strir Patra' ['Wife's Letter'] in *Śrābaṇ*[20] issue of 'The Sabūj Patra' in 1914 (1321 BE). It was a story on the emancipation of women and created a great upsurge in several sections of the Bengali society.

Tagore's travel abroad from 27 May 1912 to 27 September 1913: Significant publications and activities

Although Tagore travelled abroad on several occasions, only his literary contributions made abroad during the period he delivered the *Śāntiniketan* lectures, that is from 1908 to 1914, are mentioned here. Tagore travelled abroad from 27 May 1912 (14 *Jaiṣṭha*[21] 1319 BE) to 27 September 1913 (11 *Āśvin*[22] 1320 BE). During this time, Tagore travelled to both Europe and the USA. While in England, the beauty of Hampstead moved him to the extent that he wrote two poems in Bengali on 23 and 25 June 1913 (9 and 11 *Āṣāṛh* 1320 BE) respectively and he translated them into English and sent them to William Rothenstein. In the meantime, Rothenstein was busy preparing three copies of typed manuscript of Tagore's English version of *Gitanjali* and sent one each to W.B. Yeats, Andrew Cecil Bradley, Professor of Poetry, Oxford University and to the famous monotheistic writer, Stopford Augustus Brooke.

Tagore had thought of going to the USA just after publication of the English version of *Gitanjali* by the middle of October 1912, but due to its delay in publication Tagore started for New York only on 19 October 1912 (3 *Kārtik* 1319 BE) and reached there on 27 October 1912 (11 *Kārtik* 1319 BE). He wrote to Ajitkumar on Wednesday, 16 October 1912 (30 *Āśvin* 1319 BE): 'I am no more able to confine myself to my own writing and to the discussion about myself – my mind has become extremely eager again for mukti from the bondage of this place' (my translation) (Pal 6: 341). He had actually gone to the USA for homeopathic treatment for his piles though without much success. It was most probably on 1 November 1912 (16 *Kārtik* 1319 BE) that the India Society edition of *Gitanjali* was published in London (Pal 6: 345–346).

Tagore was requested to speak on the Upanishads by a Unitarian clergyman, Albert R. Vail. Though Tagore was reluctant to deliver the lectures, he later agreed. On Sunday, 10 November 1912 (25 *Kārtik* 1319 BE) Tagore read his essay 'World Realisation' in the Unity Club, Urbana, Illinois. This essay underwent numerous changes and was titled 'The Relation of the Individual to the Universe' and was published in *Sādhanā*: *The Realisation of Life* (1913). The second lecture was 'Self-Realisation', delivered on Sunday, 17 November 1912 (2 *Agrahāẏaṇ* 1319 BE) in the same venue. This second lecture too underwent changes and was published as 'Soul Consciousness' in *Sādhanā*. The other two lectures Tagore delivered here were 'Realisation of Brahma' on Sunday, 24 November 1912 (9 *Agrahāẏaṇ* 1319 BE) and 'The Problem of Evil' on Sunday, 1 December 1912 (16 *Agrahāẏaṇ* 1319 BE). Surprisingly the third lecture, 'Realisation of Brahma' was not featured in *Sādhanā*. Tagore read his play, *The Post Office*, before an appreciative audience on Saturday night, 14 December 1912 (29 *Agrahāẏaṇ* 1319 BE). During his period abroad both in England and in the USA, he translated some of his Bengali poems into English. The result was *The Crescent* Moon (published in the last week of November 1913 along with *Sādhanā*), *The Gardener* (1913), *Fruit-Gathering* (1916), *Lover's Gift* and *Crossing* (1918). He delivered the lecture titled 'The Problem of Evil' at two places when he went to Chicago in January 1913. 'The Problem of Self' and 'The Realisation of Beauty' were delivered at Harvard University on 7 and 9 April 1913 respectively. He left for New York on the night of 9 April and he started his voyage to England from New York on 12 April 1913 by the ship the *Olympic*.

In England, Tagore delivered 6 lectures for the Quest Society. 'Realisation in Love' his first lecture, though supposed to be read a day earlier, was read on Saturday, 24 May 1913 (10 *Jaiṣṭha* 1320 BE) in the library at Manchester College, Oxford. The second lecture Tagore delivered was 'Soul Consciousness', at Caxton Hall in London on Monday evening, 26 May 1913 (12 *Jaiṣṭha* 1320 BE). The third lecture at Caxton Hall was 'The Problem of Evil' on Monday, 2 June 1913 (19 *Jaiṣṭha* 1320 BE). The fourth lecture at Caxton Hall was 'The Problem of Self' on Monday, 9 June 1913 (26 *Jaiṣṭha* 1320 BE). With 'Realisation in Love' Tagore marked the end of the lectures he was delivering at Caxton Hall on Tuesday, 17 June 1913 (3 *Āṣāṛh* 1320 BE). On Friday, 19 June 1913 (5 *Āṣāṛh* 1320 BE) Tagore delivered his fifth lecture, 'Realisation of Brahma', at Kensington Town Hall in London. 'Realisation in Action' was read by Rabindranath Tagore on Saturday, 21 June 1913 (7 *Āṣāṛh* 1320 BE) at Notting Hill Gate for the Brahmo Samaj of London. It was his sixth lecture in England.

Tagore's views on the conception and compilation of the *Śāntiniketan* essays

Rabindranath Tagore was forty-seven years of age when he started delivering his *Śāntiniketan* lectures. These lectures started quite informally with a handful of young men at Śāntiniketan ashram among whom was Kshitimohan Sen, requesting Tagore to impart to them the knowledge attained through his dawn-*upāsanā*[23] at Śāntiniketan. Sen mentions that Tagore used to sit under the open sky at his ashram from around 3:00 a.m. to 3:30 a.m. in dhyana. Sen among others in Tagore's ashram used to ask Tagore to impart to them the spiritual wealth he gained through the dhyana, but he initially refrained from doing so as it was his spiritual sadhana and those moments were very sacred to him. Kshitimohan Sen writes about the conception of the *Śāntiniketan* talks:

> One day he came to know that the next 16 *Agrahāẏaṇ* [1 December] was a special day for me. When he was thinking about what blessings he would bestow upon me on that occasion, I begged him for a little of the *prasād*[24] of that dawn-*upāsanā*. This *Brahmamuhūrta*[25] of dawn was his highly prized possession. . . . After a lot of careful consideration but with exceeding hesitation he agreed to this for a few days.
>
> *(my translation; Pal 6: 37)*

The following was what Rabindranath Tagore himself wrote to Rani Mahalanabish on 30 January 1935 (16 *Māgh* 1341 BE) regarding the *Śāntiniketan* essays:

> Many a time my own song seemed to be the composition of someone else just heard through me. The book *Śāntiniketan* exactly appears like that – it is as if its words are beyond my sadhana and capacity. The first volume is just out – the words that I can hear while going through the proof of the second part are not mine, yet are mine . . . so I may be praised only to that extent as is done to a well-made talking machine.
>
> *(my translation; Pal 6: 38)*

This is a proof in itself that Tagore was himself overwhelmed with the *Śāntiniketan* talks that he delivered. These talks served as inspiration to his other creations, namely, *Sādhanā* and *Thought Relics*.

A brief description of Rabindranath Tagore's thought[26]

It must be understood at the outset that the word religion in the ancient Indian context refers to the Sanskrit word 'dharma' originating from its root 'dhṛ' which means 'to hold' or 'to maintain' or follow a proper code of conduct. But 'dharma' does not necessarily mean religion. Religion, as is generally understood, refers to the ritualistic worship of gods and goddesses or certain ritualistic practices among sects or it may include both. Tagore does not advocate such thought. The meaning of 'dharma' is far beyond the above-mentioned understanding of religion. 'Dharma' has several meanings, such as that which is firmly established, doing one's duty, being just or righteous, being morally upright, doing the right thing or doing the right practice to lead one's life properly. Tagore employs the word 'dharma' quite often in his lectures and writings. In *Sādhanā*: *The Realisation of Life* Tagore provides the meaning of 'dharma' as 'the innermost nature, the essence, the implicit truth, of all things. *Dharma* is the ultimate purpose that is working in our self' (*Sādhanā* 74). To Tagore, dharma is the essence of life which leads one to the ultimate Truth inherent in all things. Dharma is a way of leading life through the execution of one's duty and conduct. Tagore reveals, 'It is the function of religion not to destroy our nature but to fulfil it' (Sadhana 74). Hence to Tagore, religion brings out the best in mankind and is the path which leads one to the ultimate goal in life. To maintain dharma, one must have *darśana* ('view point') in life. Without *darśana* there can be no fulfilment of dharma. The word philosophy is regarded as 'darśana' in Sanskrit. It originates from the Sanskrit word 'dṛś' which literally means 'to see' or 'to view'. One interpretation of 'darśana' is 'to see' the Divine or holy persons. Another interpretation is how one sees the life around oneself which directs a person to reach the supreme goal. The latter interpretation is more appropriate in this context. Moreover, there can be no dharma or *darśana* in a person's life devoid of spirituality. Spirituality may be interpreted as one's communion with the Divine. From the *Śāntiniketan* essays, it is understood how Tagore stresses on being a spiritually awakened being. So, each of the three terms namely, 'religion', 'spirituality' and 'philosophy' have ontological connection with each other.

To understand the development of Rabindranath Tagore's thought as reflected in *Śāntiniketan*, it is essential to know the influences and personal experiences which led to such religious, spiritual and philosophical thoughts in him. Earlier in this book, it was observed that Prasanta Kumar Pal mentioned in *Rabijibani* (*A Biography of Rabindranath Tagore*) that the pain and agony of losing his close ones and his own failing health gradually led Tagore to explore his inner self and be inclined towards God. The mood of the *Śāntiniketan* essays became deeply embedded in his heart in this manner (Pal 6: 33).

Tagore's philosophy provides an insight into the reality around us. It has to be felt and in turn will bring joy to the individual. About Tagore, Edward J. Thompson says, 'in his [Tagore's] earlier phase as poet, he believed in two dogmas, the *love* and *joy of the Universe.* He believed in these to the end' (81). There is a reflection of that in the *Śāntiniketan* essays as well. Vishwanath Naravane, in *Rabindranath Tagore: A Philosophical Study*, observes, 'In Tagore philosophy, Love and Bliss are almost interchangeable terms. His utterances about Bliss and Joy are reminiscent of the Vaisnava stress on 'Hlādini Sakti'' (25), a concept which will be discussed later in this section. Without love there is no bliss or joy because it is only love which brings about the overwhelming feeling of joy or bliss.

Tagore was influenced by the Upanishads, Vaiṣṇavism, Buddhism, Bāul philosophy, the Gītā, the teachings of Hafiz and Sufism amongst others. In the *Śāntiniketan* essays, Tagore draws heavily from the Upanishads, though the reflection of Buddhism, Vaiṣṇavism, Bāul philosophy, the Gītā and the Bible is also evident in them. When one refers to the influence of the Upanishads on Tagore, his upbringing should also be taken into account. Benoy Gopal Ray, in his book *The Philosophy of Rabindranath Tagore*, mentions that the sloka of the Īśa Upanishad[27] which had inspired Tagore's father, formed the guiding principle of his life as well (2). The environment where he grew up was steeped in the Upanishadic tradition. As a child he used to chant the Upanishadic mantras with his father, Maharṣi Devendranath Tagore. Tagore's was a Brahmo family which itself was closely involved in the Brahmo Samaj and later he himself delivered lectures and composed prayer songs for the gatherings at the Samaj.

In the *Śāntiniketan* essays Tagore has mostly elucidated the Upanishads. In his essay 'Om' he explains the concept of Om as is mentioned in the Chāndogya Upanishad. While interpreting the slokas, Rabindrananath gave his own views regarding them. As an example, in the essay 'This Shore – the Other Shore'[28] ('E Pār-o-Pār') Tagore refers to 'parama gatiḥ' (*Śāntiniketan* 1: 53) which is part of a sloka from the Bṛhadāraṇyaka Upanishad meaning 'supreme attainment' (4. 3. 32, 2004), to be interpreted as 'supreme motion' in 'This Shore – the Other Shore'.[29] The word 'gatiḥ' both in Bengali and Sanskrit means 'motion', 'result' or 'outcome'. So, Tagore made use of the pun. He interpreted the Upanishadic words using the knowledge and experiences of the truths as perceived in his own life. This gave immediate relevance to the truths he was lecturing on. Benoy Gopal Ray reiterates this point in his book:

> What is important in Rabindranath's interpretation of the Upanisads or the Vedanta is not philological or grammatical correctness but purity and simplicity of his own realization. Sometimes we find that the poet himself discovered some truths but he tried to link them up with those of the Upanisads. Again, we find that while expounding a particular Upanisadic Śloka, he added to it some wisdom of his own.
>
> *(4)*

The example from the essay 'This Shore – the Other Shore' is one such case. The *Śāntiniketan* essays aim at the enrichment of the soul to lead us from darkness to light.

The aspect of love in Śāntiniketan *and some other Tagorean texts*

Love is a dominant theme in Tagore literature. The reader profits from just going through some of the Tagorean texts randomly. Let Tagore's novel *Gora* (1910) be taken as an example. In *Gora*, Anandamoyee's love for her adopted son, Gora, is apparent. While describing his mother, Gora says:

> Mother, you are my mother! The mother whom I have been wandering about in search of was all the time sitting in my room at home. You have no caste, you make no distinctions, and have no hatred—you are only the image of our welfare!
>
> *(407)*

This reveals how the finite love of a mother for her son reaches Infinite dimension because a mother does not discriminate against her children on the grounds of sex, caste or religion. Regarding the character of Gora, Sisirkumar Ghose in *Makers of Indian Literature*: *Rabindranath Tagore* says, 'He is not immune from change and love. And it is Sucharita rather than Pareshbabu that helps to bring about the change in Gora' (73). This 'change' is evident when Gora on discovering his identity as an Irishman is freed from the bondage of caste and creed and asks Sucharita, his 'love', to 'take my [his] hand and lead me [him] to this guru of yours [hers]' (407). So, it is 'love' which gives him the joy to proceed towards the Infinite.

Another instance of finite love leading to the Infinite can be seen in Tagore's novel *The Home and the World*. Nikhil's love for his wife, Bimala, makes him feel

> I[he] should not try to fetter my [his] life's companion with my [his] ideas, but play the joyous pipes of my [his] love and say: 'Do you love me? Then may you grow true to yourself in the light of your love. Let my suggestions be suppressed, let God's design, which is in you, triumph, and my ideas retire abashed'
>
> *(272–273)*

It is because of Nikhil's love for Bimala that he lets her venture outside of the space demarcated for her by societal norms of the times and it is this love which brings him joy.

In the play *Chitra*, the character of Chitra says to Arjuna: 'love springs up struggling toward immortal life' (*Collected Poems and Plays of Rabindranath Tagore* 234). While Arjuna says to her: 'I grope for that ultimate you, that bare simplicity of truth' (*Collected Poems and Plays* 234). Both Chitra and Arjuna are seeking a kind of love which is Infinite through their finite love for each other.

In the play, *Sanyasi, or the Ascetic*, at the beginning of the play the Sanyasi considers himself 'free': 'I am free. I have not this obstacle, this world round me. I live in pure desolation' (*Collected Poems and Plays* 605). The Ascetic is in negation of the world around him and says to the girl, 'What game of yours is this with me, little girl? I am a Sanyasi, I have cut all my knots, I am free' (*Collected Poems and Plays* 612). We find the character of the Ascetic to be a stern person aloof from the world of feelings till Raghu's daughter, Vasanti, awakens filial feelings in him and ultimately he remarks:

> Let my vows of Sanyasi go. I break my staff and my alms-bowl. This stately ship, this world, which is crossing the sea of time, – let it take me up again, let me join once more the pilgrims. . . . I am free. I am free from the bodiless chain of the Nay.[30] I am free among things and forms and purpose. The finite is the true Infinite, and love knows its truth.
>
> *(Collected Poems and Plays 619)*

In the beginning the Ascetic renounced worldly life and considered everything around him as maya[31] but it is his fatherly love which helped him to realize that it is the finite which is the Infinite and vice versa. It is love which brought about the realization in him that 'Only he is pure who has washed away the world from his mind' (*Collected Poems and Plays* 606). Hence, it was not physical alienation from the world that he should strive for but to stay detached from the world mentally. And this realization of freedom from the 'chain of the Nay' gave him joy.

In Tagore's story 'The Devotee' ('Boṣṭamī') we again see the theme of love: the love between two human beings – the devotee and the ascetic. The love between the two is finite but it is nevertheless a means of uniting with the Infinite.

In Tagore's story 'The Fruit Seller from Kabul' ('The Kābuliwāllāh'), the fruit seller's love for the five years old girl, Mini, is filial in nature. Hence, the love of a parent for his child is universal in nature, and this is another way in which love for the finite ultimately culminates in love for the Infinite. In *Śāntiniketan*, in the essay 'Detachment', Tagore explains this through Yājñavalkya's words: 'This means, not because you desire your son that he becomes dear to you, but because you yearn for the Atman alone that your son becomes dear to you'. So, the son is the finite aspect of the Infinite Atman. Hence, when a person loves his son and he 'becomes dear to you [him]' it is the Supreme Reality to whom he actually expresses his love as He is the Infinite manifestation of the finite love.

Let us explore the aspect of love in Tagore's poetry. In *Gitanjali: Song Offerings*, Sonnet XXXIV, Tagore writes 'Let only that little of my fetters be left whereby I am bound with thy will, and thy purpose is carried out in my life – and that is the fetter of thy love' (20). This is a poem with bhakti strain. It is love which gives bliss. The lines of the poem could be addressed to any mortal yet the poet addresses it to the Divine. In poem LV of *Fruit-Gathering*, a woman sat 'at the feet of the corpse of her dead husband, gaily dressed for a wedding' (75). She wished for a boon from the great poet Tulsidas who happened to be wandering about. To assert her claim to be with her husband in heaven she said, 'For heaven I do not long' (75). She pleaded, 'I want my husband' (75). Tulsidas granted her the boon and said, 'Go back to your home, my child. Before the month is over you will find your husband' (75). This again reveals how the finiteness of love transcends the Infinite. The 'husband' is a metaphor for the Supreme Reality and it is not that she longs to be with her 'husband' because she desires 'heaven' but because she cannot bear to be separated from him. Naravane says regarding Tagore's influence in poetry, 'in Vaisnava poetry Tagore found a 'transfiguration' of human into Divine love' (25). But it can be said that this 'transfiguration' of love was not simply restricted to Tagore's poetry alone but percolated to other genres in which he wrote as is revealed from the above-mentioned examples. Another instance is the character of Nandinī in Tagore's play *Red Oleander.* Nandinī's finite love for Ranjan transcends the finite bond of love when she joyfully goes to embrace death as that would bring about her union with Ranjan: 'I'd been waiting because he'd come, and he came. I'll prepare for him to come again, he'll come again' (Lal 184). While describing the God of *Gitanjali* Naravane says, 'The God of "Gitanjali" is emphatically this Upanishadic God in whom power and punishment go side by side with love' (16) – the reconciliation of 'power and punishment' on one side and 'love' on the other side – harmony of the opposites, is something that we see in the *Śāntiniketan* essays as well. In the essay 'Law', Tagore says, 'He who is the Progenitor, is Himself the Friend, again it is He who is the Lawgiver. Hence, whatever be the law, essentially there is no fear'. The 'Lawgiver' upholds the law with discipline and there are no exceptions as law is universal, while the 'Friend' is 'in the realm of love within me'. So, 'essentially there is no fear' because 'on one hand he [man] pays the dues of the King and on the other hand he arranges the basket of offerings for his Friend'. In the essay, 'The Unique', Tagore again harps on this fact when he says,

> I try to abide by all Your rules and if I fail, I accept Your punishment – but, in the form of "I", I want to know You as my sole One. There You have made me free – because, without freedom love will not be realized.

There is a reconciliation of the opposites once again. This idea which is very much prevalent in *Śāntiniketan* is present in other Tagore texts as well. This reconciliation of the opposites is possible because it is love that brings them together as one.

Earlier in the course of this study, a reference to Naravane was made who rightly points out that Tagore's concept of 'Bliss and Joy' (25) is similar to Hlādinī Śakti. 'Hlādinī [Śakti], corresponding to Ānanda (Bliss)', writes Svāmi Tapasyānanda 'is the energy by which He [Supreme Reality] enjoys His own innate Bliss and makes others enjoy the same' (*Bhakti Schools of Vedanta* 323). There are numerous examples of that in *Śāntiniketan*. In the essay, 'Detachment', Tagore says, 'the joy that is felt, is love itself. That love does not bind; that love pulls us along. That love is pure and unopposed. It is that very love which is mukti – the death of all attachments'. Tagore gives all importance to Bliss. In the essay 'This Shore – the Other Shore', Tagore says, 'It is that Bliss which has rendered that infinite motion to the universe'. In the same essay Tagore also refers to joy as 'supreme joy'. Here 'motion' refers to God's action which gives Him bliss. In this regard Svāmi Tapasyānanda says, 'The function of the Śaktis [Powers] of Kṛṣṇa [God] is to carry out His will and contribute to His sportive manifestations, which form the expression of His essential nature as Bliss' (324). In the essay, 'The Eternal Abode', Tagore says,

> The Supreme Atman is full of bliss in this individual atman. Where there is the never-ending union of that love, enter there and look at that place. Only then would you realize within the very depth of your heart what the bliss of Brahman is.

It is due to bliss that He carries on with His manifestation which is His action. He takes man (finite) and elevates him to the Divine (Infinite) and vice versa.

The idea of love is based on God sacrificing His divinity to be manifested as all-pervading humanity. In Purushasuktam it is seen that the Supreme Being, Prajāpathi, sacrifices Himself to create. There is a description of *devas* (gods), regarded as the pranas of Prajāpathi, having 'bound the *Prajāpathi* like a sacrificial animal, as it were',[32] to be offered for sacrifice. In the essay 'Three', Tagore asserts:

> To establish that welfare in the world, all self-interests get completely defeated and we understand to what extent the nature of true union is

> established by pure self-sacrifice. When we understand that completely, only then does it become possible to attain unimpeded union in love in every way with *Advaitam* who is that Supreme Atman in the form of Oneness.

Self-interests 'get completely defeated' only when there is love and when there is love, 'pure self-sacrifice' is possible and only then 'unimpeded union' with the 'Supreme Atman' becomes possible. It is not only God who undergoes self-sacrifice to attain union with the human being but it is also the human being who does the same. Though the finite and Infinite are apparently different yet they are essentially united. This brings us to Tagore's leanings towards the doctrine of *acintya-bhedābheda* (inconceivable identity-in-difference).

The word 'acintya' is a Sanskrit word with the combination of 'a', meaning 'non', and 'cintya' meaning 'logical' or 'conceivable', hence 'acintya' means 'alogical' or 'inconceivable', that is, beyond logic. The conjoined Sanskrit words 'bhedābheda' is a combination of 'bheda' meaning 'difference', and 'a' and 'bheda' meaning 'non' and 'difference' respectively. Hence, it is referred to as 'difference-in-non-difference' or 'identity-in-difference'. Svāmī Tapasyānanda, in his book *Bhakti Schools of Vedanta,* says,

> Bengal School of Vaiṣṇavism propounds the doctrine of Inconceivable Identity-in-difference (*Acintya-bhedābheda*). Śakti [power] is both identical and different from Śaktimat [Powerholder]. At the same time the element of identity makes the Supreme Reality non-dual even in the midst of difference. How these two contradictory features can co-exist is not attempted to be explained logically. For this reason it is designated as *Acintya* – alogical or incomprehensible by thought.
>
> *(315)*

That which is finite is different from the Infinite, yet it is identical to the Infinite. In the essay 'The Whole', Tagore beautifully explains this:

> When man attempts to see the whole all at once, he sees it hazily, hence he first sees it in parts and then he unites the parts into the whole. For this reason, if he sees only the parts and completely denies the whole, then he has to be seriously answerable for that; again, if he only aims at the whole and completely ignores the parts then that emptiness becomes totally futile for him.

Though apparently the 'parts [finite]' and the 'whole [Infinite]' appear different, they are inconceivably identical to each other. In another instance from *Śāntiniketan*, in the essay, 'Night' Tagore says, 'When we stay awake, there is a sport between our power and the Power. There is a union of our action with the Universal Action of Viśvakarmā'. The union between power and the Power is that oneness. This draws a parallel to Swami Vivekananda's speech 'The Open Secret' where he says, 'Take a grain of sand. Analyse it. We start with the assumption that it is finite, and at last we find that it is not, it is infinite' (*The Complete Works of Swami Vivekananda* 2: 397). It is not finite because of its identity with the '[i]Infinite' though it is different. This concept finds further elaboration in Swami Vivekananda's sermon to Madam Emma Calve regarding the immortality of the soul. A drop of water had fallen into the ocean and it mourned its loss of individuality. Swamiji explained what justification the ocean offered to the drop of water:

> When you join me, you join all your brothers and sisters, the other drops of water of which I am made. You become the ocean itself. If you wish to leave me, you have only to rise up on a sunbeam into the clouds. From there you can descend again, little drop of water, a blessing and a benediction to the thirsty earth.
>
> *(Life of Swami Vivekananda 1. 452)*

When the finite atman (the drop of water in Swamiji's sermon) becomes one with the Infinite Atman (the ocean in Swamiji's sermon), it loses its finiteness and whenever it wishes to be of service it can assume its finiteness. This brings us to the concept of *vijñāna*.

Tagore's concept of harmony between opposites bears similarity with the unique concept of *vijñāna* as propounded by Sri Ramakrishna. Tagore regards the opposites like the positive and the negative, or the finite and the Infinite existing harmoniously together. When Tagore wrote these essays, Sri Ramakrishna's doctrine of *vijñāna* was existent. To my knowledge no other research has ever attributed Sri Ramakrishna's concept of *vijñāna* and *bhāvamukha* to Tagore's philosophy as yet. My study is the first of its kind to do so. There are certain strains of thought that reveal Tagore's approach as that of a *vijñānī* in the *Śāntiniketan* essays. Who is a *vijñānī*? Sri Ramakrishna very beautifully depicts this by differentiating between a *jñānī* and a *vijñānī* while explaining the concepts to the Pundit at Dakshineshwar, he said, 'The vijnāni retains the 'I of the devotee', the 'I of the jnāni', in order to taste the Bliss of God and teach people' (*Gospel* 479). That is, after realizing Brahman or the Supreme Reality, the *vijñānī* realizes that the world is a manifestation of that Supreme Reality enclosed in name (*nāma*) and form (*rūpa*). In his essay, 'Understanding Bhavamukha: Sri Ramakrishna's Unique State of Consciousness', Swami Atmapriyananda elaborates on the function of a *vijñānī*: 'Under a Divine command, and out of great compassion and unbounded love for all beings, the *vijñānī* engages in the welfare of all beings: *sarva-bhūta-hite ratāḥ*'[33] (39). Then, who is a *jñānī*? Sri Ramakrishna says, 'The jnāni reasons about the world through the process of "Neti, neti", "Not this, not this". Reasoning in this way, he at last comes to the state of Bliss, and that is Brahman' (*Gospel* 476). A *jñānī* renounces the world of name and form and stays immersed in Brahman (sat-cit-ānanda). Since a *vijñānī* sees the world as the manifestation of Brahman, he does not see the world as unreal (*mithyā*) as the *jñānī* does but considers it as the sport (*līlā*) of the Supreme Reality. In 'Ferry Me Across', Tagore says, 'Do not presume they say, 'Ferry us from this very work of ours'. They want to stay amid their work and be ferried across and that is why their work is not being neglected as they sing' – this is like the *vijñānī*. So, according to Sri Ramakrishna, the following are the steps to reach the state of *vijñāna*,

> You realize the Nitya by negating the Līlā [state of a *jñānī*]. Then you affirm the Līlā, seeing in it the manifestation of the Nitya [state of a *vijñānī*]. One attains this state after realizing Reality in both aspects: Personal and Impersonal.
>
> (*Gospel* 477–78)

The 'Personal' aspect of 'Reality' is with name and form (*saguṇa*). The 'Impersonal' aspect of 'Reality' is without name and form (*nirguṇa*). This concept of *vijñāna*[34] can be traced to the Upanishads and the Bhagavadgītā. There are several instances of it. One such instance from the Upanishad is:

Pratibodhaviditam matamamṛtatvam hi vindate;
Ātmanā vindate vīryaṁ vidyayā vindate'mṛtam.[35]

The above sloka means 'Immortality is attained through the absolute Knowledge [*vijñāna*] of the Immortal [Brahman]. Through the Ātman [the *jñāni* attains *brahmajñāna*[36]] strength is obtained, through the Knowledge [*vijñāna*] immortality is attained'. It is not that the state of *jñāna* is considered as inferior to the state of *vijñāna* because it is absolutely necessary to attain the state of *jñāna* before reaching the state of *vijñāna*. On reaching the state of *vijñāna* one has the realization that everything is the manifestation of Brahman. It is the manifested Brahman which is termed *Śakti* (Primordial energy responsible for creation, preservation and destruction). There are other instances from the Upanishads where there are notions of the *vijñānī*. Another such instance is 'Ātmakrīḍa ātmaratiḥ kriyāvāneṣa brahmavidāṁ variṣṭhaḥ'[37] which means 'Sporting with the Supreme Atman, rejoicing with the Supreme Atman, he is fully active, he [*vijñānī*] is the greatest among all the knowers of Brahman'.

The person who has attained Brahman is blissful and on realizing that everything in the universe is the sport (*līlā*) of Brahman, he does not withdraw from the world like the *jñānī* does, he [*vijñānī*] performs duties required of him and is thus considered to be among the greatest knowers of Brahman. Tagore also explains this very sloka of the Muṇḍaka Upanishad[38] in an essay of this collection, 'Prana', 'Those that are the greatest among the knowers of Brahman, their sport lies in the Supreme Atman, their bliss lies in the Supreme Atman, and they are always active'.

In the Bhagavadgītā too there are references to the *vijñānī*.[39] Swami Tapasyananda interprets *jñāna* in the Bhagavadgīta as 'simple knowledge' of God and *vijñāna* as 'special knowledge' of God respectively (*Śrīmad-Bhagavad-Gītā: The Scripture of Mankind* 208). This is akin to Sri Ramakrishna's concept of *jñāna* and *vijñāna*. According to Swami Tapasyananda's interpretation of *vijñāna*, it is a 'higher illumination' (209) and the universe is a 'false presentation [which is] to be rejected' (208) by the *jñānī*. In the following sloka from the Bhagavadgītā 'jñānaṁ te 'haṁ savijñānam', 7.2, Kṛṣṇa mentions to Arjuna how He will impart complete *jñāna* to him and subsequently *vijñāna*. And by knowing *vijñāna* Arjuna would not thirst for any further knowledge. There is another reference among several other references in the Bhagavadgītā 18.51–53 where Arjuna is advised by Kṛṣṇa on how he should enable himself to attain *jñāna* (being one with the Supreme Being or Kṛṣṇa or God) by being unattached to the material aspects of life. Then in the Bhagavadgītā 18.54–56, the *jñānī* goes on to achieve what is beyond *jñāna*. This denotes the attainment of *vijñāna* and in such a state, a *vijñānī* 'attains supreme devotion [bhakti] for Me [Kṛṣṇa]'[40] (Bhagavadgītā 18.54). This supreme devotion after attaining *vijñāna* brings about the realization that everything is the manifestation of Brahman and hence the *vijñānī* partakes in the joy of the Divine sport (*līlā*) by various kinds of actions.

The 'Knowledge' which is derived from 'the knowers of Brahman' is that the Infinite plays through the finite. In this regard we are reminded of another such example which Swami Vivekananda offers in his essay, 'The Open Secret'. He says,

> Whoever thinks that I am little makes a mistake, for the Self is all that exists. The sun exists because I declare it does, the world exists because I declare it does. Without me they cannot remain, for I am Existence, Knowledge and Bliss Absolute – ever happy, ever pure, ever beautiful.
>
> *(Complete Works 2: 404)*

Since the finite and the Infinite are one and same, this is possible. Tagore, in his essay 'Day', says, 'We will realize the Atman everywhere – this is the only aspiration of the atman'. That is what a *vijñānī* does and that is also what staying in *bhāvamukha* consists of practically. An important gift of Sri Ramakrishna philosophy is that of *bhāvamukha*. Swami Saradananda, a direct disciple of Sri Ramakrishna, explains that Sri Ramakrishna received divine instruction to remain in *bhāvamukha*. Swami Saradananda, in *Śrīśrīrāmakṛṣṇa Līlāprasanga* (*Sri Ramakrishna*: *The Great Master*), goes on to explain the command:

> Do not remain in the Nirguṇa [devoid of name and form, purely sat, cit and ananda aspects] by the complete mergence of the I-ness [in Brahman], but live your life and do good to people, being in constant, complete and immediate knowledge of the fact that you are none other than that "limitless I"'.
>
> *(1: 443)*

It is more evident in the next example from another *Śāntiniketan* essay. In the essay, 'Beauty' Tagore remarks, 'in the unusual realm of this "I" within our inner atman, there is coming and going of that Blissful One and there is evidence of that throughout the universe'. Hence when the self-realized person is in *bhāvamukha* he is not only merged in God-consciousness but also sees everything as the manifestation of God. At that state of consciousness finite-Infinite, Real-unreal, Absolute-relative are all one and the same manifestation of the Supreme Being. In the essay, 'Night' Tagore remarks that 'self-realization' takes place in spite of the fact that the realized person is 'amidst the variety and plenty of the world', and he devotes himself to all kinds of 'work with solemnity and purity'. So, the state of *bhāvamukha* of a self-realized person is being fully merged with Brahman and also remaining fully aware that the world is a manifestation of the same Brahman, that is, *Nirguṇa* (without attributes)-*Saguṇa* (with attributes).

There is a fundamental difference between *vijñāna* and *acintya-bhedābheda.* The *vijñānī* has to pass the stage of the *jñānī* to know that all is One, and whatever duality there is, it is the sport of Brahman while in *acintya-bhedābheda* there is no such transformation in realization from *jñānī* to *vijñānī*, but an understanding that it is Kṛṣṇa's [Supreme Reality] Hlādinī Śakti which is manifesting the external realm. The followers of *acintya-bhedābheda* do not acknowledge maya in the way the *jñānīs* consider maya. To the former, maya (considered the power of manifestation) is reality. Yet, in *acintya-bhedābheda*, advaita is not compromised as there is the concept of 'identity'. Swami Vivekananda in his speech 'The Open Secret' says, 'every grain of sand, every thought, every soul, everything that exists, is infinite. Infinite is finite and finite infinite' (*Complete Works* 2: 399). This view finds expression many times in Rabindranath Tagore's *Śāntiniketan* essays. Maitreyī's prayer in 'The prayer' reveals how the finite-Infinite divide can be overcome:

> We find it [amrita[41]] where we have love. Amid this love itself we get a taste of the Infinite. It is love itself which puts the shadow of the Infinite within the finite, transforms old into new and never accepts death. When we observe the trace of love within diverse matters of the world, we get to know the Supreme Being who is beyond death. Through this we understand that His true nature is the embodiment of love.

Relevance of the *Śāntiniketan* for translation

These short pieces not only throw a challenge to a translator but also show how 'instruction' can render excellent pieces of literature as the *Śāntiniketan* essays have done.

Selections from the text, *Śāntiniketan*, were considered for translation because they are not only rich in their contents but also because Tagore had conveyed such great truth in such a simple manner, made easy for readers of all age groups, culture and race to comprehend. These essays reveal Tagore's profound philosophical and spiritual insights. Today the globalized world is steeped in consumerism. In such a case all aspects of one's life are defined in terms of material gains and material well-being, ultimately leading to a sense of void resulting in destruction and chaos. It is only through a sense of spiritual well-being that one can experience true fulfilment in life and bring about a balance. Only a strong foundation in spirituality can withstand the deluge of high-profile consumerism. It would be done as Radhakrishnan puts it, not 'by means of any set lessons about God and His existence, but by allowing the souls to express themselves freely and spontaneously' (*The Philosophy of Rabindranath Tagore* 208). Tagore's essays help one strive towards this fulfilment, this freedom. It is not that whatever he says is totally new but the manner in which he says them, coloured with his own experience, makes it easier for his audience or readers to understand. While going through the proof of the *Śāntiniketan* essays Tagore writes to Rani Mahalanabish on 25 January 1935 (11 *Māgh* 1341 BE):

> At one time when I went on uttering these words among a few worshippers daily in the morning then I indeed made myself hear them – if I had not said them then those words would not have even been heard by me, they would have remained unmanifested in me.
>
> *(my translation; Pal 6: 38)*

These lines reveal the extent to which these essays had overwhelmed him. The text is a classic piece of literature with its highly spiritual, philosophical and religious content which is no doubt relevant in a person's life and work even at the present time.

These essays can be said to be the process of development in Rabindranath's spiritual path. The essays convey a strong spiritual message which makes us aware of our situations in life by drawing our attention to our separation from the environment, the necessity of sorrow in our lives, the need for sacrifice, the nature of mukti, the attainment of unity through love and the fact that love and sacrifice go hand in hand, among others. These essays search for and conceive of a supreme philosophy of life which illuminates and shows a guided path towards hope and stability in the midst of turmoil and conflict where humankind has lost the purpose in life. The essays do not conform to any particular religion, rather they go beyond that barrier and allow the readers to interpret the essential message with respect to their own experiences. The essays are the psalms of life which inspire us to enter into the threshold of peace and bliss. And it is as if Tagore acts as a true guru and delivers guidance. As a result, we find profound solace, discover our ultimate aim in life and arrive at the right path to attain it. Kshitimohan Sen who attended those *Śāntiniketan* lectures mentions that a few of them used to gather at the verandah of the Śāntiniketan temple at 4:30 a.m. in the winter of 1908 (*Agrahāẏaṇ* 1315 BE), and Tagore used to be seated there in meditation much earlier. Sen writes:

> From 4.30 am to 5 am we used to obtain some *prasād* of his just obtained Truth relating to inner significance and get up from there. He used to sit on that seat much longer even after that. It went on like this for sometime. Those who used to go, were highly benefitted and satisfied. . . . From 2 December 1908 (17 *Agrahāẏaṇ* 1315 BE) up to 20 April 1909 (7 *Baiśākh* 1316

> BE) the words he has written about his spiritual moments have become immortal treasures in our language.
>
> *(my translation; Pal 6: 37)*

The text, with its contemporary approach, reveals the essence and applicability of the scriptural message mainly of the Upanishads. When the translator translated the Bengali text, *Śāntiniketan*, into English, she saw how best she could deliver the spirit and the cultural appeal to the readers, and tried her utmost to transfer the Source Language Text (SLT) into the Target Language (TL) one in a holistic manner.

There is a need to refer to ancient literature in contemporary era as it will not only help human race to develop to the level of perfection but would liberate mankind, to function not only within the constricting bonds of the microcosm but also realize that the macrocosm and the microcosm are intimately linked, inseparable. It is only ignorance which separates one person from the other. Here Tagore talks about the necessity to hear the inner voice in spite of performing our worldly activities in order to 'arise, awake'.

Title and compilation

In a letter dated Friday, 8 January 1915 (24 *Pauṣ* 1321 BE) Tagore wrote to Ajitkumar Chakraborty that he wanted Chakraborty to take the responsibility for compiling and publishing the collection of essays. In another undated letter to Chakraborty, Tagore suggests the probable titles to this collection of essays; they are 'Sañcaẏ' or 'Saṁgraha' or 'Āharaṇ', each of which means 'Collection'. Tagore also gave Chakraborty the liberty to suggest any other title saying that he, Tagore, would not complain whether they were good or bad. In that very letter Tagore also inquired of him if the number of essays were sufficient to be published in two volumes, if not, they should be published in one volume (Pal 7: 55). However, it is not known who actually titled the collection of essays, but it is apparent that it surely had Tagore's approval as the two volumes were compiled in 1934–1935 when Tagore was still alive.

One reason for naming the talks *Śāntiniketan* could have been that the talks had started at Śāntiniketan. Another crucial reason could be that Tagore was grooming a select group of individuals to carry on with his legacy of Śāntiniketan. Whenever a person delivers a talk, the intended audience is of primary concern to the speaker. It is in keeping with the audience that the speaker frames his speech. In this case Tagore was requested by the young residents (mostly consisting of teachers) of Śāntiniketan to deliver talks which had spiritual insight. Another reason for naming the talks *Śāntiniketan* is likely that Tagore aspired for an 'abode of peace' and it is through these talks he tried to show how that was possible to achieve.

The edition of *Śāntiniketan* used for this translation

The text used for this translation is the Visvabharati edition in two volumes. The first nine parts of the collection of essays were included in the first volume while the remaining eight parts, that is, from ten to seventeen were included in the second volume.

A note on the *Śāntiniketan* essays

Śāntiniketan (*Abode of Peace*) (1908–1914) is a group of 152 essays consisting of seventeen parts in two volumes. These essays were talks or lectures delivered by Tagore on various occasions and are named after the place in which his ashram is situated. The first thirteen parts were printed between 1908 and 1912 (1315 BE–1318 BE) and the last four parts (14–17) were published between 1915 and 1916 (1322 BE–1323 BE). The first eight parts were serialized lectures delivered at Śāntiniketan after his dawn-*upāsanā* which were later written and were concluded within six months of their commencement, from 2 December 1908 to 20 April 1909 (17 *Agrahāyaṇ* 1315 BE to 7 *Baiśākh* 1316 BE). The other nine sections of the collection were talks conferred on different occasions by Tagore. From 1909 to 1916 the essays were first published in seventeen individual volumes before being compiled into two volumes in 1934–1935. The first of the two volumes contains the initial nine parts with 107 essays while the second volume contains the last eight parts with the remaining forty-five essays. All 152 essays were delivered over a period between 1908 and 1914. Tagore was fifty-five years of age by the time all the seventeen parts were published. However, it is important to note that not all the essays that Tagore delivered till *Māghotsav*[42] of 1915 (1321 BE) were included in the collection. One such essay is 'Ātmasampad' ('Self-wealth') delivered on Sunday, 3 January 1915 (19 *Pauṣ* 1321 BE) addressed to the students. It was published in the *Caitra* issue of 'Tattvabodhinī' in the same year. The reason for such omission is not known.

The first part[43] of *Śāntiniketan* consisted of eleven essays delivered from Tuesday, 1 December 1908 (16 *Agrahāyaṇ* 1315 BE) to Thursday, 17 December 1908 (2 *Pauṣ* 1315 BE). The first part of *Śāntiniketan* was published on Sunday, 24 January 1909 (11 *Māgh* 1315 BE).[44]

The first two lectures 'Arise! Awake!' ('Uttiṣṭhata jāgrata') and 'Doubt' ('Saṁsay') were delivered at the Śāntiniketan temple but were written in Kolkata. This was understood as Kshitimohan Sen mentioned in his letter that on his request Tagore started those lectures on Sen's birthday on 2 December 1908 (17 *Agrahāyaṇ* 1315 BE) at the Śāntiniketan temple from 4 a.m. at dawn to 5 a.m. That the essays were written in Kolkata was evident from the cashbook entry which mentioned the cost of conveyance from Howrah station to the house at Jorasanko (Pal 6: 37). Tagore used a diary of 1908 as the manuscript of these serialized lectures and started writing from the page dated 1 January 1908 (Pal 6: 38). The essay 'Lack' ('Abhāb') appeared without date in the *Rabindra Rachanāvalī*, but Kanai Samanta, who edited the manuscript of the New Edition published in 1984 [*Śrābaṇ* 1391 BE], confirmed the date from Tagore's manuscript and the essay was published with a date. Both the essays 'Lack' and 'Vision of the Atman' ('Ātmār Dṛṣti') were delivered at the Śāntiniketan temple on Tuesday, 8 December 1908

(23 *Agrahāyaṇ* 1315 BE). The rest of the lectures which follow did not have such confusion with the dates as Tagore himself wrote the dates at the end of each essay (Pal 6: 38). In the initial editions it was mentioned that the lectures delivered by Tagore from 13 to 14 December 1908 (28 to 29 *Agrahāyaṇ* 1315 BE) were titled 'The Fruit of Renunciation' ('Tyāger Phal'), 'Love' ('Prem') and 'Harmony' ('Sāmañjasya') but in the manuscript it was observed that these essays were titled as 'Love' on Sunday, 13 December 1908 (28 *Agrahāyaṇ* 1315 BE) and 'The Harmony of Conflicts' ('Birodher Sāmañjasya') on Monday, 14 December 1908 (29 *Agrahāyaṇ* 1315 BE). Kanai Samanta conjured that this confusion regarding the dates was probably caused during the correction of proof by Tagore when he might not have checked the press copy and might have changed the titles of the essays to bring about harmony among them. This guess is quite logical. So, by following this logic, in the following edition it was possible to provide the date of the lecture 'Love' (Pal 6: 41).

Lectures of the second part were delivered between Friday, 18 December to Sunday, 27 December 1908 (3 *Pauṣ* to 12 *Pauṣ* 1315 BE), starting with 'Fear of Perversion' ('Bikārśankā') on Friday, 18 December 1908 (3 *Pauṣ* 1315 BE) and concluding with 'This Shore – the Other Shore' ('E Pār-o-Pār') on Sunday, 27 December 1908 (12 *Pauṣ* 1315 BE). This second part was published on Wednesday, 24 February 1909 (11 *Phālgun* 1315 BE) and consisted of twelve lectures.

There were twelve lectures in the third part of *Śāntiniketan* and they were delivered from Monday, 28 December 1908 (13 *Pauṣ* 1315 BE) as well. The first essay of this part began with 'Day' ('Din') Monday, 28 December 1908 (13 *Pauṣ* 1315 BE) and ended with 'Nature' ('Prakṛti') on Thursday, 7 January 1909 (23 *Pauṣ* 1315 BE). In the earlier editions the lecture, 'Three' ('Tin') was referred to had been delivered on Wednesday, 5 January 1909 (21 *Pauṣ* 1315 BE) but the essay was dated 6 January 1909 (22 *Pauṣ* 1315 BE) in the manuscript. This error was corrected in the 1984 edition (1391 BE) (Pal 6: 43). The third part was published on Friday, 5 March 1909 (21 *Phālgun* 1315 BE).

Out of the twelve lectures of the fourth part of *Śāntiniketan*, 'Pervading the Universe' ('Viśvavyāpī') and 'Manifestation of Death' ('Mṛtyur prakāś') were delivered in Calcutta. All twelve talks were compiled between Saturday, 9 January 1909 (25 *Pauṣ* 1315 BE), starting with 'Attainment' ('Pāoyā') and Tuesday, 19 January 1909 (6 *Māgh* 1315 BE), ending with 'Manifestation of Death' ('Mṛtyur prakāś'). The last essay of this part was published in the *Phālgun* issue of 'Tattvabodhinī', 1908 (1830 *Śakābda*[45]) and printed in the fourth part of *Śāntiniketan*. The fourth part was published on Friday, 12 March 1909 (28 *Phālgun* 1315 BE).

The fifth part of *Śāntiniketan* consisted of eight essays. This part began with the essay 'The Festival of New Age' ('Nabayuger Utsav'). Tagore read this essay at Maharṣi Bhavan,[46] Śāntiniketan, in the evening *upāsanā* on Sunday, 24 January 1909 (11 *Māgh* 1315 BE) and it was published in 'Baṅgadarśan', 1909 (*Māgh* 1315 BE), and also in 'Prabāsī', 1909 (*Phālgun* 1315 BE). The next seven lectures were delivered from 14 February to 21 February 1909 (2 to 9 *Phālgun* 1315 BE).

He delivered 'Thoughtfulness and Purity' ('Bhābukatā o Pabitratā') on Sunday, 14 February 1909 (2 *Phālgun* 1315 BE), and 'Marriage' ('Pariṇaẏ') on Sunday, 21 February 1909 (9 *Phālgun* 1315 BE). The fifth part was published on Thursday, 15 April 1909 (2 *Baiśākh* 1316 BE) and consisted of seventy-five pages.

The sixth part of *Śāntiniketan* was also published on the same day as the fifth, that is, Thursday, 15 April 1909 (2 *Baiśākh* 1316 BE). It was of ninety-eight pages consisting of fourteen lectures. The first lecture of this part is 'Three Levels' ('Tintalā') written on 22 February 1909 (10 *Phālgun* 1315 BE), and the last one was 'Fruit' ('Phal') on Thursday, 4 March 1909 (20 *Phālgun* 1315 BE). The essay 'Dedication' ('Niṣṭhā') which was published in the *Baiśākh* issue in 1316 BE of 'Bhāratī' was actually the combination of 'Dedication' and 'The Function of Dedication' ('Niṣṭhār kāj') of the sixth part of *Śāntiniketan* essays. In this collection the date given to these two essays was Monday, 1 March 1909 (17 *Phālgun* 1315 BE).

The seventh part of this collection of essays contained fourteen lectures and was published on Wednesday, 2 June 1909 (19 *Jaiṣṭha* 1316 BE). This part[47] consisted of ninety-eight pages. After his return to Śāntiniketan, Tagore resumed his lectures on Tuesday, 16 March 1909 (3 *Caitra* 1315 BE). The first lecture of this part was 'To See the Truth' ('Satyake Dekhā'). This part ended with 'The Omnipresent' ('Bhūmā') on Saturday, 27 March 1909 (14 *Caitra* 1315 BE).

Tagore began to deliver the lectures of the eighth part of *Śāntiniketan* from Sunday, 28 March 1909 (15 *Caitra* 1316 BE) to Tuesday, 20 April 1909 (7 *Baiśākh* 1316 BE). This part began with the essay 'Om' and concluded with 'The Path of Mukti' ('Muktir Path'). The essay 'To Obtain and Not to Obtain' ('Pāoẏā o Nā-Pāoẏā') and 'To Become' ('Haoẏā') were combined as 'To Obtain and to Become' ('Pāoẏā o Haoẏā') and was published in the *Jaiṣṭha* issue 'Bhāratī', 1909 (1316 BE). From 'Om' to 'Mukti' the lectures were inscribed in a particular note book while 'The Path of Mukti' was written in loose sheets and attached to the note book to form the manuscript of the eighth part of *Śāntiniketan*. But while writing the part, Tagore made a mistake and wrote "seventh part" which he later rectified as the eighth (Pal 6: 56). This part[48] was published on Tuesday, 15 June 1909 (1 *Āṣāṛh* 1316 BE). It consisted of 145 pages. This part contains twenty essays.

On Tuesday evening, 13 April 1909 (31 *Caitra* 1315 BE), Tagore conducted worship at the Śāntiniketan temple on the occasion of the End of the Year. The speech he delivered was named 'End of the Year' ('Barṣaśeṣ'). Tagore wrote 'Mukti' and 'The Path of Mukti' on the same day he arrived in Calcutta on 20 April 1909 (7 *Baiśākh* 1316 BE) as is evident from the cashbook entry.

The serialized lectures that commenced on Tuesday, 1 December 1908 (16 *Agrahāẏaṇ* 1315 BE) came to a culmination after this. These lectures were compiled in the initial eight parts of *Śāntiniketan*.

The essay 'Hermitage' ('Tapovan') was read on Wednesday, 1 December 1909 (15 *Agrahāẏaṇ* 1316 BE) at Overtoun Hall at 6 p.m. (Pal 6: 113) and was published in 'Prabāsī', 1909 (*Pauṣ* 1316 BE). 'After the Holiday' ('Chutir Par') was published in the *Āśvin* issue of 'Tattvabodhinī', 1910 (1831 *Śakābda*). When the school at Śāntiniketan resumed at the beginning of 1909 (*Āṣāṛh* 1316 BE) Tagore welcomed the students and teachers possibly with the speech 'After the Holiday'. Ajitkumar

Chakraborty wrote an essay in the *Bhādra* issue of 'Prabāsī' based on 'Tolstoy's Last Message'. Viewing the similarity between Ajitkumar Chakraborty's essay and 'After the Holiday', it might be deduced that Tagore had read that essay as there was a reflection of it in 'After the Holiday' (Pal 6: 79). 'Contemporary Age'('Bartamān Yūg') was published in the *Agrahāẏaṇ* issue of 'Tattvabodhinī' 1910 (1831 *Śakābda*). It is not known when this lecture was delivered.

On Tuesday, 25 January 1910 (12 *Māgh* 1316 BE), the ninth part of *Śāntiniketan* was published. The book consisted of 115 pages.[49]

The tenth part of the *Śāntiniketan* essays began with 'Devotee' ('Bhakta') on Wednesday night, 22 December 1909 (7 *Pauṣ* 1316 BE). 'Devotee' was published in a periodical, 'Suprabhāt', at the beginning of 1910 (*Māgh* 1316 BE). This essay dealt with Maharṣi's sadhana and about the ashram. 'The Ever New' ('Ciranabīnatā') was published in the *Phālgun* issue of 'Tattvabodhinī' 1910 (1831 *Śakābda*) and also in 'Bhāratī' in the first quarter of 1910 (*Phālgun* 1316 BE). But before its publication elsewhere it was already included and published in the tenth part. 'Perception of the Universe' ('Viśvabodh') was published in the first quarter of 1910 in 'Prabāsī' (*Phālgun* 1316 BE) and also in the *Caitra* issue of 'Tattvabodhinī', 1910 (1831 *Śakābda*).

'Devotee' was delivered on the night of the nineteenth annual celebration at Śāntiniketan. ' The Ever New' was delivered on Monday morning, 24 January 1910 (11 *Māgh* 1316 BE) at the third storey of the Adi-Brahmo Samaj which was full of people. Both Tagore and Priyanath Shastri were seated on the dais at the right time. 'Perception of the Universe' was delivered on the same day in the evening at the Maharṣi Bhavan (Introduction, *Śāntiniketan*, 2: 515–516). The tenth part of *Śāntiniketan* was published on Saturday, 29 January 1910 (16 *Māgh* 1316 BE). It was of 107 pages.[50]

The eleventh part consisted of six essays. It began with 'The Dharma of Essence' ('Raser Dharma'). Possibly this lecture was delivered at the Śāntiniketan temple, without any date but was probably written on Wednesday, 30 March 1910 (16 *Caitra* 1316 BE). It was printed in the *Baiśākh* issue in 'Bhāratī', 1910 (1317 BE) (Pal 6: 132). The essay titled 'Being in a Cave' ('Guhāhita') was published in the middle of 1910 (1317 BE) in the *Āṣāṛh* issue of 'Prabāsī' and *Bhādra* issue of 'Tattvabodhinī', 1910 (1832 *Śakābda*). 'Birth Celebration' ('Janmotsav') was published in the Bhādra issue of 'Bhāratī', in the third quarter of 1910 (1317 BE) (Pal 6: 151). 'Rare' ('Durlabh') was published in 'Bhāratī' in the middle of 1910 (*Āṣāṛh* 1317 BE). On his birthday Tagore delivered the lecture 'Birthday Celebration' before the students of Brahmavidyālaẏ at Bolpur on Sunday, 8 May 1910 (25 *Baiśākh* 1317 BE). The essay 'An Evening in *Śrābaṇ*' ('Śrābansandhyā') was published in 1910 CE (*Bhādra* 1317 BE) issue of 'Prabāsī'. This part concluded with the essay 'Hesitation' ('Dvidhā') published in 'Bhāratī', 1910 (*Āśvin* 1317 BE).

As per the Bengal Library Catalogue, the eleventh part was published on Saturday, 8 October 1910 (21 *Āśvin* 1317 BE). It consisted of 114 pages.[51]

The twelfth part of *Śāntiniketan* consisted of five essays. It began with 'Complete' ('Pūrṇa') on Wednesday, 27 July 1910 (11 *Śrābaṇ* 1317 BE) and was published in 'Prabāsī', 1910 (*Āśvin* 1317 BE). Other essays from this part were 'The Śrāddha[52]

Ceremony of Mother' ('Mātṛśrāddha') delivered on Monday, 12 September 1910 (27 *Bhādra* 1317 BE), and published in 'Prabāsī', 1910 (*Kārtik* 1317 BE); 'End' ('Śeṣ') published in 'Mānasī', 1910 (*Āśvin* 1317 BE). 'Harmony' ('Sāmañjasya') was published in 'Bhāratī', 1910 (*Māgh* 1317 BE) and *Phālgun* issue of 'Tattvabodhinī', 1910 (1832 Śakābda). The last essay of this part was 'Awakening' ('Jāgaraṇ') published in 'Prabāsī', 1910 (*Māgh* 1317 BE) and *Phālgun* issue of 'Tattvabodhinī', 1910 (1832 *Śakābda*). The twelfth part of *Śāntiniketan* was published on Tuesday, 24 January 1911 (10 *Māgh* 1317 BE) and consisted of 107 pages.

In 'Complete', the young friend referred to in the essay was Tagore's biographer, Prabhatkumar Mukhopadhyay and it was on his birthday that Tagore delivered this talk. Tagore conducted a special *upāsanā* on Saturday, 3 September 1910 (18 Bhādra 1317 BE), on account of the third death anniversary of Mathurnath Nandi's wife who was also the mother of the ashram students Hitendra, Hirendra and Narendra Nandi. This lecture was titled 'The Śrāddha Ceremony of Mother' (Pal 6: 173). The essay 'Harmony' was delivered by Tagore on Mukhopadhyay's birthday at Śāntiniketan temple. At the Maharṣi Bhavan at Jorasanko he delivered this lecture once again on the day of his father's *śrāddha* anniversary held on Friday, 20 January 1911 (6 *Māgh* 1317 BE). It was not clear whether he delivered this lecture in the afternoon or in the evening. 'Awakening' was delivered in the evening of the annual celebration at Śāntiniketan on Thursday, 22 December 1910 (7 *Pauṣ* 1317 BE).

The thirteenth part of *Śāntiniketan* essays contained three essays namely, 'Karma Yoga' ('Karma Yog'), 'Self-realization' ('Ātmabodh') and 'Success of the Brahmo Samaj' ('Brāhmosamājer Sārthakatā'). 'Karma Yoga' featured in 'Bhāratī', 1911 (*Phālgun* 1317 BE) and *Caitra* issue of 'Tattvabodhinī' 1911 (1832 *Śakābda*). This essay was actually read by Tagore on the occasion of the 81st Brahmo Festival at the Adi Brahmo Samaj in Calcutta on Wednesday, 25 January 1911 (11 *Māgh* 1317 BE). After leaving out certain portions of this essay, Surendranath Tagore translated it as 'Realisation in Action' and this translated version was read by Rabindranath Tagore on 21 June 1913 at Notting Hill Gate for the Brahmo Samaj in London. 'Self-realisation' was printed in 'Prabāsī' in 1911 (Phālgun 1317 BE), and Caitra issue of 'Tattvabodhinī', 1911. The essay 'Success of the Brahmo Samaj' too was published in the *Baiśākh* issue of both 'Tattvabodhinī', 1911 (1832 *Śakābda*) and 'Prabāsī', 1911 (1318 BE).

On the occasion of the *Māghotsav* on Wednesday, 25 January 1911 (11 *Māgh* 1317 BE), the essay 'Karma Yoga' was read by Tagore in the morning and 'Self-realization' was read by him in the evening (Introduction, *Śāntiniketan*, 2: 189, 191). Perhaps these essays were written by Tagore at Shilaidaha. 'Success of the Brahmo Samaj' was an essence of the lecture delivered at the Prayer Hall of the Sadharan Brahmo Samaj (temple) at 6:30 p.m., on Thursday evening, 26 January 1911 (12 *Māgh* 1317 BE) (Pal 6: 192). This part[53] was published on Friday, 10 May 1912 (27 *Baiśākh* 1318 BE).

The fourteenth part[54] of this collection of essays contained nine essays. This part was published in 1915.[55] In the year 1915 (1322 BE) Tagore only published one book of his and that book happened to be the fourteenth part of

Śāntiniketan essays (Pal 7: 153). The part began with the essay 'Beautiful' ('Sundar') on Wednesday, 29 March 1911 (15 *Caitra* 1317 BE) and concluded with 'The Uniqueness and the Universe' ('Biśeṣatva o Viśva'). 'Sundar' was published in 'Bhāratī' (*Āṣāṛh* 1318 BE) as well as in 'Tattvabodhinī' in the middle of 1911 (*Āṣāṛh* 1833 *Śakābda*). 'The End of the Year' ('Barsaśes') was published in the *Jaiṣṭha* issue of both 'Bhāratī', 1911 (1318 BE) and 'Tattvabodhinī', 1911 (1833 *Śakābda*). 'New Year' ('Nababarṣa') was brought out in the *Jaiṣṭha* issue of 'Tattvabodhinī' in 1911 (1833 *Śakābda*) and also of 'Prabāsī' (1318 BE) in the same year. 'An Evening of a Northwester' ('Baiśākhī Jharer Sandhyā') was published both in 'Tattvabodhinī' 1911 (1833 *Śakābda*) and 'Bhāratī', 1911 (1318 BE) in the *Śrābaṇ* issue. 'Realization of Truth' ('Satyabodh'), 'To be True' ('Satya Haoẏā'), 'To See the Truth' ('Satyake Dekhā'), 'Purity' ('Śuci') and 'The Uniqueness and the Universe' were essays without any date. These five lectures were delivered on various occasions in 1911 (1318 BE) by Tagore. The essays were published in 'Tattvabodhinī' and the year in which the last of these essays were published is 1912 (1319 BE) (Pal 6: 307). At the end of the text of 'Purity' the date provided was Wednesday, 5 April 1911 (22 *Caitra* 1317 BE) (*Śāntiniketan* 2: 425), but in the Introduction rendered by Kanai Samanta it was understood that in Tagore's manuscript, the date and 'Wednesday' were inscribed, the year was confirmed from the almanac (Introduction, *Śāntiniketan*, 2: 516). 'Realization of Truth' was published in 1912 (1834 *Śakābda, Bhādra*), 'To be True' in 1912 (1834 *Śakābda, Pauṣ*), 'To See the Truth' in 1912 (1834 *Śakābda, Māgh*), 'Purity' in 1912 (1834 Śakābda, *Āśvin*), 'The Uniqueness and the Universe' in 1912 (1834 *Śakābda, Agrahāẏaṇ*).

The essay 'Beautiful' was the theme of the speech he delivered on Wednesday, 29 March 1911 (15 *Caitra* 1317 BE). In the morning of the New Year, on Friday, 14 April 1912 (1 *Baisākh* 1318 BE), Tagore conducted worship at the Śāntiniketan temple. The essay 'New Year' was the essence of the lecture he delivered. When that essay was published in 'Tattvabodhinī' it had the title 'The New Year Within' ('Antarer Nababarṣa') (Pal 6: 215). Tagore delivered the talk 'An Evening of a Northwester' on Wednesday evening, 19 April 1911 (6 *Baiśākh* 1318 BE), at the Śāntiniketan temple (Pal 6: 215). The essays 'Realization of Truth', 'To be True', 'To See the Truth' and 'Purity' were the substance of the talks delivered at the Śāntiniketan temple. The essay 'The Uniqueness and the Universe' was also the theme of the lecture delivered at Śāntiniketan.

The fifteenth part of *Śāntiniketan* included three essays namely 'Realization of the Father' ('Pitār Bodh'), 'The Claim of Creation' ('Sṛṣtir Adhikār') and 'Small and Big' ('Choto o Baṛo'). All these essays were published in 'Tattvabodhinī'. 'Realization of the Father' was published in 1911 (1833 *Śakābda, Phālgun*) while 'The Claim of Creation' and 'Small and Big' were published in 1913 (1835 *Śakābda, Phālgun*). The last essay of this part, 'Small and Big', was also published in both 'Prabāsī' and 'Bhāratī' in 1914 (*Phālgun* 1320 BE).

'Realization of the Father' was delivered on Thursday morning, 25 January 1912 (11 *Māgh* 1318 BE) at Māghotsav. 'The Claim of Creation' was the gist of the lecture delivered in the morning of 24 January 1914 (11 *Māgh* 1320 BE) at the

Adi Brahmo Samaj temple and 'Small or Big' was delivered in the evening of the same day of Māghotsav at the Adi Brahmo Samaj.

The sixteenth part of *Śāntiniketan* consisted of five essays. This part began with the essay 'The Compassion of Beauty' ('Saundaryer Sakaruṇatā') in the morning of 25 January 1915 (11 *Māgh* 1321 BE) and ended with 'One Mantra' ('Ekti Mantra') on Wednesday, 28 January 1914 (15 *Māgh* 1320 BE). All the essays were published in 'Tattvabodhinī' and only 'One Mantra' was simultaneously published in the 'Prabāsī' in 1914 (*Caitra* 1320 BE) as well. 'The Compassion of Beauty', 'The Child of Amrita' ('Amṛter Putra'), 'The Festival of the Traveller' ('Yātrīr Uṯsav'), 'The Acquaintance with Sweetness' ('Mādhuryer Parichaẏ') were all published in 1914 (1836 *Śakābda, Phālgun*).

'The Compassion of Beauty' and 'The Child of Amrita' were delivered in the morning while 'The Festival of the Traveller' and 'The Acquainta with Sweetness' were delivered on Monday evening, 25 January 1915 (11 *Māgh* 1321 BE) (Introduction, *Śāntiniketan*, 2: 517). The orally delivered lecture in the temple of the Sadharan Brahmo Samaj in the evening of 28 January 1914 (15 *Māgh* 1320 BE) was the written version of 'One Mantra'. Tagore was not too satisfied with the written version (Pal 6: 463).

The seventeenth part of *Śāntiniketan* contained eleven essays starting with 'Awakening' ('Udbodhan') delivered on Monday, 22 December 1913 (7 *Pauṣ* 1320 BE) and concluded with 'Innermost Peace' ('Antaratara Śānti') delivered on Tuesday, 22 December 1914 (7 *Pauṣ* 1321 BE). All eleven essays were published in 'Tattvabodhinī'. 'Awakening', 'The Initiation of Mukti' ('Muktir Dīkṣā'), 'Waiting' ('Pratīkṣā') and 'A Summons to Move Forward' ('Agrasar Haoẏār Āhvān') were published in the *Māgh* issue of 'Tattvabodhinī' in 1913 (1835 *Śakābda*). The essays 'Do Not Harm Me' ('Mā Hiṁsīḥ') and 'Forgiveness of Sin' ('Pāper Mārjanā') were published in the issue of 1914 (*Āśvin-Kārtik* 1836 *Śakābda*). 'The Work of Creation' ('Sṛstir Kriya') was published in 1914 (*Agrahaẏāṇ* issue of 1836 *Śakābda*). 'The Day of the Initiation' ('Dīkṣār Din'), 'More' ('Āro'), 'Advent' ('Ābirbhāb') and 'Innermost Peace' were published in 1914 (*Māgh* issue, 1836 *Śakābda*). The talks 'Awakening' and 'The Initiation of Mukti' were delivered by Tagore in the morning at Śāntiniketan temple on Tuesday, 22 December 1914 (7 *Pauṣ* 1320 BE). The lecture 'Waiting' was delivered in the evening of the very same day. None of the three essays were written prior to Tagore's lectures. Ajitkumar Chakraborty happened to transcribe them at the time Tagore delivered those lectures. The lectures were later corrected by Tagore and were printed in 'Tattvabodhinī'. After that these lectures were published in the seventeenth part of *Śāntiniketan* with minor corrections. 'A Summons to Move Forward' was an abridged version of the discussion Tagore had on Tuesday noon, 22 December 1914 (7 *Pauṣ* 1320 BE), with the teachers at Śāntiniketan and this was also transcribed by Ajitkumar Chakraborty. In this discussion Tagore followed the message given in Stopford Brooke's *Onward Cry* (Pal 6: 458). 'The Day of the Initiation' and 'More' were delivered on Tuesday morning, 22 December 1914 (7 *Pauṣ* 1320 BE) while 'Advent' and 'Innermost Peace' were delivered in the evening. However, in volume two of the compilation of essays, 'night' was stated after the end of the essay 'Innermost Peace'. 'Innermost Peace' was based on Tagore's song 'Tumi ye ceye ācho ākaś bhare/ Niśidin animese dekheca more' ('Your gaze indeed pervades the entire sky./ You see me with steadfast gaze day and night' [244]), written on Tuesday, 24 March 1914 (10 *Caitra* 1320 BE).

Selection of the fifty essays

The fifty essays selected for translation contain the essential ideas of this collection. Thematically all fifty essays are linked together; one after another they journey onwards and reveal the means to arrive at the abode of peace, 'Śāntiniketan'. There is also something which is very unique about these fifty essays, that is, in the nature of examples Tagore has cited to reveal, explain or support what he has said. Tagore has used examples from all walks of life – ordinary life as well as the natural sciences, the Bible, the Upanishads, the Gītā and other sources – to explain great truths of life. This selection of fifty essays forms a very practical guide as to how to overcome adversities and to turn them all in favour of our fulfilment in life and to make our existence on earth as meaningful as possible.

The links among the fifty selected essays

Each of the fifty essays follows a pattern. Tagore makes use of certain words or phrases and keeps repeating them. Even those words fall under certain categories, for instance, he uses economic terms like 'wealth', 'save', 'need', 'want', 'poverty', 'lost', 'lack', and 'borrow', uses words which deal with celebration like 'festival' or 'celebration' or 'mela' or 'fair', employs words denoting the time of day like 'day', 'night', 'morning', 'evening', 'dawn' and 'dusk', utilizes legal terms such as 'justice' and 'injustice' and uses terms consisting of spiritual discipline like 'sadhana', 'bliss' and 'renunciation' and a host of others. Sometimes he uses certain words in a particular essay or in several essays and he employs those words as titles of other essays such as 'lack', 'sin', 'sorrow', 'renunciation', 'power', 'prayer', 'beauty', 'prana', 'end', 'mukti' and 'more'.

If the collection of the selected essays is considered to be a single sentence then each of these essays functions like a part of speech. Each of these fifty essays is necessary in the collection of translated essays as it enhances the flow towards the goal, that is, the 'abode of peace'.

The first essay of the collection, 'Arise! Awake!', seeks 'peacefulness'. To attain peace one has to 'awaken the consciousness in the midst of the Infinite within'. The title of the essay 'Arise! Awake!' itself is considered the 'awakening mantra'. The word 'awake' has been repeated several times in this collection of fifty translated essays. The time of day mentioned in this essay is 'morning', 'night' and 'evening'. In this essay Tagore posites the idea that one lacks 'the effort to even doubt the existence of that Truth [which is 'liberated, pure and eternal Truth'] if one does not 'arise awake'. The next essay of this selection is titled 'Lack' and it delves further into this idea. Attaining God will put an end to the worldly restlessness and will bring about peace.

'Lack' explores the concept of uniting mankind with God. Worldly persons are not even aware that they 'lack' God daily and do not know the consequences of leaving God out from their daily lives. In this essay Tagore talks about the mind being fully 'awakened' while searching for that 'voice and touch' of the Mother. 'Mother' is the finite aspect of the Infinite God through which Tagore tries to make one understand the relationship between the finite and the Infinite. The journey towards peace begins the moment one is receptive enough to seek God. Here Tagore has employed economic terms like the title itself which is 'lack', other such terms found in the essay are 'loss', 'quarter of a pice', 'wealth', 'wants', 'storehouse' to convey the essence of his message in this essay. The time of day mentioned in this essay, 'dawn and dusk', 'day and night', are images which recur several times throughout the selected fifty essays. So, human beings have to awaken their consciousness to see that they lack the touch of God in their daily activities and should seek God and find Him.

It is not enough to seek God. A person should also be aware of that which obstructs his union with Him. In the essay 'Sin,' it is revealed what happens when the finite (man) tries to unite with the Infinite (God). 'Sin' is nothing but an obstacle towards man's union with the Infinite. When there is a pull between the finite 'atman' and the Infinite 'Atman' to unite, it is 'sin' which comes in the way. The variation of the usage of the word 'awake' occurs in this essay as well: 'when the atman awakens, it seeks the Atman in the universe'. God is referred to as 'Supreme Love' in this essay. Time of day again finds mention here as 'dawn', 'night' and 'daybreak'. The word 'mukti' finds its first mention in this essay of the collection of fifty translated essays, and 'beauty' gets a mention too. These are words which will recur in other translated essays of this selection as well.

In the essay 'Sorrow', Tagore talks of the acceptance of sorrow as a prerequisite for getting in touch with Truth, otherwise 'we deprive ourselves of coming in perfect contact with Truth'. This is the next step after identifying 'sin' as an obstruction in the path to 'perfect contact with Truth'. In this essay, Tagore employs scientific terms and concepts as examples like 'centripetal and centrifugal forces'. He makes use of biological terms and processes like 'organ', 'digestion', 'breathing', 'health', 'strength', 'body', 'nourishment', 'limbs', 'food', 'organs of digestion' and 'organs of rejection'. There are economic terms in this essay too just as in the essay 'Lack', such as, 'lack', 'allowance', 'dealings', 'accounts', 'buy', 'paid', 'book of accounts' and 'settle up accounts'. There are binary opposites like 'acceptance and rejection' as well. There is the use of legal words like 'law', 'justice' and 'injustice', 'right and wrong' and 'wrong and unjust'. Also, there are inclusions of words like 'happiness', 'beauty', 'prana, 'sorrow', 'power' and 'renounce' – variations of or the same words which feature as titles of the subsequent essays. Sorrow is necessary to unite with Brahman and it is considered to be positive because it unveils the Truth. Hence in order to unite with the Infinite, sin has to be dispelled, and that is when one encounters sorrow.

The next translated essay is 'Renunciation' and it expounds the necessity of 'renunciation'. When 'sorrow' wears itself out, it is then that one realizes the necessity of 'renunciation'. This is because when a person lets go, he moves towards attainment. The time of day referred to in this essay is 'morning'. The words 'law', 'completeness' and 'mukti' are included in this essay and they later on become the titles of three different essays. The word 'tune' is repeated in another essay titled 'The Bonds of the Mantra'. The words 'demands', 'poverty', 'save', 'sell' and 'wealth' are economic terms used in other essays of this collection of fifty essays. The word 'renunciation' is repeated many times in this essay as well as in others in the collection. The word 'blissful' is a variation of 'bliss' and it occurs in majority of the essays of this collection. There is the word 'amrita' which is mentioned here and it is used both in the literal and mythical sense in the next essay 'Prayer'. The word 'renounce', as Tagore uses it here, has a positive connotation. A person encounters 'sorrow' because he has to renounce, or give up, 'sin'. Sin is the obstacle to our union with God. So in 'Renunciation' Tagore says, 'When we do work by being unattached to our work, only then do we attain complete claim over it'. It is only when one gives up the fruits of one's labour 'by being unattached' that one actually attains God.

The essay, 'The Prayer', can be said to be an extension of the previous essay. Here Maitreyī discards the finite (husband's material possessions) for the Infinite (immortality which she regards as 'love'), and she pines for 'love' as she knows that is the only way to reach Him. It is only through love that she, a finite being, can attain the Infinite as she says, 'Amid this love itself we get a taste of the Infinite'. Merging of the finite into the Infinite is achieved only through love. Words like 'awakened', 'sin', 'beautiful', 'endless', 'necessities', 'prayer', 'beauty', 'wealth', 'savings', 'save', 'love', ' more', 'lack', 'happy', 'amount', 'want', 'need' and 'power' find mention in this essay. These words have either been mentioned in the previous essays of this collection of fifty translated essays or will be mentioned in the remaining essays of this collection. Some of the words that Tagore uses within individual essays are also turned into essay titles: 'Power', 'Sin', 'End', 'Beauty', 'Prayer' and 'More'. One faces 'sorrow' when one renounces all that which causes 'sin' (obstructing the union of mankind with Brahman), but how does one unite with the Infinite after renouncing all one's attachments? It is through love that the finite unites with the Infinite. Love is beyond reason and self-interest.

In the previous essay, 'The Prayer', Tagore referred to love being instrumental in the union of the finite and the Infinite. Here in 'Dispersed Fair', Tagore expounds one such Upanishadic concept (of the finite and the Infinite being linked) using everyday examples. The main theme of this essay is that the finite and the Infinite are intrinsically linked. The first word of the title is 'bhāṅgā' which literally means 'broken' (depicting finiteness) in Bengali. This denotes fragmentation, something which was initially a complete whole, Infinite, is now manifested in its finite entity. In its English translation, the word used is 'dispersed', this is to convey the sense of the essay. The times of day mentioned in the essay are 'day', 'night' and 'dawn'. These serve as the titles of three other essays of this collection. There are also words like 'mela', 'needs' and 'wants' which are repeated in several other essays. At one moment these 'wants' are extremely essential, and in the very next moment they are treated as 'waste' ('aborjonā'), 'load' ('bojhā') and 'burden' ('bhār'). These words convey the finiteness of all 'wants' and with that there is a human aspiration to go beyond them. Tagore makes use of several metaphors and formal elements to reveal the finiteness of things around mankind, yet in the last paragraph Tagore clearly reminds one that all dispensable 'wants' are contained in the 'indispensable' ones as he says, 'if there were no dispensable wants within the indispensable ones, could we then have survived?' Hence, the finite and the Infinite are intrinsically linked and are united with themselves. The finite is a necessity because without the finite there would be no question of its union in love with the Infinite. It is by means of the finite that mankind becomes one with the Infinite. God carries on with His sport of uniting with His bhakta.

In the essay 'End of Festival', Tagore talks of the man who 'saves a little every day', the finite trying to connect with the Infinite, and this propels one towards the search for an 'abode of peace'. Here too Tagore uses 'amrita' in its literal sense, as in 'the pot of amrita held in Its [Dawn's] hand'. Economic terms and expressions have also been used in this essay, like 'wealth', 'settling up accounts', 'saves', 'poverty', 'bankrupt', 'miserliness', 'debts', 'abundance', 'borrow' and 'wasted'. The word 'renunciation' is used in this essay, the title of a previously mentioned essay of this selection. The time of day mentioned here is 'dawn'. The word 'festival' occurs several times in this essay which also finds mention in other essays of this collection. Tagore tries to bring harmony between opposites, citing love as its uniting function: 'At least once a year man ceases to be miserly and tries to forge a relation of sharing with that generous One'. The 'relation' is the relation of love. Tagore positions two opposites together like the terms 'king' and 'beggar', 'rich' and 'poor', 'miserly' and 'generous', 'poverty' and 'wealth', 'invited' and 'uninvited' in this essay. Here festival is a metaphor for uniting with God. The word 'end' in this essay reveals the bankruptcy of spiritual wealth. On a daily basis if one prepares to attain God then the festival will not 'end', every day will be the day of festival. This essay subtly reveals how essential it is to prepare oneself daily to attain the union between the finite and the Infinite, so that when it is actually time for human beings to unite with God, their love for Him should be awakened.

'Ferry Me Across' starts with 'On that very day, when the mela had dispersed at dawn'. The first line itself has a link with the essay titled 'Dispersed Fair', because there is a reference to the mela which had dispersed, and with that titled 'At Dawn', as the time of day depicted is 'dawn'. The essay features words and phrases like 'renounces', 'ferry me across', 'sea', 'shore', 'boatman', 'bondage', 'loss', 'fair', 'day and night', 'completeness' and 'O Sea of Bliss' which figure in several other essays of this collection. One does not 'ferry across', that is, attain God, by renouncing his work, it is the individual's work which helps a person to attain God and be ferried across: 'Whenever he [man] is able to make his house as Your house, then by being in his [man's] house itself he is ferried across'. One does not need to go elsewhere to attain God, one attains Him by performing one's daily tasks by realizing that these are God's work: "It is Your [God's] work". The essay answers the question: How should a person be ferried across by awakening his love for Him? It is by doing his regular duties with love for Him, realizing that it is actually His work and not the work done for his self-interest.

In the essay 'This Shore – the Other Shore', the use of the phrase 'ferry across' continues from the previous essay and Tagore explores the essence of this phrase. Here the phrase 'ferry across' too has the same meaning as in the previous essay. Tagore reflects on the fact that all beings are essentially connected: 'That pride builds a wall from all sides to keep a distance between us even though we are very close to each other'. This 'pride' is the finiteness, the 'sin', which creates obstacles in one's attainment of the oneness with God. So, whenever mankind is able to transcend this 'sin' of finiteness through 'renunciation', by overcoming 'sorrow', through regular practice and by awakening love, mankind is 'ferried across' and finds God to be within them and not somewhere else. Tagore repeats words in Bengali which in English translate into 'money', 'wealth', 'lose', 'joy', 'sea', 'shore, 'burden', 'power', 'distance', 'motion' and 'Bliss' which he had already employed in previous essays. The times of day mentioned in this essay happen to be 'night' and 'morning'.

In 'Day' man tries to know the ways in which he can realize that God is not far away but near. This essay answers that question as to the consequences of being separated and united. In man's union with others he attains union with the Supreme Reality. God pervades the whole universe and so, wherever man is able to go beyond the finiteness of his atman and go towards the many, he unites with God: 'When we are only occupied with ourselves we are unconscious, when we move towards all, we are awake. It is only then that we know ourselves'. When people are united with others they actually attain God: 'That is why by being alienated, by being insignificant, we just drift along being futile in all respects; that is why neither does our knowledge perfectly unite with Knowledge, nor does the heart unite with the Heart, nor does effort unite with Effort to create an appropriate temple of the human atman – by no means is our atman able to assume its great form worthy of uniting with that Great Being, Viśvakarmā'. Staying within the narrow concerns of the atman is a failure. So, it is by overcoming the finiteness that we achieve oneness with God. There are words like 'power', 'lose', 'lack', 'dearth', 'poverty', 'joy', 'happiness', 'love', 'end', 'renunciation', 'lost', 'amount' and 'steal' in this essay. Some of these words are titles of other essays of this collection while the others are economic terms. Tagore uses his theme of opposition once again here: 'light and darkness', 'sleep and wakefulness', 'contraction and expansion' and 'once it ebbs, again it flows'. The words 'awake' and 'whole' have been repeated in this essay as well. The times of day mentioned here are 'morning' and 'night'.

The essay, 'Night' answers the question: How does one achieve the harmony that prevails in God's universe in spite of the diverseness in one's lives? In 'Night',

Tagore reveals it is by uniting with the Supreme Atman that one attains harmony with everything: 'we need to establish a perfect harmony with the Supreme Atman for some time' or else, we will find ourselves alienated from every other thing. By meditating upon the Supreme Atman one will be able to 'transform the realm of work of the world into the realm of joy'. Tagore employs the theme of opposition once again: 'night and day' and 'sleep and awakening'. The words which have been used in previous essays are repeated once more: 'power', 'sleep', 'slumber', 'awake', 'ended' 'day', 'joy', 'peace', 'love', 'beauty', 'beautiful', 'surrender', 'tune', 'wastes', 'accumulated', 'needs', 'light' 'pay for damages' and 'casting the net'. There is mention of scientific terms and musical instruments as in 'scientific laboratory' and 'tānpurā' respectively. The times of day mentioned are 'dawn', 'night', 'day' and 'morning'.

The essay, 'At Dawn', is a carry-over of the idea in the essay 'Night'. It answers the question: What do we achieve by this union with the Supreme Atman? By this true union with the Supreme Atman one may find one's true identity. A person should see himself as being one with the Omnipresent, or else he will consider himself 'small' and 'weak'. He should go beyond his finite self and unite with the Infinite. So, in the essay 'At Dawn' Tagore says, 'may the entire distance between them [atman and Supreme Atman] dissolve'. If that is not so then 'we do not know our true identity' ('At Dawn'). The word 'dawn' also explains the realization of our 'identity' of being 'completely enclosed within the Supreme Atman'. The phrase 'at dawn' was mentioned in the essay 'Ferry Me Across'. The word 'messenger' is mentioned in the essay, 'At Dawn' which is once again used in the next essay of this collection, 'The Unique'. The time of day referred to 'At Dawn' is 'dawn' ('daybreak') and 'night'. There are also words like 'power' and 'rule' which find mention in other essays of this collection. The word 'night' occurs several times in this essay. And the essay, 'At Dawn', is a direct follow up of the previous essay 'Night' as it highlights the union of the finite with the Infinite. Always one should realize oneself as being immersed in God.

In the essay 'The Unique', the following question is asked: How is our identity different from those of others? It is different in the way that it has a unique relation with God in spite of having a general relationship with all: 'In this very abode of "I" lies Your divine sport'. So in 'The Unique' Tagore says, 'of all my sorrows, my supreme sorrow lies in being separated from You and that is the sorrow of pride; of all other joys, my supreme joy lies in my union with You and that is the bliss of divine love'. This reveals that though man has unity with God as with everything else, there is a place where his relation with God is one-on-one. It reveals to us how man actually goes beyond his finite self by uniting with God. There are repetition of words like 'saved', 'creation', 'unique' and 'bliss'. Oppositions like 'general' and 'unique', 'sorrow and joy', 'separation and union', 'immortality and death' also find mention in this essay.

In the essay, 'Beauty', there is the continuation of the idea as in 'Unique'. It reveals how the 'unique' 'I' is special and answers the question: How does man transcend his finiteness? It is by accepting God out of his 'free will' that one can transcend finiteness, because it is 'in the unusual realm of this "I" within our inner atman, there is coming and going of that Blissful One and there is evidence of that throughout the universe' ('Beauty'). So, this 'I' transcends the finiteness and becomes the Infinite. It is in this 'unique' 'I' that man has to accept Him with love. The identity of the Infinite is with the finite. Tagore mentions that God gives mankind a chance to decide and accept Him out of love, only then can mankind see His love for us, as in 'Beauty' Tagore says: 'May there be joy between you and me; accept me of your own accord'. There are words like 'dawn', 'beauty', 'beautiful', 'joy', 'bliss', 'peaceful', 'love', 'sin', 'awaken' and 'sorrow' being repeated in this essay as well. Bliss is felt through love.

The idea that Tagore has presented in the essays 'Unique' and 'Beauty' has been developed further in 'Law', that is, the idea of the general (Lawgiver) and unique (Friend), two contradictions residing in one place, in the 'I', but Tagore does not just stop at that idea, the idea progresses:

> On the side in which I am equivalent to a brick, a piece of wood, a tree and a stone, in that general direction God's all-pervading Law does not in the least allow me to be different from the ordinary entity. Again in that direction where I am uniquely 'I', in no way does God's unique bliss allow me to unite with all.
>
> *('Law')*

As seen in 'Law', the finite is always linked with the Infinite when 'each [finite] one of us is united with the whole [Infinite]'. When man transcends finiteness he discovers that God could be both a Friend and a Lawgiver. As Lawgiver He treats mankind like every other thing as 'wood and stone, sand and dust' ('Law') and one has to follow the Universal Law. But what seems more emphatic in the essay 'Law' is God's manifestation as a Friend because 'His manifestation as a Friend is certainly not within the realm of law – where else will that manifestation be if not in the realm of love within me?'. This is because the 'realm of law' is general, but it is in 'the realm of love' that the self, 'I', becomes 'unique' and attains God. There are repetitions of the words like 'want', 'law', and 'bliss' as in the other essays of this collection.

In the essay 'Three' Tagore continues his idea of the general and unique from the previous essay: 'Towards nature there is rule and towards our atman there is bliss' ('Three'). It inquires of the function of 'nature' in seeking the Supreme Atman. Here 'nature' is 'general' whereas atman is 'unique'. But in the essay, 'Three', Tagore reveals that the two are not contradictions, following rules can also lead one to God: 'When we understand that [true union is established upon pure self-sacrifice] completely, only then does it become possible to attain unimpeded union in love in every way with *Advaitam* who is that Supreme Atman in the form of Oneness'. In Tagore literature, it has been observed that love is treated as the ultimate. To Tagore, immortality is 'love'; he asserted this view in the essay, 'Prayer' as well, where the word 'love' has been repeated a number of times in reference to Maitreyī. Words like 'rule' and 'end' are also repeated in this essay. Again in 'Three' it is found that the finite is linked with the Infinite: 'everyone [finite] has taken eternal refuge in Him [Infinite]'. Actually 'everyone' here refers to every being that appears to be 'different' from the Infinite and yet is 'identical' with It due to love. Here the nature of relation of the finite with the Infinite is reflected upon.

'The Whole' carries forward the idea of the previous essay. In this essay Tagore delves further into the question of 'part' and 'whole'. Here Tagore asks the question: Why is it necessary to see in parts and then see from the point of wholeness? It is important to do that as there is bound to be distortion of truth if that is not done. Tagore uses the example of the spiritual and physical sides of man and says in 'The Whole', 'it is necessary to see these two [parts] as perfectly united within absolute wholeness'. Tagore repeats the use of the words 'awakened', 'beauty' and 'morning' in this essay.

In the essay, 'Power', Tagore picks up the thread from the previous essay, 'The Whole', when he says, 'The moment there is separation, there is suffering as well'. So, when the 'parts', that is, a part like 'self-interest', gets transformed into doing selfless action, it goes towards the 'many' and by doing that it gets liberated. Here 'part' can be taken as 'self-interest' and 'Whole' or 'Infinite' as 'Supreme Truth', and there is only one way to achieve that, and it is through 'action'. It is 'action' that liberates a person from the finite and helps him to transcend from the finite to the Infinite. Here Tagore expouses further on 'power' and 'action': 'Our power wants to get liberated within action – not only for external necessities, but for internal revelation'. This 'internal revelation' renders 'bliss'. The words which are found in other essays are also being repeated here such as 'law', 'rules', 'sorrow', 'renunciation', 'mukti', 'lack', 'completeness', 'power' and 'bliss'. The times of the day mentioned is in this essay are 'day' and 'night'.

In 'Prana' one sees a direct link with the essay 'Power'. In 'Power' Tagore talks of the necessity of unselfish 'action' which liberates and brings about 'bliss'. In 'Prana' there is the manifestation of bliss and action that work in tandem. As Tagore says, 'In prana, both bliss and action remain united together'. Prana has been equated with Brahman here: 'He [knower of Brahman] takes Brahman, the manifestation of Prana of the universe, within his prana'. So, it is the internalization of the Infinite Prana into the finite prana of the devotee, the knower of Brahman. Bliss is within while action is without, and both of them are in the prana. The Prana is being manifested in the individual prana: 'He who is manifested in the whole universe in the form of Prana, manifested at the same time in the forms of bliss and action, is that very Prana which the knower of Brahman manifests through his own prana itself'. Words like 'bliss', 'action', 'manifestation' and 'prana' are repeated in this essay as well.

In 'Place for Pilgrimage' too Tagore picks up the thread from the previous essay of this translated collection, 'Prana', about the need to delve within. So in 'Place for Pilgrimage' Tagore says, 'meditate on He who resides within!' He justifies the need to delve inside:

> When I know that I am within the Supreme Atman and that the Supreme Atman is within me, then as I see another person I will surely be able to see that he too is within the Supreme Atman and the Supreme Atman is within him.

In this essay, the target of mankind as Tagore reveals, is the transition from the outside to the inside and mankind ultimately achieves it. There are repetitions of economic terms such as 'need', 'end' and 'loss'. There are repetitions of words like 'touchstone', 'fear', 'power', 'happiness', 'uproar' and 'sins' in this essay.

After the transition from the outside to the inside, Tagore's concern in the subsequent essay, 'Observer', is to save the inside from the attacks of the outside and he mentions ways in which one can keep one's heart from the turmoil of the outside world. So a person should see the inner atman as an 'observer', and the inner atman does not get involved but is beyond every worldly attachment: 'He [one's inner atman] indeed pervades the world, the body, the intellect and the heart, yet our inner atman transcends this world, this body, this intellect and this heart. He [one's inner atman] is the Observer'. There are repetitions of words like 'peaceful', 'noise', 'uproar', 'joys', 'sorrows', 'detached', 'mukti' and 'renouncing'.

What happens when a person sees the Supreme Brahman within oneself? The person ceases to fear. In 'The Eternal Abode' Tagore instructs one to look within oneself to see the bliss of the inner atman so that there will not be any fear. That which is outside is narrow and finite, the atman which is inside is Infinite:

> see the atman in the inner abode, in the midst of the Eternal, in the midst of Brahman; only then will the entire power of pleasure and grief go away. Why then is there any fear of harm, criticism, sickness, death or anything else at all? The atman is ever triumphant.

There are words recurring in this essay which also appear in other essays of this collection of fifty essays such as 'bliss', 'pleasure', 'sorrow' and 'love'.

'Three Levels' carries forward the idea of the previous essay. The essay, 'Three Levels', also resembles another essay, 'The Whole', where it is mentioned that seeing things in parts is important, only then can one understand the 'Whole'. Similarly, here in 'Three Levels' it is seen that Tagore gives the answer to the question: What happens when one delves deep into the 'innermost cave' within? The answer is 'all the conflicts between the inside and the outside become resolved. Then there is no victory but joy; no struggle but sport; no separation but union; not "I" but all; neither outside nor inside, then It is Brahman'. So, three levels, 'the physical, the religious and the spiritual', are seen and all three have their respective purposes. The recurring words: 'awakened', 'surrendered', 'sufferings', 'sorrows', 'day', 'night', 'love', 'power', and 'grief', 'wants', 'sorrow' and 'happiness' are also present in the essay.

'Philosopher's Stone' takes up the idea from the previous essay. This essay provides answers to the questions: How do conflicts between the inside and the outside get resolved? How is there a harmony between the two? In the essay,

'Philosopher's Stone', Tagore makes it clear that it is not by 'renunciation' of a person's daily activities that he will know the Supreme Being. Amidst a person's day-to-day activities he meditates upon Him and he offers the fruit of his labour to Him: 'at all times, in all actions, I will let the *upāsanā* go on in the immovable court of that secret chamber within my heart'. No matter what duties a person performs, the *upāsanā* continues 'within my [his] heart'. Words such as 'awakens', 'peace', 'uproar', 'rejoicing' and 'renunciation'; times of day such as 'dawn' and 'morning'; and economical terms such as 'lose', 'saved' and 'wants' are repeated in this essay as well.

In the next translated essay, 'Prayer', Tagore carries forward the idea of the previous essay by providing the answer to the question: What is found in that heart after allowing *upāsanā* to go on? One finds the 'endless Truth' in that heart after allowing *upāsanā* to go on. The words 'sinless', 'beauty' and 'bliss' are repeated in this essay.

'Detachment' answers the question: What is Truth? This is also a propagation of thought from the previous essay. The answer to this is given in the essay 'Detachment': 'when we know the Truth then it is within that undivided Truth itself we know all the fragments'. So, Truth is both finite and Infinite. Here the finite, 'fragments', leads to the Infinite, the 'undivided Truth', the 'Whole'. Hence the son (finite being) becomes dear to a person solely because of his quest for God (Infinite Being). Words like 'sins', 'joy', 'whole' and 'beautiful' recur. Tagore makes use of examples from linguistics: 'letters', 'words', 'part of speech' and 'syntaxes'.

'Collectedness' also takes up the thread from the previous essay when it inquires: How does one find Truth? The answer this essay, 'Collectedness', provides is that Truth is found by pursuing single-minded sadhana:

> there is a need to awaken this very faith in the first place that the goal is true; then it has to be known whether the goal is within or without, whether it is at the periphery or at the centre; then there is need to learn to follow the right path.

The words 'lack', 'power', 'happiness' and 'awakened' which are titles of other essays or titles with variations in the word are repeated in this essay.

In 'Dedication' it is as if the essay itself provides the answer to: What happens in the path of sadhana? There are trials and tribulations in the path of sadhana but it is Dedication which helps one to undertake the journey successfully to the end: 'along the desert path of dryness and emptiness, without taking any food or even without getting anything'. In this essay the words 'prana' and 'unending' find mention as well.

The essay 'The Function of Dedication' is a continuation of the thought as reflected in the previous essay, 'Dedication'. The function of Dedication is to see that a person reaches the desired destination and does not lose track: the Dedication which 'overcomes hopelessness, the Dedication which has the capacity to withstand shock, the Dedication indifferent to external encouragement and the Dedication unmoved by criticism – at no cost, for no reason should that Dedication renounce us'. Some of the words which occur in this essay and are also found in other essays are: 'energy', 'power', 'joy', 'love', 'awake', 'stop', 'peace', 'night', 'beauty', 'sea', 'end', 'lack' and 'renounce'. A majority of the repeated words are either titles of essays in this collection or are variations of or parts of those titles.

'The Obverse' espouses the need to locate the right destination in life and is a continuation of the idea presented in 'The Function of Dedication'. What happens when one looks at the wrong direction? When one looks at the wrong direction, the destination is lost. The destination which is reached through dedication is, in fact, 'within' and not outside: 'For once, turn your gaze within; only then would you be able to understand all the meanings'. Words like 'joy', 'power', 'night', 'day', 'blissful' and 'dawn' are again mentioned in this essay.

'To see the Truth' is to see the 'essence' of everything a person sees around himself and does not see them on the 'surface' in a superficial manner. In order to do that in 'To see the Truth', Tagore says, 'Amidst the entire array of events we direct our gaze inwards to behold the One who is the fundamental power of the universe'. So, one has to meditate on the 'One' within to understand the essence of everything. This essay is an elaboration of the thought of the previous essay which reveals how we tend to look in the wrong direction, neglecting the right one. There are repetitions of the words like 'joy', 'awake', 'end', 'awaken' and 'bliss' in this essay as in several other essays of the collection.

In the previous essay Tagore talked of seeking the 'essence' of everyday events and in this essay, 'Creation', this idea is carried forward. What does a person see when he looks within? He sees the 'Creator' engaged continuously in the process of creating his inner realm, that is, preparing his realm of *upāsanā*, just as He is doing for the outer realm: 'He who is seated amidst this world and beyond, is seated in this courtyard [at the seat of *upāsanā* within]' ('Creation'). So, He is preparing us to be able to see the manifestation of His 'incessant bliss'. The word 'Truth' is repeated in this essay.

The word 'manifested' of the previous essay has been taken up by Tagore in this essay the 'Loaded Boat' and he builds upon it: 'The little field of his [a person's] life is like an island surrounded by the unmanifested from all directions, only that little part has been manifested in him' ('Loaded Boat'). So in order to get 'incessant bliss' ('Creation') a person in whom 'that little part has been manifested' ('Loaded Boat') has to give up his ego. The 'fruit' of his labour (which may be termed as *upāsanā*) is not 'wasted'. Economic words such as 'accounts', 'tax', 'saved' and 'cost' too find mention in this essay.

So, after a person renounces his 'ego' he attains his nature as is espoused in the essay, 'Attainment of Nature'. But, what is a person's nature? It is the same as that of the 'Supreme Atman'. In 'Attainment of Nature', Tagore mentions that a person's atman 'is not joyful while receiving, it is joyful while giving'. This gives it bliss. The following words once again occur in this essay as in several other essays of this collection: 'creates', 'sorrow', 'awakens', 'creation', 'renunciation', 'bliss', 'joy' and 'love'.

In the essay, 'Commandment', Tagore elaborates on manifesting one's atman. The ultimate outcome of manifesting the atman is bliss, but how does one manifest the atman? One manifests the Atman by 'propagation of this love'. Lack of sin leads to the propagation of love. As the Supreme Atman is all-pervading, so also is the atman. There is also a link between this essay and the essay, 'The Prayer', in reference to Maitreyī's prayer where she wants only 'love'. The following words also occur in this essay: 'sorrow', 'love', 'bliss', 'renounce', 'sin' and 'bondage'.

In the next translated essay, 'Completeness', Tagore takes up the idea of love from the previous essay and builds on it. Love for all (finite beings), both 'neighbours' and 'enemy', is necessary for the attainment of the 'Omnipresent' (Infinite). And to love a person one has to go beyond the obstruction of 'ego, self-interest, anger and greed'. Only then can one love all and be united with all. Union with all is the union with Brahman. So, 'The person who aspires for the *Brahmavihāra* has to attain this level of love'. Economic terms such as 'cost', 'necessities' and 'needs' and other words like 'love', 'completeness', 'ego', 'awaken', 'renunciation', 'desires' and 'complete' recur in this essay.

The essay 'Om' elaborates on the idea of the essay 'Completeness'. In 'Om', Tagore shows how the fragments are all inclusive: 'The One in whom nothing has been excluded, within whom all the fragments have become a whole, all contradictions have become resolved, it is only to Him that our atman wants to accept as "Yes" with folded palms'. This is 'completeness', this is Om. This essay also repeats the words 'completeness', 'prana', 'peacefully' and 'sin'.

'Supreme Obtainment' carries the idea of inclusiveness in the previous essay with a different vein and deals with an understanding of how Brahman can be obtained. Just as in 'Om' Tagore talks of the inclusiveness of the fragments or the finite in the Whole or the Infinite, here he talks about man's longing for the Infinite which is within the finite. So, when the atman longs for obtaining God, it does not think He is another entry in the inventory of things, but He is 'the Infinite within the finite, our atman aspires to realize that Infinite' ('Supreme Obtainment'). Not only that, people have to understand that whatever they enjoy have been bestowed upon them by God: 'whatever there is in the universe He pervades them all, it has to be known that whatever you have attained have been bestowed upon you by Him' ('Supreme Obtainment'). So, the Infinite pervades the finite. The following words are again repeated in this essay: 'obtaining', 'wants', 'inventory', 'account', 'lost', 'adding', 'accumulating', 'garbage', 'refuge' and 'bliss'.

The first line of 'Self-surrender' follows from the first and second sentences of the previous essay, 'Supreme Obtainment'. Tagore picks up the theme of obtaining Brahman from the previous essay and explores the idea in this essay, 'Self-Surrender'. Instead of trying to obtain God one should surrender oneself to Him by getting rid of the obstacles such as the 'ego', only then would one realize 'that I am [one is] truly within Him and there is no separation from Him anywhere' ('Self-surrender'). This again draws upon the all-inclusiveness of 'Om' when each entity is actually within Brahman and everything that is enjoyed is by 'His bestowal'. The following words are repeated in this essay: 'lacking', 'joy', 'love', 'happiness', 'sorrow', 'ego', 'power' and 'happiness'.

The essay 'Self-confidence' asks the question: Why do we try to 'obtain' God? Tagore through the essays says, 'the reason that we seek the Supreme One is solely for the yearning of our own "one"'. It is because our atman considers itself as one with the 'Supreme One' that it wants to stay united with It. As a single atman it is separated from the others and eventually from the Supreme Atman but as the atman longs for completeness and oneness, it tries to unite with the others and thus 'transform[s] this small one [atman] into the greater One [Supreme Atman]'. The following words are repeated in this essay: 'prana', 'completeness', 'love', 'joy', 'power' and 'bliss'.

What is the way in which one can find fulfilment in seeking God? How does a person manifest that he has a father? It is with the help of the mantra. In 'The Bonds of the Mantra', Tagore asserts that the 'mantra' is a means to attune ourselves to God and he says, '*Pitā nohasi*: is one such mantra'. The following words recur in this essay as well: 'awaken', 'special [as in biśeṣ]', 'unique', 'attune', 'tune', 'joy', 'sorrow' and 'blissful'.

The essay 'The End of the Year' carries forward the idea of the previous essay where one has to attune oneself to God to understand the finiteness of life and not hold on to anything. Tagore conveys the fact that there is oneness and continuation, there is only an apparent separation: 'There is no separation between the end of the year today and the beginning of the year tomorrow – this end enters into that beginning with complete silence and with utmost ease' ('The End of the Year'). In this essay the justification of 'end' or 'death' is being made. It is death which lets go while life firmly tries to hold onto everything. When the finiteness of life is revealed to mankind only then does mankind respect death. The following words are repeated in this essay: 'end', 'beautiful', 'renunciation', 'wants', 'miser', 'savings', 'piled up', 'tune', 'sin', 'sorrow', 'detachment', 'accumulated', 'seashore', 'self-surrender', 'evening' and 'peaceful'.

In 'Mukti' Tagore conveys the idea that the finite reveals the Infinite following the idea of the previous essay that there is no separation: 'Wherever we see the Infinite within the finite, we see the Immortal, there itself lies our bliss'. Tagore equates the Infinite with Truth in the essay 'Mukti': 'This Infinite itself is the Truth; to see It is to see the Truth'. To see finite as Infinite, and to see the Infinite as Truth, is mukti. So, to see the Infinite, mankind does not have to renounce the world but to accept it as the manifestation of God's bliss. Here, habitual work is considered as finite, but it is through work that mankind will attain mukti. In this essay too there are repetition of words like 'joy', 'morning', 'bliss', 'love', 'awakens', 'power', 'completeness', 'detachment' and 'renunciation'.

In 'After the Holidays' Tagore picks up the idea from the essay, 'Mukti', about the term 'habit' which tries to make everything mundane. In 'After the Holidays', Tagore says, 'to gain an opportunity to see our regular work anew, we at times distance ourselves from it'. What is the ultimate goal of doing work? The goal is, as Tagore mentions in 'After the Holidays', 'when we see the inner truth of work, we see that entity which is much greater than work. Then just as our pride fades away and our heads bow down in reverence, our chest swells with joy'. Whatever be the work, one has to see the 'One' beyond everything. Working for the sake of doing the work or to achieve the fruit of one's labour is not joy in the true sense. A person sees the ultimate essence of work by going beyond the work itself; in such a case even when there are obstacles in the path of accomplishing that task, the obstacles actually help one to get closer to God. That which is beyond is God. In this essay too there are repetitions of the words 'joy', 'blissful', 'energy', 'power', 'peace', 'miser', 'lack', 'end', 'beautiful', 'evening', 'pain' and 'beauty'.

In the essay 'End', Tagore reveals the justification for stopping: 'A river stops where it does because the sea begins there – so, there is no harm in its stopping'. After work and action, as evident from the previous essay, 'After the Holidays', one has to stop. In 'End' Tagore glorifies 'pause' because it does not only denote an 'end' but also marks a beginning. Tagore employs linguistic metaphors like 'terminal point of a measure', 'full stops', 'caesura', 'words', 'poem' and 'writing' to drive home his point. In this essay too there are repetitions of words like 'renounce', 'end', 'poverty', 'renouncing', 'saving', 'save', 'miserliness', 'end', 'poverty', 'wealth', 'bankrupt', 'renunciation', 'beautiful' and 'bestowing'.

A unique day of festival is the very day human beings see God. Though God can be seen daily, human beings do not make the effort to do so. In the essay, 'Awakening', there is again the concept of the 'unique' and the 'general' as in a previous essay of this selection titled 'The Unique'. Every day is a day of festival, but as human beings do not call upon God earnestly they do not see Him. But if they did so earnestly even for a moment they would certainly have fulfilment of seeing God: 'Let us awaken the power which is within us. If we get its response even for a moment then its fulfilment lasts for ever' ('Awakening'). Here too the words 'awakened', 'festival', 'special ('biśes')', 'uniqueness', 'joy', 'accumulated', 'lack', 'amounts', 'habit', 'lacking', 'storehouse', 'waste', 'stock', 'tune', 'loss', 'power', 'dawn' and 'beauty' are found as in the other essays.

The previous essay deals with a 'unique' day for mankind to be able to see God. Though that day is 'unique', one has accumulated one's spiritual wealth on a daily basis in order to make the day 'unique'. 'The Day of Initiation' maintains this strain of thought and answers the question: How can we see Truth? Tagore in this essay mentions it is 'only through joy that it is possible to see the Truth, not by any other means. Through our extreme attachment we grasp everything externally. It is for this very reason that a certain day comes for us [human beings] to see the inner form of joy by getting rid of that attachment'. So, the day of initiation is that day when human beings can see the 'the Eternal Life within'. Words like 'festival', 'love', 'awakened', 'bliss', 'renounces', 'joy' and 'sin' are repeated.

In the previous essay, 'The Day of Initiation', Tagore referred to the Supreme Will pervading the universe and realization of God within. In

'More' Tagore shows how ordinary human beings go beyond their finite existence and become Infinite by answering a great summons: 'See it as being pervaded by God – that abode of bliss will be revealed everywhere'. Hence, Tagore reveals in the essay that external conditions no longer affect humans. Words like 'more', 'festival', 'storehouse', 'power', 'joy', 'wealth', 'sorrow', 'celebration', dawn', 'amass', 'tune', 'endless', 'commandment', 'business and trade', 'money' and 'bliss' mentioned in previous essays are repeated in this essay as well.

'Innermost Peace' is the last essay of the collection. Here too words and phrases like 'awaken', 'bliss', 'uproar', 'noisy', 'festival', 'noise', 'peace', 'mela' and 'buying and selling' recur as in some other essays of the collection. There is the reference to the music of the *ektārā* in both the first and the last essay of this collection. In the first essay of the collection, 'Arise! Awake!', Tagore writes about the 'uproar' of activities, and in the last essay, 'Innermost Peace', too he continuously talks of 'uproar'. In the first essay 'Arise! Awake!' Tagore makes an attempt to awaken the consciousness of mankind even in uproar and in the last essay of the collection, 'Innermost Peace', he implores the yogi to wake up in order to seek the eternal peace in the midst of uproar, as in the last essay he says,

> Ye yogi, wake up, your asana for yoga is ready, take your own asana – sit where there is uninterrupted peace in the midst of this uproar, amidst distress, agitation and conflict of the inherent six cardinal sins. Light the lamp of your festival there.

Thus these fifty essays reveal the state of awakening of human consciousness in search of the 'abode of peace'.

Methodology adopted in this translation

Bengali date system

The Bengali date system was retained within parentheses at the end of the individual translated essays. Equivalent dates from the Gregorian calendar were also provided at the end of each translated essay for the benefit of the Target Reader. The conversion of *Bangābda* or Bengali era to the Christian era is calculated based on the following accepted method.

1. From months falling under the second half of April to December: subtract 593 from AD to get *Bangābda*.
2. From January to the first half of April: subtract 594 from AD to obtain *Bangābda*.

The Bengali calendar has six seasons during a year with two months corresponding to each season. They are specified as follows:

Names of Bengali seasons	Names of the corresponding Bengali months
Grīṣma (Summer)	*Baiśākh* and *Jaiṣṭha*
Barṣā (Monsoon)	*Āṣāṛh* and *Śrābaṇ*
Śaraṯ (Autumn)	*Bhādra* and *Āśvin*
Hemanta (Pre-Winter)	*Kārtik* and *Agrahāẏaṇ*
Śīt (Winter)	*Pauṣ* and *Māgh*
Basanta (Spring)	*Phālgun* and *Caitra*

Readership

The first step for a translator is to determine the target readership. By keeping the Target Reader (TR) in mind, the translator was able to devise methods for translating the Bengali Source Text (ST) into English Target Text (TT). The translation of the *Śāntiniketan* essays is aimed at both the national (non-Bengali) and the international target readership. For the Indian readership, certain culture-specific terms and quotations were retained in transliteration. But for the non-Indian and Indian diaspora (by birth) readers, endnotes and a glossary were furnished.

Over the years there has been a paradigm shift in the practice of translation. It has become more of a target-centric than source-centric exercise. Each method employed keeps the TR in mind. The two most important shifts in theoretical developments in translation theory over the past three decades have been (1) the shift from source-text-oriented theories to target-text-oriented theories and (2) the shift to include cultural factors as well as linguistic elements in the translation training models. Those advocating functionalist approaches have been pioneers in both areas (Gentzler 70).

It was quite apt when a critic said,

> When language and culture are both alien to target readers, innumerable hurdles need to be crossed on the way before optimum communication through translation becomes possible. . . . But still, the gap in human experiences across cultures, is an in-built problem in cross-cultural translation.
> *(Datta 120–121)*

In this translation too there were certain 'hurdles' which were overcome while translating the text to bring about effective 'communication through translation'. The slokas from the Upanishads, the Gītā and other scriptural texts, for instance, were retained and transliterated in this translation, and their meanings and references were provided in the endnotes. This was to enable the TR to have the feel of the cultural authenticity and flavour of the Source Culture. Thus, in the course of translation, a dialogue between the two cultures takes place in the 'Third Space' (Bhaba 38) to assist communication.

Linguistic aspects

Regarding translation Susan Bassnett-McGuire says,

> . . . translation involves the rendering of a Source Language (SL) text into the Target Language (TL) so as to ensure that (1) the surface meaning of the two will be approximately similar and (2) the structures of the SL will be preserved as closely as possible but not so closely that the TL structures will be seriously distorted.
>
> (2)

Translating a text is akin to tight-rope walking. A slight loss of balance can result in a disaster. In a text like *Śāntiniketan*, there is always a tussle between transferring 'the surface meaning' of the ST and the TT along with the transference of the TT of the underlying meanings that Tagore so playfully has woven from the ST to the TT as well as striking a balance between the structures of the SL and TL.

Whenever a highly culture-specific text like *Śāntiniketan* is being translated, it is equipollence which is given priority over equivalence in this respect.[56] In fact, Sukanta Chaudhuri considers translation as 'the encounter of two equipollent forces, the mutual reflection of light between two opaque objects that the trained eye [the eye of the translator] alone can recognize and render, not the view through a transparent lens' (63). Due to culture-specificity there is bound to be some sort of opaqueness. Here the equipollent forces are the two languages, cultures, histories, civilizations trying to assimilate what they can from each other through the activity of translation. The main challenge in translating this text is to keep it aesthetically literal, meaningful, to maintain fidelity and to conform to the basic rules of English grammar and syntax. Nowhere has any sentence, clause or phrase from the ST been rooted out of the Translated Text. Basudeb Chakraborti says, regarding Jibanananda Das's self-translation of his poem 'Banalata Sen', 'there are certain lexical items in the Source Language Text (SLT), which are untranslatable, certain nuances of meaning that are impossible to translate' (65). Such nuances impossible to translate are observed in the *Śāntiniketan* essays as well. For instance, Tagore employed the 'chalitbhasha', that is the 'common' or 'current' language in the Bengali *Śāntiniketan* essays, but in no way can that linguistic nuance be conveyed in the English translation. In some cases of translating *Śāntiniketan*, when literal translation posed a barrier to convey the spirit of the original, alternative steps were taken to reveal the meaning of the ST. In an essay of this selection, 'Detachment', letters from the Bengali alphabet were provided by Tagore – ka (ক), kha (খ), ga (গ) – and then two such letters were combined to form a word as an illustration of a concept such as, 'kara', 'khala'.[57]

But it was not possible to do the same for the English translation. So, transliterations of the same were provided in the Roman script instead of turning those letters into their 'supposedly' English equivalents.

The names of mythical Indian Gods not entered in *Concise Oxford English Dictionary* (henceforth *COD*), such as Lakṣmī,[58] Rudra,[59] Śiva[60] and Viśvakarmā[61] were retained and annotations in the form of footnotes were provided and the names were also included in the glossary. But where 'Agni' (the name of a God) implied fire and not the fire-God, the word fire was inserted in the translated text to make it less cumbersome for the readers.

There are some words which have layers of meaning in terms of their usages depending upon contexts. One such example would be the Bengali word 'kāj', which literally could mean work, task or function. The translator would have to select the appropriate word in the Target Language keeping in mind the context in which the original word was put and then think out the suitability of selecting a word for it in English. Another such word was 'Āro', literally translated as 'more' but which could either be used as an adverb or as an adjective depending on the context in which it would be placed. There are numerous such instances in the translated text.

Syntax and usage

Bengali and English syntaxes are no doubt different in their patterns. In Bengali the basic syntactical pattern is 'Subject-Object-Verb' while in English it is 'Subject-Verb-Object'. An instance of this could be:

> Bengali [transliteration]: *Āmi* [I] *dābā* [chess] *kheli* [play].
> As per Bengali syntax – Subject Object Verb: I chess play.
> As per English syntax – Subject Verb Object: I play chess.

The translator had to keep in mind the syntactic patterns of the SL and the TL without which no syntactic transfer would take place between the two languages.

As the English Language usage does not necessarily follow the pattern of the Bengali one, a change had to be incorporated in the translated version. For instance, in the essay 'More' instead of the literal translation of the Bengali phrase into English as 'affection and love', it has been changed to 'love and affection'. There is another such case in the essay 'The Function of Dedication', where instead of writing 'to myself and to everyone' as was the syntax in the Bengali ST, it was written as 'to everyone and to myself' in the English translation. There are many such instances in the TT.

Some linguistic nuances in Bengali

Many a time throughout the text we find Tagore using the suffix '-i' ['-ই'] to give emphasis to a particular word. English does not require such frequent emphasis, but in keeping with the tone of the words of the source language text words such as 'only', 'alone', 'indeed', 'too', 'very', 'itself' and 'at all' are incorporated in the English translation to convey the emphasis. Another case in the Source Text was that of the suffix 'o' ['-ও'], an adverb, used quite randomly unlike in English to mean 'too', 'also' and 'even'. One more such instance was in the frequent application of the word 'to' ['তো'] in the Bengali text which is used both in the case of an adverb and as an interrogation in Bengali. Sometimes it is employed in asking a question, making a request, as in 'if', 'in case' and sometimes it is placed at random in a speech without meaning anything in particular except for emphasis. All these particulars of Bengali Language have been incorporated in the translated version to give the readers a feel of the original.

Notes on some Bengali pronouns

In English Language if first, second and third classes of personal pronouns are present in a particular sentence, the order of placing the pronouns is the following: the third person pronoun comes first, followed by the second person, lastly the first person. In order to conform to the patterns of the grammar in English in the essay 'Om' instead of the literal 'I and you' as in the Bengali sequence, 'you and me' has been rendered in the translation conforming to the sequence of English grammar. A similar case was observed in 'The Function of Dedication' where instead of the literal 'to myself and to everyone', 'to everyone and to myself' has been rendered in the translation to avert the distortion of English grammar.

Bengali pronouns like 'ini' ('he' or 'she or 'this person') is used for a person as a mark of respect; 'tini' which is (another version of 'se', meaning 'he' or 'she' or 'that person') also used in reverence, 'yini' ('who') is also used to show respect. The word 'tā̊r' denotes 'his' or 'her' and is used in reverence for a person or God. But in contemporary English there is no such word to express that manner of respect. So, the translator had no choice but to use the current English pronouns.

Prose style

Tagore has employed long sentences in many instances and long sentences in this collection are mostly retained in the English translation of *Śāntiniketan*, as they would convey the feel of the ST and reveal Tagore's prose style in the TT. While discussing Tagore's prose style in general, Buddhadeva Bose said,

> . . . no two consecutive sentences begin or end in the same way, and closed and open sounds caressingly alternate. And Tagore does all this intuitively, with an apparent ease which baffles all. . . . The syntax of the English Language clearly influenced him.
>
> *(112)*

This syntax is clearly evident in the *Śāntiniketan* essays. To a great extent, a reading of the English translation of the *Śāntiniketan* essays will reveal Tagore's prose style as well.

Though it is generally the norm to use shorter sentences in English than the cumbersome compound or complex versions, the author had definitely had some sort of intention in writing the long Bengali sentences. It was observed that a particular idea was very carefully and beautifully interwoven in a long sentence and by simply breaking that sentence into smaller ones, the charm, the flow and the emphasis of the original would invariably be lost. However, whenever there were major difficulties in translating a longer Bengali sentence into English, it was broken down into smaller ones without disrupting the unity of the original, but such occasions were quite few. About Tagore's prose style Bose again observes,

> . . . in Tagore the unit is the paragraph, and the link between the paragraphs and the sentences of which they are composed, is provided not merely by grammar or logical coherence, but by another element, less easy to define, which remains off stage as it were and yet animates the whole.
>
> *(112)*

This trend is very much observed in the *Śāntiniketan* essays. At times a sentence consists of several lines to contain the unity of the idea. For instance the following is one such example from the essay, 'End of Festival', 'Our mind becomes dispirited over the scattered leavings of food, melted candles and withered garlands seen on the day following the festival; then the heart loses its magnificent generosity; the mind becomes pained at the thought of settling up accounts'. In this long sentence the idea flows through the sentence geared by the punctuation marks. Mutilating this long sentence into smaller ones would have disturbed the strain of the flow of thought that Tagore wanted to convey. Hence, in the TT too Tagore's style of paragraphing of the Bengali ST was retained.

Orthography

Capitalization

Apart from proper nouns and words at the beginning of a sentence, the first letter of words signifying the Infinite Being or Supreme Reality or Brahman and other such terms synonymous with God have been capitalized. The first letters of words which have been personified have also been capitalized along with proper nouns. Also, the first alphabets of the transliterated slokas have been capitalized. This is to familiarize non-native speakers of Sanskrit to understand where a sloka begins.

Punctuation

The translated essays of this collection in most cases maintain the punctuations of the ST as rendered by Tagore keeping the rules of English punctuation intact.

Regarding Tagore's use of punctuation, Buddhadeva Bose said, 'it was Tagore who showed how much Bengali can gain in speed, strength and richness by adopting parentheses, inversions and several other devices which are common in English and all other languages which have developed a prose literature' (112). The sentences of the original essays made liberal use of 'dash', 'exclamation', 'comma' and 'semi-colon', amongst others. It was evident from the usage that Tagore followed the rules of English punctuation. In the course of translating the essays, whenever it was deemed necessary to alter the punctuation of the ST, changes were made, but in most cases the punctuation pattern of the ST was retained.

In the TT, single quotation marks were provided for those words, phrases and sentences in which Tagore himself had used quotation marks in the ST. For other words, phrases and sentences which did not have quotation marks in the original but were used in the form of direct speech, double quotation marks were provided for them. This strategy has been maintained throughout the TT. In the case of annotations, only single quotation marks were employed whenever necessary.

Sound

As the *Śāntiniketan* essays were originally lectures and were primarily meant for the audiences rather than for the readers, they have rich tonal quality when read aloud in Bengali. There is no doubt that the Bengali ST has a distinctive sound pattern which is bound to be lost in translation, in spite of great efforts on the part of the translator to retain it. But an alternative method was adopted whereby the translated pieces were read out aloud – great care was taken to make the essays sonorous. Every single word of this translated version was placed in such a way that the essays not only retained the spirit of the original but also maintained a certain sound pattern which had the capacity to appeal to the ear of the listener. Also, if a reader wishes to read the translations of these essays aloud, the words threaded together will not have a tongue-twisting effect. And by closely following Tagore's punctuation pattern in the ST with minor variations, the translator has ensured that the orator pauses at the right moments and would have chances to draw ample breaths as the orator reads it aloud. Buddhadeva Bose very aptly points to certain characteristics of Tagore's prose when he says,

> Tagore makes full use of the natural rhythm of spoken Bengali; neither stuffily nor loosely colloquial, it is rather an idealized form of the living speech of his countrymen. The very inflexions of our voice, ranging from assertion to the whispered word, from dejection and doubt to passionate belief – all this is heard in the prose of Tagore.
>
> *(112–113)*

A similar effect was tried by the translator to be reflected in the TT.

Culture-specific words and italics

Culture-specific Indian words included in the *COD*, eleventh edition, in keeping with their meaning as regards the context of the essays, have neither been italicized nor underlined, nor were they included in the glossary as they have already been entered into English vocabulary. Examples of some such words are: bhakti, dharma, dhyana, mantra, mela, puja, rishi, sadhana, sloka, yoga and yogi. In this case no diacritical marks were added to these words either. Culture-specific Indian words not included in the *COD*, eleventh edition, have been transliterated and italicized throughout the TT. In such cases the translator has provided their meanings in the first endnote and in the glossary.

There are words which have been entered in the said dictionary and specified, but their meanings as provided in the *COD* do not suffice for or are different from those applicable to the context of these essays. These words are neither italicized nor are they transliterated. In such cases the translator has provided their meanings in the endnote and in the glossary by retaining the spelling of the appropriate words as in the said edition of *COD*. An exception to this rule is the word 'karma' as it is synonymous with another word 'kāj' of the SL. Due to this, 'karma' was translated into English and an endnote was included to elaborate on this. The word 'karma' was employed only twice in these essays.[62]

Annotations and glossary

As there are many culture-specific words in the text, there was a need to maintain a glossary. It contains SL transliterated terms to which no appropriate equivalents were found in the TL as well as those terms that are repeated often in the course of translation of the essays. As it is not possible to annotate the words every time they appear, they are explained in the glossary apart from being explained in the endnotes on their first appearances both in the sections of 'Introduction' and in the translated text. Scriptural quotations are annotated only on their first appearance and are not included in the glossary except in the case of single words. When the Bengali months are mentioned in the TT, the same rule applies except that they are endnoted in the 'Introduction' to the TT but not in their subsequent mention at the end of each essay in the TT as their English translations are provided along with them.

Other aspects of this translation

It is a conscious stance on the part of the postcolonial translator to carry out the strategy of foreignization (Hatim and Munday 339).[63] Due to incompatible elements of the ST and the TT, alienness is generated. There are several aspects which reflect postcolonial elements in writing. In the Introduction to *The Empire Writes Back* it is mentioned that 'One of the main features of imperial oppression is control over language. The imperial education system installs a "standard" version of the metropolitan language as the norm, and marginalizes all "variants" as impurities' (Ashcroft, Griffiths, and Tiffin 7). As the translation was kept as aesthetically literal and as close as possible to the original sentence by sentence, even word for word where possible, and also punctuation by punctuation in majority of the cases, by that it has been possible to portray certain inherent usage of the Bengali Language in English. So, this particular translation of fifty essays maintains fidelity to their original as much as possible in terms of form, meaning and essence. For example, in a translated sentence of the essay 'Ferry Me Across' there is an expression which is not common in English as in the last paragraph 'within the fair of our activities'. In 'standard' English one would have used some other expression, but this translation refrained from doing so to make the translated version a 'standardized' English one. The translated text was full of such instances. The expression 'touchstone in her mind' in TT of the essay, 'Prayer' while referring to Maitreyī is not an expression commonly observed in English but such an expression as is observed in the ST is commonly used in Bengali. In some other expressions such as, 'Amid this love itself we get a taste of the Infinite' in the same essay, 'Prayer' or 'complete taste of friendship' as in the essay, 'Sorrow', one does not make use of 'taste' in such a manner in English but the usage employed here is different so as to convey the feel of the Source Culture, the alienness in the translated version. Gayatri Chakravorty Spivak asserts, 'The history of the language, the history of the author's moment, the history of the language-in-and-as-translation, must figure in the weaving as well' (375). It is hoped that through the translation of the fifty essays of *Śāntiniketan*, the 'intimacy' (Spivak 373) of the translator with the ST has been revealed in the TT. 'Translation is the most intimate act of reading. I surrender to the text when I translate' (Spivak 370). Hence, through the activity of translation one can go as close to the ST as possible.

Notes

1 This is a collection of Tagore's translation of Bengali poems from various poetry collections such as 'Kheyā' into English prose verse. It is not to be confused with the Bengali 'Gitāñjali' published in 1910.
2 The title is the English translation of the Bengali play *Prakṛti Pratiśodh* published in 1917.
3 The title is the English translation of the Bengali short play *Chitrāngadā*, published in 1914.
4 The title is the English translation of the Bengali Source Text *Rājā*, published in 1914.
5 It was first translated into English in September 1924 in 'Visva-Bharati Quarterly' (Special Autumn Number). This was the same translation that was printed as a book by Macmillan (London) in 1925 as *Red Oleander*.
6 The novel was later translated into English and published with the same title in 1924.
7 The Bengali title is 'Postmaster'.
8 This is not to be confused with the collection of essays having the same title in English.
9 *Man* is a compilation of lectures Tagore delivered in Andhra University.
10 Here Maharṣi refers to Debendranath Tagore. The word 'Maharṣi' has been entered in the *Concise Oxford English Dictionary* (henceforth referred to as *COD*), eleventh edition, as 'Maharishi', a noun, meaning 'a great Hindu sage or spiritual leader'. See 'Maharishi' in *COD*, 11th ed.

11 *Kārtik* is the seventh month of the Bengali calendar, lasting from the second half of October to the first half of November.
12 *Phālgun* is the eleventh month of the Bengali Calendar, corresponding to the second half of February and first half of March of the English Calendar.
13 *Caitra* is the last month of the Bengali year as per the Bengali Calender, and it corresponds to the second half of March and the first half of April.
14 In this context, 'devi' is an honorary title bestowed upon women during Tagore's times and also much before. The term is still used, but rarely. It also means a goddess.
15 *Āṣāṛh* is the third month of the Bengali Calendar, corresponding to the second half of June and first half of July.
16 *Bhādra* is the fifth month of the Bengali calendar, lasting from the second half of August to the first half of September.
17 *Māgh* is the tenth month of the Bengali calendar, corresponding to the second half of January and first half of February.
18 *Agrahāẏaṇ* is the eighth month of the Bengali Calendar, corresponding to the second half of November and first half of December.
19 *Pauṣ* is the ninth month of the Bengali Calendar, corresponding to the second half of December and first half of January.
20 *Śrābaṇ* is the fourth month of the Bengali year corresponding to the first half of July and the second half of August.
21 *Jaiṣṭha* is the second month of the Bengali calendar, lasting from the second half of May and ending on the first half of June.
22 *Āśvin* is the sixth month of the Bengali calendar, corresponding to the second half of September and first half of October.
23 The word *upāsanā* means worship.
24 The remnant of the food (or articles) spiritually tasted or accepted by a deity when offered to it (becomes *prasād*). Whatever is tasted or accepted by the deity becomes spiritually enhanced. It can also be the remnant of food (or other things) tasted or partaken of by a revered person.
25 Four at dawn is considered *Brahmamuhūrta*. Among the Hindus this period is considered to be most auspicious for spiritual practices such as dhyana, *japa* (repetition of a mantra or divine name usually silently) and the like.
26 This section (title slightly changed) including 'The Aspect of Love in *Śāntiniketan* and Some Other Tagorean Texts' was written by me published as follows: Bhattacharyya, Medha. 'A Brief Description of Rabindranath Tagore's World View.' In *Twentieth-Century Literary Criticism*. Detroit: Gale, USA, 2016. Vol. 324. 301–306. Print.
27 See *Rabīndra Rachanāvalī*, vol. 1, p 22.
28 All the English translations of the *Śāntiniketan* essays in this book are mine.
29 See 'This Shore – the Other Shore'.
30 'Nay' here stands for the concept of 'neti neti' ('not this, not that').
31 It is maya which makes one see Brahman as the phenomenal world, having name and form.
32 Purushasuktam 7.
33 This is the concluding part of the sloka from The Bhagavadgītā, 12.4. This means 'intent upon the welfare of all created beings'.
34 There are references to *vijñāna* or its variations in several of the Upanishads. The following are some of them: Chāndogya Upanishad: 'Vijñānaṁ' (7.7.1), 'vijñānena', 'vijñānavato', 'vijñānādbhūya', 'vijñānādvāva'(7.7.2); Muṇḍaka Upanishad: 'vijñānādyadvariṣṭthaṁ'(2.2.1), 'vijñāmayaśca'(3.2.7); Taittirīya Upanishad: 'vijñānamayaḥ'(2.4).
35 Kena Upanishad, 2.4.
36 The Sanskrit term denotes the Knowledge of Brahman.
37 Muṇḍaka Upanishad, 3.1.4.
38 See note 37.
39 The words *jñāna* and *vijñāna* are present in the Bhagavadgītā along with their grammatical variations. The following are some of the references in the Bhagavadgītā: 'pāpmānaṁ

prajahi hy enaṁ/ jñāna-vijñāna-nāśanam' (3.41), 'jñānaṁ te 'haṁ sa-vijñānam' (7.2), 'Jñāna – Vijñāna Yoga' (Chapter 7).

40 Bhagavadgītā 18.54. The line is 'madbhaktiṁ labhate paraṁ'.

41 Amrita is referred to as the Divine nectar of immortality obtained by the churning of the ocean. It is from the myth of the *Samudra Manthana* (*Churning of the Ocean*). Amrita had to be obtained by the Gods to regain their lost power being continuously defeated by the demons. Tagore makes a pun on 'amrita'; at one instance he gives the literal meaning of the word and again he gives the mythical meaning. Whenever the literal meaning is applicable, it has been translated either as 'immortal', or 'immortality' and whenever its mythical meaning is implied by Tagore, 'amrita' has been transliterated. Here the word 'amrita' has been retained as it connotes the mythical drink of immortality. The translation of the word or its transliteration in any given place depends on the context.

42 A festival celebrated by the Brāhmos in the month of *Māgh*.

43 It consisted of '2 + 2 (Index) + 89' pages (Pal 6: 41). This part consisted of eleven essays. One thousand copies were made, and priced at four annas each. The publisher was Indian Publishing House at Sukia Street.

44 The date of publication is according to Bengal Library Catalogue.

45 *Śakābda* or Śaka era is counted from the reign of Kaṇiṣka I in 78 A.D.

46 The word 'bhavan' means a residence or mansion in Bengali.

47 One thousand copies were printed and priced at four annas each.

48 It cost four annas. A thousand copies of it were printed.

49 It was priced four annas per copy.

50 It cost four annas per copy.

51 The eleventh part was priced four annas per copy.

52 *Śrāddha* ceremony is a Hindu rite held a few days after a person's death to pay respect to him or her. The number of days after which this ceremony would be held varies from caste to caste.

53 Its price was four annas per copy and one thousand copies were made.

54 The following was written on its title-page in Bengali: '*Śāntiniketan* / (fourteenth part) / Śrī Rabindranath Thākur / Brahmacharyasram/ Bolpur/ 1915/ Price 4 annas. [Next page:] Available at – /Indian Press, – Allahabad/ Indian Publishing House/ 22 Cornwallis Street, Calcutta/Allahabad – from Indian Press/ Printed and Published by Apurvakrishna Bose/ Number of Pages: 2+2+117' (Pal 7: 154)

55 Since the book was printed in Allahabad, the date of publication was not documented in the Bengal Library Catalogue (Pal 7: 154).

56 See more input on 'equivalence' from *Routledge Encyclopedia of Translation Studies*.

57 See 'Detachment'.

58 Lakṣmī is the Hindu goddess of fortune and the consort of Viṣṇu.

59 Rudra is the Vedic God of the storms. See glossary.

60 It is the third god of the Hindu Trinity, Maheśwara, known as the destroyer.

61 In the Hindu mythology Viśvakarmā is considered to be the 'Divine Architect'. See glossary.

62 See 'Arise! Awake!', note 2.

63 Foreignization is 'A translation which seeks to preserve "alien" features of a ST in order to convey the "foreignness" of the original' (Hatim and Munday 339). See *Translation: An Advanced Resource Book* for a better understanding.

PART II

Translation of the fifty selected essays

Arise! Awake![1]

Arise, awake! In the morning we are spontaneously awakened from our sleep by Divine light – we wake up from the deep slumber of the entire night at once. But who will dispel the delusion of the evening? We find ourselves in an enclosure of deception emanating from the thoughts and practices of the whole day. How can the mind be redeemed from that into pure, noble peacefulness? The whole day, like a spider spreading web one after the other, has surrounded us from various directions – has completely veiled the Eternal, the Omnipresent. How shall I remove all these webs to awaken the consciousness in the midst of the Infinite within? O dear, arise! Awake!

If we do not caution our consciousness from time to time when the day goes on tying us down from all directions through various acts,[2] thoughts and desires, creating a veil between the universe and our atman – if this awakening mantra 'arise, awake' is not chanted time and again from the inner core of our atman amidst all the diverse activities of the day, then by being repeatedly entangled and being extremely bewildered time and again we would become numbed in the end. In such a situation we no longer have the desire to pull ourselves out of this lethargic state. We consider all that surrounds us as the ultimate Truth. We even fail to believe that the liberated, pure and eternal Truth lies beyond this. In fact, we lack the effort to even doubt the existence of that Truth. Hence, when the whole day is uproar of various activities, then it is as if in the innermost core of our heart an *ektārā*[3] plays on:

'Ye arise awake!'

Kolkata
2 December 1908
(17 *Agrahāyaṇ* 1315 BE)

Lack[4]

If we were to incur the worldly[5] loss[6] of even a quarter of a pice[7] by getting on without God day and night, we would immediately become alert to this fact. But that danger is not there; the sun provides us with light, the universe provides us with food, the vast human community fulfils our innumerable wants through its innumerable life-giving veins. What do we lack then by excluding God from our world? Alas! So long as we do not know that there is a lack, we live at ease free from any doubt, and while leading an affluent lifestyle we think we are the ones who are specially favoured by God.

But how can that manner of loss be explained?

Here, let me give the example of a dream I had. I lost my mother quite early in my childhood. My mother's presence was not felt during the days of my adult life. Last night I had a dream that I was still in the days of my childhood. Mother is sitting in a room at the garden house by the side of the Ganges. Mother is there in every respect – but her presence is not always uppermost in my consciousness. So, without paying any attention to Mother, I walked past her room. On reaching the verandah, I do not know what happened to me all of a sudden – a thought dawned upon me that Mother is there! I immediately went to her room, took the dust of her feet and offered my *praṇām*[8] to her. She held my hand and said: "You have come!"

At that very moment the dream broke off. I continued to think: "I live in my Mother's house, I walk past her very door ten[9] times a day – I know without any doubt that she is there, but household activities continue as if she is not there. What harm is there in that? She has not closed the door of her storehouse, she continues to serve food and her fan continues to fan me even when I am asleep. Only one little thing is missing: she is not holding my hand and saying, 'You have come!'" Food, drink, wealth, people, everything is there, but where is that voice and that touch? When the mind becomes fully awakened, and does not get the voice and touch that it longs for, it only searches from room to room filled with goods, then food and drink no longer appeal to it.

Think carefully but once: rarely in life do we come close to something or someone. No doubt we visit our close relative daily, but it is only by the grace of God that we reach him even for a moment. How many days have we conversed with him privately and walked together in the glow of dawn and dusk, but out of all these days, perhaps I remember only that single day when my heart became full and I felt: "I have reached him!" There are hundreds and thousands of people who have never come close to anything or anyone even for once in their entire lifetime. Though born into this world, they have failed to make any direct contact with it. They are not even aware of the fact that they have not made this contact. While laughing, playing, gossiping with everyone, giving and taking, coming and going with different people, they think: "Ah, I'm together with everyone!" This form of togetherness is so utterly trivial that it lies beyond their comprehension.

Śāntiniketan
8 December 1908
(23 *Agrahāẏaṇ* 1315 BE)

Sin[10]

We clearly know what this entity called sin is when an atman longs for the Atman in such a manner that nothing can stop it in any way. When our consciousness wants to gush forth like a waterfall of melted ice, only then can it fully realize the obstacle of sin – it cannot forget sin even for a moment. To defeat that sin, to remove that sin, our ailing consciousness tends to float like froth around it. In fact, when our mind continues to work, due to the impact of that work it discerns even a small pebble, nothing remains concealed from it any more.

Prior to that we only regard piety and sin as objects of social good and evil, convenience and inconvenience. We mould our character in such a way that it befits the society, so that the ideal of courtesy is maintained. Once we succeed to that extent, there remains no hesitation in our minds; we feel that the purpose of the code of moral conduct has been fulfilled by us.

Then on one occasion when the atman awakens, it seeks the Atman in the universe, it then sees that the practice of mere politeness would not do, nor would it do to even preserve the social norms – the need is much greater, the obstacle is far graver. We have cleared and paved the way on the surface, it is not obstructing our worldly path, no one is able to notice it; but all the roots have been ingrained within, they have internally got entangled with each other in the form of a web, there cultivation of spirituality gets stunted at every step. Even the minutest, the finest root holds on to it and creates a veil. Then we also see that sin which did not come to our notice before and understand to what extent the entity called sin acts as an obstacle in the path of our ultimate fulfilment. Without paying any heed to man or any social wants, we then consider sin only as vice and push it away with all our hearts – it becomes impossible to bear sin. With all its forces, sin, in fact, is occupying the path to our ultimate union with Supreme Love – deceiving others or one's own self regarding it will not do any more – there is no longer any comfort in being good to people – then with all our heart we will have to pray to that Pure Form: *Viśvāni duritāni parāsuva.*[11] Dispel all sins, send them far away in every possible way from the universe – not even a trace of them should be left – because you are *śuddhaṁ apāpaviddham*[12] – the atman seeks only You, that is its only true aspiration, that is its ultimate wish. Ye the Omnipresent, *sarvataḥ prāpya,*[13] at present I cannot even conceive of such good fortune that I will be united with Your Atman and attain It from all directions and will manifest myself within all. But I have to pray for this little grace that even if I am not worthy of Your complete manifestation, may the merest fraction of Your light still enter through a slit of my closed door to enable me to know the enclosed darkness of the room as nothing but darkness. With doors and windows shut, I was sleeping deeply at night. At daybreak, when light entered through the slit in the door and I lay motionless in bed, the appearance of the perfectly pure dawn outside struck my drowsy mind all of a sudden. Then the heat of the bed became unbearable, the air of the room defiled by my own breath began to suffocate me; it became really impossible to stay inside; then the pleasantness, clarity and purity of the unbounded universe – the indication of all beauty, fragrance and music summoned me out of doors. In the like manner, send Your messenger of light, Your messenger of mukti[14] through a few slits of my veil – only then will the affliction of my confinement, sin and darkness no longer allow me to be perfectly calm, the bed of comfort will continue to torment me, I will surely then have to utter: *Yenāhaṁ nāmṛtā syam kimahaṁ tena kuryām.*[15]

Śāntiniketan
10 December 1908
(25 *Agrahāẏaṇ* 1315 BE)

Sorrow

The mantra of our worship states: *Namah sambhavāya cha mayabhavāya cha!*[16] Let us give namaskar[17] to the Bestower of happiness and to the Bestower of benevolence. But we only give our namaskar to the Bestower of happiness, we cannot give our namaskar to the Bestower of benevolence all the time. The Bestower of benevolence is not only the cause of happiness but of sorrow as well. We know only happiness to be His bestowal and consider sorrow as the irony of some ill-luck.

Afraid of sorrow and afflicted with pain, we create different kinds of veils to shield ourselves from it. We only want to hide ourselves. What happens due to that? Due to that we deprive ourselves of coming in perfect contact with Truth.

The rich who live in luxury keep themselves away from all discomfort, they live a life only surrounded by comfort. What happens due to that? Due to that they make themselves crippled; they cease to have any control over their limbs. All those strengths[18] with which they were born into this world cannot develop due to the lack of action – they become withered and distorted. They live in an artificial world within a self-created enclosure. An artificial world can never provide our nature with all its normal nourishment; so, in such a situation our nature becomes like that of a home-made doll, it does not attain perfection.

If out of utter fear we keep trying to shield our mind from the infliction of sorrow, then we have to live in the world in an imperfect manner. Consequently, that never ensures our good health and ultimate development of strength. In spite of being in this world, if a person does not undergo sorrow then that person does not obtain all that he deserves from God – his allowance falls short.

All relatives and friends keep away from the one who is too sensitive to sorrow by nature. Just because he considers some trivial matter to be grave, people say, 'There is no use for him' – their talk and behaviour concerning him do not remain normal at all. Neither does he listen to every word nor does he listen to the right words – neither does he get all of what he deserves nor does he get them in proper measure. This can never do him any good. That unfortunate soul who is never hurt by his friends and is only treated with indulgence, is deprived of the complete taste of friendship – friends in their dealings with him cannot become his friends in the true sense of the word.

In this world the sorrow which is our due will not necessarily be fully justified. We have to accept even that we consider wrong and unjust. Just like opening the book of accounts, to pay a careful attention only to that which is rightful in order to make us proper human beings – does not really happen and even if it does, it does not do any good to us. We must have the ability to properly accept that which is wrong and unjust as well.

Do we obtain our share of happiness in this world even in its right measure? Do we not many a time buy more than what we have actually paid for out of our own pockets? But I never feel I am unworthy of that. I just grab all of it quite well without the slightest hesitation. Is it only then in the case of sorrow that I have to settle up accounts in terms of right and wrong?

There is a reason why in spite of our accurate assessment we do not get what we want. The action of our prana goes on through acceptance and rejection – both the centripetal and centrifugal forces are of equal importance to us. In our prana, in our intellect, in our perception of beauty, in our inclination to do welfare, in fact, in all the aspects of our excellences, the fundamental principle is that, it will not only accept, but will also renounce.

Hence the food we take does not contain the essential ingredients in the right proportion, just as it has an edible portion, it has a nonedible portion too. The body rejects this nonedible portion. If we take only the edible portion of food in the right measure then it does not do us any good and the body becomes diseased. This is because not only do we have the power and organs of digestion, we also have the power and organs of rejection. We have to engage that power and those organs in action too, only then the prana will attain completeness due to harmony between acceptance and rejection.

Similarly, it is not a law that in the world we would get only justice and none should do us an injustice. In the world, it is essential for our nature that justice be fused with injustice. Just as in the act of breathing, our nature too must have such spontaneity that we can accept with ease the little we deserve and can give up that little which is to be renounced without resentment.

Hence, whether just or unjust, the utmost effort to completely shield ourselves from sorrow and hurt weakens our humanity and makes it diseased.

This cowardice not only gives rise to frailty and weakness of luxury, but also defiles the purity of those people who are oversensitive to sorrow by nature and shield themselves for fear of getting hurt. Under the veil they accumulate a lot of filth. The more they want to conceal that publicly for fear of people, the more that becomes polluted and continues to impair health. Those who can accept criticism, injustice, sorrow and pain of the world freely and unhesitatingly, not only become strong but also become pure. In an unveiled life, the full impact of the world continues to wear away their defilement.

Hence, be prepared with all your heart and soul – offer *praṇām* to the One who is the Bestower of happiness and also to the One who is the Bestower of sorrow – only then would you attain health and strength – *praṇām* will be offered only to the One who is benevolent,[19] the One who is the most benevolent.[20]

11 December 1908
(26 *Agrahāÿaṇ* 1315 BE)

Renunciation

If there is a little truth in the *upāsanā*[21] we perform every morning then with the help of that we prepare ourselves for renunciation day by day. We must truly be prepared for it because there is a dharma of renunciation in the world whose law is infallible. It does not allow us to pause anywhere; it only talks of renouncing and moving forward. We do not ever reach any such place where on reaching it we can say – everything culminates here itself, everything is fulfilled, hence we would never move away from here anymore.

Since the dharma of the world is not to hold on to anything, but to set aside, to propel forward, if we do not harmonize our will with the world then there will be repeated conflicts between the two. If we go on asserting 'We will remain here', 'We will retain this' while the world says, 'You have to renounce that', 'You have to move on', then unbearable pain continues to be generated. Our will gets defeated – that which we do not want to give up, is snatched away from us. Hence we have to tune up our will with the strain of this universal dharma.

The instant I unite my will with that of the universal dharma, I truly become free. That indeed is the law of freedom. If I do not willingly join in with the universe, the universe will then forcefully make me obey it. I will then be left with no joy or glory, the world will then pull me by the ear like a slave.

Hence, someday the world should not get a chance to say, 'I will snatch it away from you', may I rather be able to say, 'I will renounce it'. But if we do not prepare our will towards this renunciation daily, we will feel like evading them somehow when we are confronted with the enormous demands of death and damage, yet no deception will work at all – that will be a sorrowful day indeed.

We should never think that through renunciation we would suffer from poverty and emptiness. Our renunciation is to attain something with completeness.

We will not obtain[22] what we do not forsake. While enclosed within the womb the baby is unable to attain its mother – when it is born by severing the bond of the placenta, when it becomes free, only then does it attain its mother completely.

Likewise, we too have to be free from the enclosed womb of this world – only then will we truly obtain the world, because we will obtain it by being free. By being confined like a foetus we are unable to see the world; only those who have become free know the world and obtain it.

Hence the person who is attached to the world is not necessarily worldly; the one who has renounced the world is indeed worldly, because he no longer belongs to the world, the world rather belongs to him. Only he can truly say, 'This is my world'.

The horse drives the carriage being tied to it by the reigns, but can the horse say, 'The carriage is mine'? Is there, in fact, any significant difference between the carriage wheels and the horse? The coachman who by remaining free drives the carriage, it is he who has the authority over the carriage.

If I want to be the master, I have to be free.[23] This is the reason why the Gītā terms that yoga as the Karma Yoga,[24] the yoga in which we do work by being unattached. When we do work by being unattached to our work, only then do we attain complete claim over it; otherwise we get entangled in it and become embodied in work itself, we do not become a karma yogi.[25]

So, to gain the world we have to renounce it, and to accomplish a work we have to forgo attachment while doing it.

This certainly means that harmony has to be brought about between these two opposing aspects of dharma of give and take – within these two if one ever becomes predominant then that leads to misfortune. If taking is given the sole priority then we get attached, and if giving becomes solely prominent then we ourselves get deprived. If work is devoid of mukti then we become slaves and if mukti is devoid of work then we become extinct.

In fact, renunciation is not emptiness, it is the completeness of claim. When a minor does not obtain complete claim over a property, he cannot donate or sell it. He then has the limited claim of enjoyment, he does not have the noble claim of renunciation. In a situation where we can only save and cannot give from our heart's content, in that situation we do not have freedom regarding those items we save.

Hence Christ said that it would be very difficult for a rich man to gain mukti.[26] That is because the little wealth he is unable to give away is the wealth which, in fact, binds him. Whoever has made this bondage greater has indeed fallen into greater danger.

All these bondages are becoming weakened day by day, renunciation is becoming easy for us daily – may we obtain this fruit from our *upāsanā*. Due to the intense attraction of various attachments, our nature has become hard like a stone. During our *upāsanā*, may the fountain of amrita[27] keep falling – may it infiltrate into our very pores – may it erode this stone day by day and continue to soften it. Then by wearing it away, by removing it gradually, may it create a vast space within life and fill that space up. Observe, look within yourself once – 'The narrowness of mind is getting transformed into the broadness of mind daily due to the impact of His name, everything is becoming favourable and calm, work is becoming easy, the relationship with all is becoming true and simple, and my life is being blessed by the glory of God'.

12 December 1908
(27 *Agrahāýaṇ* 1315 BE)

The Prayer

In *Bhāratvarṣa*,[28] the Upanishad is the greatest tree[29] of the Knowledge of Brahman. Not only is it beautiful, green and shady, it is huge and firm as well. Not only does the wealth of attainment grow within it, there is also the soaring firmness of *tapasyā*[30] in it. Amid that lofty unwavering firmness, a beautiful flower has bloomed – its fragrance has made us ecstatic. It is that very prayer-mantra of Maitreyī.

At the time of renouncing worldly life, when Yājñavalkya was about to give away his entire property to his two wives, Maitreyī asked him: 'Well, tell me, will I be immortal by taking all these?'[31] Yājñavalkya replied, 'No, you will not be so. But you will possess all the paraphernalia necessary to lead your life. The way householders lead earthly life comfortably with their homes, domestic animals, food and clothing, you too will be able to lead a life like that'.[32]

At that very moment Maitreyī cried out: *Yenāhaṁ nāmṛtā syam kimahaṁ tena kuryām!*[33] What will I do with that through which I shall not be immortal? These words have not emanated from any austere knowledge. She uttered them neither by virtue of thought, nor out of dhyana, nor by discriminating between the eternal and the transient. She had a touchstone in her mind upon which she rubbed all the paraphernalia of earthly life just once and said instantly, 'That which I aspire for is certainly not this'.

In the Upanishads, amidst the profound voice of wisdom of all the male rishis, there is only a lone female voice which has been uttered with extreme yearning and that voice has not faded away. Amidst their grave voices resembling the rumble of clouds, that sound has awakened an unprecedented sweetness suffused with tears. In the Upanishads, through various ways and means we come across only the man within the human race. Then all of a sudden it is seen that at one end there is the woman within the human race who also stands alone and radiates beauty.

We have a woman in our inner nature too. We bring all our savings to her. We bring her wealth and say, 'Take this'! We bring her fame and say 'Save this'! With utmost efforts throughout his life, the man in us brings so many things from so many directions that there is no limit to it indeed. He says to the woman, 'With all these set up a home; be a good housewife and be happy with these'. The woman ascetic within us is not yet able to say clearly, "All these will be of no use to me". She thinks: "Perhaps that which I want is just this". Yet, even after obtaining all these, she is unable to accept at heart: 'I have obtained all'. She thinks that perhaps the extent of want has to be increased further – she feels that there is need for more money, more fame and it would not do without more power. But there is no end to that "more". In fact, one day she will have to realize that she wants only amrita and that these paraphernalia are not amrita. One day in a moment she will have to push aside like garbage all that she has accumulated throughout her life and say: '*Yenāhaṁ nāmṛtā syam kimahaṁ tena kuryām!*'[34]

But, Maitreyī said, 'What will I do with that through which I will not be immortal'? What does that really mean? Does it mean that to be immortal we have to maintain this physical body for an endless period of time? Or is it to exist in some other life or in some other form even after death? It is certain that Maitreyī did not aspire for the immortality of the physical body and that there was no concern in her mind regarding the eternal nature of the atman. But how then did she wish to become immortal?

This is what she said, "In this world we are constantly moving from one thing to another – by no means can we stay still. The things that occupy my mind also shift focus, my mind too gets diverted. When I let go of that which occupies my mind then it is as good as dead to me. Gradually in this manner we proceed from one death to another – this very succession of deaths has no end indeed".

Yet my mind aspires to something from which it will never have to waver ever again, on obtaining which it can say, 'I need nothing beyond this', and by obtaining whom there will be no possibility of separation any more. Only then can we completely avoid the clutches of Death. Where is that person by obtaining whom or that thing by obtaining which I can say, "I have attained this support for life – there is nothing else that I need"?

That is why Maitreyī discarded all the forsaken property of her husband and said, 'What will I do with all these? I aspire only for amrita'.

Well, if paraphernalia are not amrita what then is amrita? We do know what amrita is. It is not that we never had the taste of it on earth. If we had not got the taste of it, we would not have wept for it. Among all the aspects of the world, it is that alone we go on seeking, because time and again it touches us.

Where through death do we find a touch of this amrita? We find it where we have love. Amid this love itself we get a taste of the Infinite. It is love itself which puts the shadow of the Infinite within the finite, transforms old into new and never accepts death. When we observe the trace of love within diverse matters of the world, we get to know the Supreme Being who is beyond death. Through this we understand that His true nature is the embodiment of love. When we discover the true yearning of our inner atman to obtain this very love completely then we can easily renounce all paraphernalia and say: *Yenāhaṁ nāmṛtā syam kimahaṁ tena kuryām.*[35]

When this very utterance has emanated from a woman, it appears so clear, so true and so pleasant. By being free from all thoughts and reasons, how easily these words have been voiced. 'O dear, I don't want any house or property, I want love'[36] – what a cry is this!

Maitreyī's simple cry has taken the form of a prayer and has become awakened. Has such a wonderful perfect prayer ever been heard anywhere in this world? This earnest prayer of all mankind, eagerly voiced by this woman, has become immortal for all time to come. This very prayer is the only prayer of each one of us, and it is this very prayer which is being uttered through succession of ages in the vast history of the human race.

Yenāhaṁ nāmṛtā syam kimahaṁ tena kuryām[37] – by uttering these words with great force, that *brahmavādinī*[38] stood up with folded hands and with her face drenched in tears looked up towards heaven and said –

Asato mā sadgamaya
Tamaso mā jyotirgamaya
Mṛtyormamṛtaṁ gamaya,[39]
Āviravirma edhi[40]
Rudra[41] *yatte dakṣiṇaṁ mukhaṁ*
tena māṁ pāhi nityam.[42]

In the Upanishads, we have heard about many utterances of profound realization through the male voice. But this is the only female voice through which we have attained such a deep prayer. The supreme realization of what we truly want, yet what we lack, has been manifested very easily from the heart of a lovelorn woman – O Truth, take me away from all that is not True and accept me within You, otherwise our love will remain starved! O Light, deliver me from deep darkness and take me within You, or else, our love will remain imprisoned! O Immortality, accept me through ceaseless deaths, or else our love will be sick of roaming shelterless like travellers in the approaching night! O Manifestation, be manifested unto me, only then will all my love be fulfilled. *Āviravirma edhi*[43] – *Ye Āviḥ*,[44] O Manifestation, You are ever manifested, but be mine for once, be manifested as my own – may Your manifestation be fulfilled in me. O Rudra, O the most Terrible, You are that unbearable Rudra in the darkness of sin, in the form of estrangement, *yatte dakṣiṇaṁ mukham*,[45] reveal to me Your graceful, beautiful and loving countenance – *tena māṁ pāhi nityam*,[46] protect me by manifesting that, save me eternally – that manifestation of Your love, that very grace of Yours is my salvation for eternity.

O Maitreyī, the female ascetic! Come hither, today place your pair of holy feet in the hearts of those that are afflicted with paraphernalia. With your melodious deathless voice chant your prayer of immortality in my heart. May there not even be the faintest doubt in my mind as to how I would protect myself for all eternity.

17 December 1908
(2 *Pauṣ* 1315 BE)

Dispersed Fair

Man's mind only keeps saying, 'I want this, I want that, I want that', following that, it says, 'I don't want this. I don't want that. I don't want that'. At this moment it says, 'I cannot do without it', but the very next moment it says, 'There's no need for it'.

Last night, people of the dispersed mela said, 'It would certainly do us good if we could secure some firewood and dry leaves'. At that time it was as if they could not do without them. To build a small shelter in that wintry open field seemed to be the most important need to be accomplished in the world. There was also a great effort to make an oven somehow and to light a fire with dry leaves and try to cook whatever meal one could manage to have. All other worldly matters became trivial compared to these needs and efforts.

Somehow these firewood and dry leaves were procured. But, today even before the night is over, we hear, 'Hey! Where are the carts? Yoke the bullocks to them'. We have to go, we have to go back to the village now. This very necessity to depart is now the urgent need. The pressing necessities of the previous night are left as waste today; what they had said to be indispensable the previous day, they are fretfully busy to desert that today.

In this very manner the universal man[47] also prepares to move from one age to another. When the new dawn sets in, when the night is just about to show the first light of the day, then they shove each other, saying, 'Hey! Let's go! Where are the bullocks? Where are the carts?' Then the items of utmost necessity of that night are discarded as garbage and are rendered worthless in daylight. Smoke is still rising from the dry leaves, their ashes are still getting accumulated. The whole field is littered with broken earthen pots and cups, and sal[48] leaves. The rest huts being abandoned by their occupants are left in quite ugly and dilapidated condition. All is being left behind – the eastern sky has taken on a crimson hue, now they have to set out on their journey after invoking the gods.[49] Once again they will have to secure the needs for another age.[50] Then it will seem as if the needs of the present will be the final ones, they will never again have to venture out at dawn to harness the bulls to the carts. Saying this, they again proceed to collect branches, twigs and leaves. But, even then, of those immediate needs yet to be met, there comes the message through a doleful tune of *Bhairavī*[51] which plays, 'There is no need for it, there is no need for it'.

If this tune had not been present, if there were no dispensable wants within the indispensable ones, could we then have survived? If the want was truly overwhelming, then who would have been able to put up with its terrible pressure? Just because the days and nights of extremely dispensable wants have taken away the burden of these extremely indispensable wants, we are able to keep moving around in spite of the strong gravitation of wants. That is why just on seeing the light of dawn, dumping the piled up burden anywhere and anyhow, we are able to get on the cart again. Saying, 'nothing remains' we heave a deep sigh; likewise, saying, 'nothing moves' we do not fall into despair. It remains yet it does not, but in between these two conditions we have got space as well as refuge – we have got a house, light and air have not been lost as well.

23 December 1908
(8 *Pauṣ* 1315 BE)

End of Festival

Many a time, we go bankrupt holding festivals. Much of our days are spent in paying off our debts. When a person of modest means tries to fulfil his desire to be a king for a day, then there is no other option for him than to spend some days of his life in a beggarly fashion.

So, the day following the festival is extremely glum to us. On that day brightness of the sky is lost and our heart grows heavy with fatigue.

But, we have no choice. At least once a year man ceases to be miserly and tries to forge a relation of sharing with that generous One. Through wealth he wants to realize that God.

There are two kinds of realizations. One kind is like that of the poor man who realizes the wealth of the rich man through the gift he receives from him.

In this realization, the disparity felt is more. Another kind of realization is that of equality. In that case I do not have to sit outside the door, it is somewhat possible for me to sit on the same *jajim*.[52]

Every day when we are in a miserable state, our cheerless mind goes on to beg the Blissful One. On the day of the festival it tries to say, 'Today is not a day only to take, but also to rejoice as You do – today I have no poverty, no miserliness, my joy and my renunciation are as boundless as Yours'.

In this manner, if I realize what wealth means and what is meant by infinite abundance, then I understand and demonstrate to myself that God not only grants me grace, but is my very own.

But, in order to understand and to proclaim this, one has to suffer on many occasions in the end. Our mind becomes dispirited over the scattered leavings of food, melted candles and withered garlands seen on the day following the festival; then the heart loses its magnificent generosity; the mind becomes pained at the thought of settling up accounts.

But the person who saves a little every day, makes preparations daily to hold a festival, keeps no distinction between the day of the festival and every other day – rather retains a close connection between the two, does not have to endure suffering.

If that is not so, then we have to borrow to hold a festival. It is true that we rejoice, but the major part spent on that enjoyment is not exactly with our own money,[53] fifteen annas[54] of it is managed on borrowings. We borrow from the invited guests; from the flower garland, the lighting, the decoration of the hall; from the song, the music and the speech. Amid the excitement of that day we never remain conscious that we have borrowed. On the following day when the flowers wither, the lights are extinguished and the guests depart, at that instant the massive void of debt becomes apparent and makes the mind restless.

In this utter misery of ours, we immerse[55] the God of the festival as soon as the festival is over, we make no attempt to establish this very Lord of the festival at the helm of affairs in our everyday life.

It was our privilege that a few of us used to go to the temple premises every day at dawn and save a little together. We have not come to this festival like uninvited strangers,[56] and our daily morning savings have not been immediately spent as incidental expenses. It seems that we have been able to say to the Lord of the festival, 'I have a little acquaintance with You and have received Your invitation'.

Then we will not let our festival come to an end in a day all of a sudden, we will let this festival flow into our daily celebration. Every day at dawn this festival of a handful of us will go on. Amid all the trivialities of our daily life and in self-oblivion, at least once at the beginning of the day we will continue to realize the wealth of the eternal festival of the universe. Every day when Dawn will appear in the east holding Its light in Its hand, the few of us will calmly sit and realize that each day of our life is indeed glorious, full of wealth – the trivialities of our life have not in the least soiled It. Every day It is novel, It is luminous, It is that supreme wonder. Not a drop of its content gets depleted from the pot of amrita held in Its hand even when it is completely upturned.

24 December 1908
(9 *Pauṣ* 1315 BE)

Ferry Me Across

On that very day, when the mela had dispersed at dawn amidst various fun, frolic and gossip, a song was in the air: 'O God,[57] ferry me across!' I simply cannot forget that song. It amazes me even today.

It is surprising that for so long man has consistently been uttering these words 'ferry me across'. I cannot even understand whether he himself knows his wish fully or not.

If a *sādhaka*[58] renounces all worldly efforts and stands on the bank of his sea of sadhana and says, 'O Benefactor of attainment, ferry me across to the shore of attainment!' then I can understand the meaning of that. But, a person who has no aim, no sadhana before him – where is his boatman, where is his sea, what does he want to ferry across? Where exactly lies his this shore and where else lies his other shore?

Amidst a wide variety of activities that we perform, we say, 'O God,[59] ferry me across!' As the coachman drives his coach he says, 'ferry me across', when the grocer weighs the rice and pulses he too says, 'ferry me across'.

Do not presume they say, 'Ferry us from this very work of ours'. They want to stay amid their work and be ferried across and that is why their work is not being neglected as they sing.

O Sea of Bliss! This very shore is Yours, the other shore too is Yours. But, when I term one shore as mine then there arises a separation between this shore and the other. Then it is deprived of the realization of its completeness, inwardly its heart keeps wailing for the other shore. The "I" of my shore is estranged[60] from the "You" of Your shore. That is why there is so much outcry to be ferried across.

Considering this to be my house, the person "I" toils endlessly for it day and night. Until that person "I" is able to say, 'This is Your house too', there is no limit to the immense suffering, severe bondage and acute loss that he undergoes. Until then as he performs his duties at home, his inner atman cries out, "O God, ferry me across!" Whenever he is able to make his house as Your house, then by being in his house itself he is ferried across. When the person 'I' hurries about breathlessly day and night thinking that whatever he does is his own work, he not only gets hurt, but also hurts others in turn, only then he sings, "Ferry me across". The moment he can say, "It is Your work", he has already been ferried across.

You and I can unite only when I make my home as Your home, my work as Your work. This utterance that I shall leave my home for Your home, leave my work for Your work, is not the utterance of our hearts. It is because this too is the utterance of separation. The 'I' devoid of You, and the 'You' devoid of 'I', both appear the same to me.

That is why within our home itself, within the fair of our activities, day and night there is the cry of 'O God, ferry me across!' Here itself lies the sea, here itself lies the shore.

26 December 1908
(11 *Pauṣ* 1315 BE)

This Shore – the Other Shore

The person with whom I have only a nodding acquaintance, even if he sits right beside me, there lies a sea of distance between the two of us – that distance is the sea of ignorance, the sea of indifference. If someday that person happens to become my closest friend, just then do I ferry across the sea. Then the spatial[61] distance becomes untrue, even the distance between the bodies does not remain a distance anymore, so much so that even the estrangement caused by death does not create any distance. That pride builds a wall from all sides to keep a distance between us even though we are very close to each other, the person for whom that pride makes way becomes our very own.

That is why I said yesterday that to ferry across the sea is not simply a matter of going across a far-off place, it is to bring that which is indeed close to us, even closer.

In fact, the object which is so very close to us when kept at the farthest possible distance, its distance too is so very terrible indeed. It is for this very reason when we make our relative a stranger, we distance him farther than even the one who is unrelated to us. When we do not even have feeling for the person with whom we are in close contact, then that passivity is more severe than the inertness of death.

It is for this very reason, when we know the One who is the closest to us in the whole universe as being far away, He gets farthest away from all the people of the world; He who is the Heart of our hearts stands even farther than that gross wall, then He goes farthest away from all the distances in the world. Though we do not clearly feel the pain of this distance, it is due to the burden of this distance that our daily existence, our household, our activities and all our social relations become burdensome.

Yet, the seashore for which we are wailing about, is so very near – it is even nearer than this very side of the shore and those who know about it have stated that very clearly. We are utterly amazed when we come to hear of it – we feel, that which we had regarded to be so very distant is, in fact, so very close. This is what we had termed as unreachable, shoreless and impossible!

What do the persons that have ferried across the sea say? They say, "*Eṣāsya paramā gatiḥ, eṣāsya paramāsampat, eṣāhasya paramo lokaḥ, eṣohasya param ānandaḥ.*[62]" *Eṣaḥ*[63] means He – the person who is truly before us, the one who is really close to us. *Asya* means its – that is also very close. It is He who is its supreme motion.

He who is the Supreme Motion is not in the least away from it.[64] He is so close that He can be termed as "this person", there is no need to call Him even by His name – apart from saying, 'This is He', He does not need any further introduction. He Himself is its everything. In fact, who "He" is and whose is "its" is ever left untold. One who is on this side of the shore does not just address the one on the other shore of the sea as *eṣaḥ*, does not call him "He".

He Himself is its supreme motion. It is true we move, but who makes us move? We think money makes us move, fame makes us move, human race makes us move. He who has been ferried across says, "It is He who is 'its' motion" – it is by His pull that it moves – there is pull of money, pull of fame, pull of human race, but amongst all the pull, the supreme pull is His – all the pull may go but His pull will remain – because in all the movements, the urge to go to Him is inherent. Even Money does not say, 'You remain here'; neither does Fame nor does human race say so – all say, 'You move on'. He who is the Supreme Motion Himself is providing motion, who else then would dare to create obstruction in the path of that motion permanently?

Perhaps we may think that the earth that pulls me is the pull of the earth itself. But, if that be so, who pulls the earth? Who pulls the sun? The fact that this very universal pull through which the planets, the stars and the constellations are made to revolve and none is allowed to remain static, the centre of that vast centripetal pull is, in fact, not there within the earth. There is one Supreme Motion, that Motion is also my motion, also the motion of the earth, the motion of the sun as well.

Keeping this Supreme Motion in view, the Upanishads said, 'kohyevānyāt kaḥ prāṇyāt yadesa ākāśa ānanda na syāt'[65] – if the space were not completely pervaded by that Bliss then who else would have cared to make even the least effort? It is that Bliss which has rendered that infinite motion to the universe. It is because there is Bliss throughout the space that I am able to open my eyes.

So I say, my supreme motion is not far away, it is within all my minute movements. For instance, there is the universal force of gravitation in the falling of the apple to the ground. In all the movements of my body, and in all the efforts of my mind, He who is the Supreme Motion, is *eṣaḥ*, is this He. The centre of that motion is not far – it is here itself.

After that, He who is our supreme wealth, our supreme refuge, our supreme joy – He Himself dwells within all our glory, all our refuge and all the joys of our everyday life. Amidst our men and money, our household and the very essence of our entire enjoyment, the One who is there in His Supreme Form is *eṣaḥ* – He is indeed this person – He is here itself.

I will know all my motion as that supreme motion, all my wealth as that supreme wealth, all my refuge as that supreme refuge, all my joy as that supreme joy and will know it as *eṣaḥ* – this itself is said to be ferried across.

27 December 1908
(12 *Pauṣ* 1315 BE)

Day

Every day our life move on through light and darkness, sleep and wakefulness, contraction and expansion – once it ebbs, again it flows. At night when we sleep, all the powers of our sense organs and mind withdraw within us. In the morning they rush towards the whole world.

Do we know ourselves more and attain ourselves more when power is accumulated within us? Again, do we then just lose ourselves when in the morning our power starts getting dispersed towards others in all directions?

It is just the opposite. When we are only within ourselves we are unconscious, when we move towards all, we are awake. It is only then that we know ourselves. When we are alone we have no identity.

Our true significance does not lie within us, it pervades everything in the world. That is why with our intellect, with our heart, with our action, we are only in search of the whole; we are continuously trying to unite ourselves with the whole; or else we do not attain ourselves. We will realize the Atman everywhere – this is the only aspiration of the atman.

When the *jñānī*[66] observed this force of the falling apple in all things of the universe then his intellect was immensely satisfied. That is because when Truth is observed everywhere it is only then that its true form is manifested and that form itself gives us joy.

Similarly, when we see ourselves pervaded everywhere, only then do we see us in our true form. The more we know of the pervading nature of this truth, the more joy we obtain. Whoever brings our inner self outwards and manifests it to us in its truest form is our very own and gives us joy.

That is why from ancient times whatever man has been creating in terms of home, society and state, the only inner significance of all those is that by avoiding loneliness, by extending his diverse powers through different connections, man will realize himself in a vast realm amidst the many, amidst the variety – that is his true happiness. That is why it has been said 'bhūmaiva sukhaṁ, nālpe sukhamasti'[67] – that which is Infinite is happiness, there is no happiness in the finite. This is because within the finite the atman too becomes finite.

Just because the society which is civilized connects the many with the atman in diverse ways, it becomes the glory of the society. Otherwise, only the abundance of paraphernalia and the mere accumulation of facilities are not its fulfilment.

In a civilized society where knowledge, love and effort to do work are always active in the far-extended sphere, the man who lives there does not remain insignificant. Even if the power of that person is limited, that power easily gets the opportunity to attain its own fulfilment. That is why through the union with all, through the union with the Omnipresent, each inhabitant of a civilized society becomes strong as much as possible.

In an uncivilized society, even the person who is strong by nature becomes weak. That is because the people of such a society do not realize their own selves in enough measure. All the institutions that exist in that society are suitable only for the home and the village. There is no connection of the Omnipresent with those narrow institutions – the vast expanse of mind like the high tide of the sea does not reach there. That is why man cannot attain power by realizing his own truth, his own glory, he remains defeated everywhere. There lies no end to his poverty.

It is only for this reason that we have to practise sadhana for the sake of civilization, not for the sake of railway or telegraph. This is because man is also the ultimate destination of railway and telegraph – not any particular local station.

The fundamental concept of this sadhana for civilization is the knowledge of dharma. The lesser the degree of progress one makes, the lesser it does for him to have the knowledge of dharma. When we work in a confined place in our own homes it does not do us much harm even if the knowledge of dharma is narrow. But, the knowledge of dharma must be strong where innumerable people are to be bound in numerous bonds. There all these qualities like patience, might, perseverance, renunciation, service to others, benevolence are absolutely necessary in considerable measure. A thing can never become great if the appropriate dharma used to bind it is also not great. Whenever dharma is weak, it is only then that the vast society gets disintegrated and scattered in all directions, never ever can one bind it together.

Hence, whenever we observe some civilized society which is quite eventful, vast and is extremely powerful, then initially we have to assume that there lies a strong knowledge of dharma within it – or else, not even for a moment there can be any mutual faith and mutual bond among so many people.

In the society of our country too, if it is not possible to establish the Omnipresent through knowledge, love and action by dispelling all smallness and alienation, then the atman can never be strong and joyful. The more the union of a common man gets obstructed with everyone due to various customs and practices, the more our sadness, inability and poverty go on increasing. If we cannot create various opportunities for union with the many in our country, our *tapasyā*[68] for greatness will be fruitless.

We are making efforts to create such opportunities from various directions. But whether big or small, if we always observe disjointedness in whatever we want to bind together, then surely we have to understand that at the root of it all there is weakness in the knowledge of dharma – definitely there is lack of Truth, dearth of renunciation and lethargy of will. Certainly respect has lost its power and from the articles of puja, our self-conceit is trying to steal away a large amount for itself; surely there is a feeling of mutual jealousy; there is no element of forgiveness; and being unable to consider welfare as the ultimate fruit of welfare itself, our perseverance is repelled even by a small obstacle.

Hence, we must be careful. Where success gets obstructed, may we not try to be unworried by accusing the mute articles. There is sin so nothing binds, there is lack of dharma and so we cannot hold on to anything. That is why by being alienated, by being insignificant, we just drift along being futile in all respects; that is why neither does our knowledge perfectly unite with Knowledge, nor does the heart unite with the Heart, nor does effort unite with Effort to create an appropriate temple of the human atman – by no means is our atman able to assume its great form worthy of uniting with that Great Being, Viśvakarmā.[69]

28 December 1908
(13 *Pauṣ* 1315 BE)

Night

Yesterday, I did not cover a topic about night and day, sleeping and waking. That itself is the main topic.

When we stay awake, there is a sport between our power and the Power. There is a union of our action with the Universal Action of Viśvakarmā. It is by directing our efforts through those diverse chains of numerous divisions of the Power of the One who is 'bahudhā śaktiyogād varṇānanekānnihitārthodadhāti',[70] that we discover the wonderful flow of our powers and become joyous. At one time we thought power had got exhausted at a point, but as we proceed we see from that point the path has taken a new turn again. In this way, within the diverse powers of the universal phenomena, diversifying our own powers as well, our mind gets encouraged to attain equal motion with that in every respect.

In this manner our awakened consciousness fulfils itself by means of various motions, touches and gains by casting the net of all the powers of the senses and of the mind in all directions.

But, the fisherman cannot survive merely by casting the net. The net gets knotted, gets almost torn and gets soiled. Then in order to mend the net again, the practice of casting the net has to be totally stopped.

At night, during sleep, we completely stop casting the net of our prana, of our consciousness. That is the time to mend and to pay for damages. At that time we have to surrender our torn, knotted and soiled net into His hands, 'Ya eṣa supteṣu jāgarti kāmaṁ puruṣo nimirmāṇaḥ',[71] to the One who is creating all the necessary things by being awake when everyone has fallen into a slumber.

Hence, for once, by restraining all our efforts, we have to completely surrender our prana to the hands of that Universal Prana – at that time we become identical with the vegetation, there remains no alienation between nature and us, our ego gets completely suppressed, only then do we attain the profound ease that prevails within the entire universe. On waking we realize that the repose we enjoyed for so long was not simply a form of emptiness, but of fullness. It is the ease even in the midst of our inactivity and unconsciousness – that is the fundamental ease of this vast universal nature. The image of greenness and silent manifestation of that ease we see amidst the sprouting foliage of a calm and very large tree.

The very manner in which we surrender our prana to nature every night to get prepared again for new efforts to regain prana the following morning, likewise, during the day there is a need for us to completely surrender our atman to the Supreme Atman at least once. Otherwise, wastes start to pile up, the broken pieces never get mended, the passions go on increasing – by exceeding their needs, the desires of lust, anger, greed, among others, rise in revolt both internally and externally.

That is why at dawn during *upāsanā*, by stopping all our efforts and by calming all our inherent cardinal passions, we need to establish a perfect harmony with the Supreme Atman for some time. At that time, we have to completely make way for the Supreme Atman within our hearts; if that happens then in that opportune moment of profound peace gained from extreme self-sacrifice, there will be an infusion of health into our ailing mind. Only then will all the contractions be relaxed and all the knots in our hearts will gradually loosen.

After that, by being fragmented and pervaded through various ways and means when our inner nature calmed by *upāsanā* gets engaged in self-realization amidst the variety and plenty of the world, then it will be able to devote itself to all work with solemnity and purity; it will not continue to hurt all things around it every now and then; peace will then prevail over all its efforts. As there is an amazing harmony within the diverse phenomena of this vast universe and the existence of which has made all forms of efforts to be peaceful and all forms of power to be beautiful – the presence of which has neither turned the universe into a rigid form of a scientific laboratory nor an enormous factory building – that harmony should be there in our efforts, that beauty should be reflected in our work. We shall learn that supremely beautiful manner in which God works by surrendering all our ego to Her for a while. We shall bring ourselves at Her feet and say, 'O Mother! Do touch us once with Your able hands at dawn, then whatever wounds that have been received by us due to the blows of the world of yesterday will all be healed'.

If every day at daybreak we receive the touch of Her holy hands upon our foreheads and if we remember that fact, then we will no longer let our foreheads be soiled with dust. May the tune of this *upāsanā*, like the tune of a tanpura, continue to play within us all day long – so that we may match and weigh up every word and action of ours with that tune and by turning the whole day into pure music, we can transform the realm of work of the world into the realm of joy.

29 December 1908
(14 *Pauṣ* 1315 BE)

At Dawn

At this pure and serene hour of dawn, for once see your atman as completely enclosed within the Supreme Atman, may the entire distance between them dissolve. Let us be completely engrossed and deeply absorbed, let us derive complete fulfilment from this realization that He has accepted our atman intimately and intensely.

Otherwise, we do not know our true identity. If we do not see ourselves as one with the Omnipresent, we are under the illusion that we are small and under the false notion that we are weak. Great men of the human race have proved that we are in no way small or weak – their attainments are, in fact, the attainments of each one of us – the power of our individual atman has been manifested in them. When the upper portion of the candle has been lighted, then that benefit is shared by the entire candle. Even the lowest portion of the candle has the capacity to burn – when the time comes it too will burn, till then, it will continue to support the burning of the upper portion.

Every day during *upāsanā* at dawn, may we be able to see the greatness of the atman within us devoid of any hindrance. May we be able to dispel the very illusion that we are utterly destitute. May we dispense with the notion that we have only been born at the corner of a room and clearly realize that this body of mine is born in the realms of *bhūrbhubaḥ svaḥ*.[72] That is why, from millions of miles away from us, our family of the effulgent heavenly bodies send their messenger of light to enquire about us. Again, it is not true that the ultimate abode of my atman lies within my very ego itself – the spiritual realm in which that dwells is the *Brahmaloka*.[73] We have come to the court of this world, our claim here is to rule and not to serve as slaves. It is the Supreme Being who has sent us with the royal tilak[74] on our forehead. Hence, let us not feel ourselves inferior and hang down our heads in shame and move around in this world with unease – may we be able to secure our esteemed place in the glory of our eternal nobility.

Just as the darkness of the night sky has given way to the light of dawn in an instant like an imaginary object, let all the stock notions in our minds dissolve in a moment. May our atman, like the rising sun, manifest its liberated effulgent form in our mindscape – let our earthly realm be completely illuminated everywhere in its effulgent consciousness, in its holy light.

30 December 1908
(15 *Pauṣ* 1315)

The Unique

In a general way, I have similarity with the people of the world; I have similarity with the fine dust particles and stones, I have similarity with the grass and tree; I have similarity with the animals and birds; I have similarity with the common man; but at one point I have similarity with none at all – there I am truly unique. The one I address today as 'I' has no second. Amidst the infinite universal creation of God, this creation is completely wonderful – this is only I, I alone, incomparable and unparalleled "I". The world of this "I" belongs only to me. In the realm of this utter solitariness no one has the opportunity to enter except my Indweller.

O my Lord! In that very lone "I", in that unique "I", lies Your unique bliss, Your unique manifestation – that unique manifestation is not there in any other time and place. Lord, I will fulfil that uniqueness of mine! That You have such an absolutely independent unique sport named "I", I shall join You in this particular sport. I will unite here as one unites with the One.

On earth, let my existence as a human being consciously bear that unique sport of Yours with beauty, music, purity and greatness. May it never, by any means, be forgotten that You have a unique abode in me. This very 'I' which exists in this infinite universe, may this "I" attain fulfilment in human life.

Since time immemorial You have borne this 'I' along as distinct from others. Holding hands You have brought it along with you through the sun, moon, planets and stars, but You have involved it with none. You have manifested this "I" in me today through innumerable developments, changes and evolutions, by shifting atoms and molecules from the luminous stream of vapours of a certain nebula. That association with You since ancient times has been saved in this body of mine. From time immemorial to the present day, in the midst of this infinite creation, a unique line has been traced, that is the mark of this very "I" – I have treaded that linear path by walking beside You all along. You are the guide of my eternal path, the only friend in the endless path, I will realize You as that lone friend in my life. May nothing else equal You, nor be greater than You. And, this very mundane life through which I experience various kinds of hunger and thirst, thought and effort, along with all the trees, creepers, animals and birds, may it never become overwhelming from various directions – may my life not veil the fact that within me there is Your unique touch, unique action, unique joy, as the eternal friend and guide. Where I belong to this universe, I acknowledge You as the Supreme Lord. I try to abide by all Your rules and if I fail, I accept Your punishment – but, in the form of "I", I want to know You as my sole One. There You have made me free – because, without freedom love will not be realized, will shall not unite with Will, there will not be any union between sport and Sport. That is why in the freedom of this realm of "I", of all my sorrows, my supreme sorrow lies in being separated from You and that is the sorrow of pride; of all other joys, my supreme joy lies in my union with You and that is the bliss of divine love. Meditating upon how to dispel the sorrow of this pride, Buddha practised *tapasyā* and proclaiming how this sorrow of ego could be dispelled, Christ sacrificed his life. O dearer than the offspring, dearer than wealth! O the Indweller! O, the Dearest! In this very abode of "I" lies Your divine sport. Hence here itself there is so much of intense sorrow and such boundless cessation of that sorrow; here there is death, and amrita springs out by rupturing the bosom of that death. The very joy and sorrow, union and separation, immortality and death are Your right and left arms – may I completely accept them and be able to say, 'All my wants have been fulfilled, I just don't want anything else'.

31 December 1908
(16 *Pauș* 1315 BE)

Beauty

God is 'Satyam.[75]' We are bound to accept His Truth. We would not have any freedom if we do not accept even this little Truth. Therefore, we see the infallible Truth everywhere – in water, land and sky.

But, He is not just Truth, He is 'ānandarūpamṛtam'.[76] He is the form of bliss, the form of immortality. Where do we see that form of His bliss?

I have already given a hint earlier that by its nature itself bliss is liberated. No force can be applied to it, no estimate can be made of it. That is why on the day when we celebrate the festival of bliss, we ease off[77] the routine of our daily life. On that day we minimize our self-interest, lessen our need, relax the difference between oneself and others, ease off severe constraint of the world – only then within our abode a little free space is created where the revelation of bliss is possible. Truth accepts only bonds while bliss accepts none.

That is why in the universal nature we see the image of Truth in rules, and the image of bliss in beauty. So it is essential for us to know the form of Truth, we may even do without knowing the form of bliss. It is extremely necessary to know and to make use of the fact that there is light at dawn when the sun rises. But it does no harm to any of our activities if we fail to know this little thing that dawn is beautiful and so very peaceful.

Water, land and sky confine us in various bonds. But in water, land and sky, the arrangement of the vast variety of beauty in its various colours, fragrances and music does not compel us to appreciate anything. If we go away without paying any attention to it, it does not even abuse us for our lack of appreciation.

Hence we see that in this universe we are bound in the realm of Truth and liberated in the realm of beauty. We can prove Truth irrefutably through logic, but there is no other means to prove beauty except through our boundless joy. When a person says with disregard, 'Fie upon your beauty!' even Lakṣmī[78] of this great universe has to remain completely quiet before him. No law, no bailiff can compel him to accept this beauty.

Hence, this very arrangement of God's amazing mysterious beauty throughout the universe does not collect any fees or dues from us, it desires our free will – it says, 'May there be joy between you and me; accept me of your own accord'.

That is why I was saying, in the unusual realm of this "I" within our inner atman, there is coming and going of that Blissful One and there is evidence of that throughout the universe. Indeed everywhere His footprints are seen in the blueness of the sky, in the greenness of the forests, in the fragrance of the flowers. If He had arrived there in the attire of a king I would have obeyed Him with folded hands; but, He, in fact, comes gently in the image of a friend, He comes all alone, none of his infantry holding the symbol of authority and beating drums of victory comes along with Him – that is why the slumber of sin never gets shaken off, the door continues to remain closed.

But, surely this will not do. If that unfortunate being does not willingly accept his obligation towards love just because he has no obligation towards rules, then through a succession of births he will only wander about aimlessly and be the slave of a slave. He will never know that human birth is, in fact, a birth of joy. O dear! In that very innermost abode where the rays of the sun and the moon do not reach, where even the most intimate person cannot gain access, where only His seat is placed, open the door of that place, turn the lights on. Just at dawn I clearly see that His effulgence has surrounded my whole being, may I be able to directly perceive that His bliss, will and love have enveloped my life closely and deeply in all respects. He too has made a firm resolve that He will not reveal His image of bliss to us by force – rather He would return daily again and again, rather His manifestation of this universal beauty would seem futile to me every day, yet He would not force me in the least. The day when my love would awaken, on that day His love will not in the least remain concealed from me anymore. The very reason why this "I", in spite of being 'I', wandered from door to door for so long with so much sorrow, the mystery behind that sorrow of estrangement will be unveiled in an instant on that day.

3 January 1909
(19 *Pauṣ* 1315 BE)

Law

Whenever the topic of will, love and bliss is raised, its opposite topic continues to strike the mind. It says, 'Why then is there so much of discipline and restriction? Why do I not get what I want? Why do I get burdened by that which I do not want?'

Here man has tried to answer this not by means of reason, he has tried to answer this only through faith. He said: *Sa eva bandhurjanitā sa vidhātā.*[79] It means He who has manifested me 'sa eva bandhuḥ',[80] is bound to be my friend. If His bliss had not been manifested in me then I would never have existed. Again, 'sa vidhātā',[81] God is second to none – He who is the Progenitor, is Himself the Friend, again it is He who is the Lawgiver. Hence, whatever be the law, essentially there is no fear.

But, it would not do if the law is inconsistent. It cannot be that today it is of one sort, tomorrow it is different, one law for me and another for others, there is no constancy in time and manner – this is certainly not law. Law is in fact the Universal Law.

From the dust of this earth to the stellar region, all are wreathed in an unbroken thread of this law. If for my own comfort and convenience I say, 'Sever the link of Your law at one place, at another place draw a special distinction between the law meant for others and for me', then indeed it means, 'While crossing the mud, my clothes are getting soiled. Hence tear away the connecting link of this universal necklace and scatter all the suns and stars on the path'.

This law is never meant for any individual and for any particular fraction of time – it is due to this connection of the Universal Law that each one of us is united with the whole, and at no point in time will this union get separated. The Upanishads said, "He who is the Lord of this universe, He is 'yathātathyatoharthān vyadadhāt śāśvatībhyaḥ samābhyaḥ'".[82] He has been making all laws appropriately since time immemorial and for all eternity. The root of this law is eternal – this law is without beginning or end. After that, once again this law conforms to 'yathā tathyataḥ';[83] from beginning to end, it is accurate, nowhere is there any break or inconsistency. Modern science has not stated anything with more force and clarity than this regarding the Universal Law.

But, if that be so, if He only sits on the iron-throne of that infallible law as the Lawgiver, then we only become equivalent to wood and stone, sand and dust before Him. In that case, we just become captives kept in chains.

But He is not only the Lawgiver, 'sa eva bandhuḥ',[84] He is indeed the Friend.

In fact, I see the manifestation of God throughout the universe, but where is His manifestation as a Friend? His manifestation as a Friend is certainly not within the realm of law – where else will that manifestation be if not in the realm of love within me?

The realm of God's action is within this universal nature, and the abode of bliss of the friend is within my individual atman.

Man is on one hand nature and on the other hand atman – on one hand he pays the dues of the King and on the other hand he arranges the basket of offerings for his Friend. On one hand with the help of Truth he has to attain welfare, on the other hand he has to become beautiful through welfare.

Nature lies in the direction in which God's will gets manifested in the form of law and the atman lies in the direction where God's will gets manifested in the form of bliss. The dharma of nature is bondage while the dharma of atman is mukti. Truth and bliss, bondage and mukti, represent His left and right arms. It is with these two arms that He has held mankind.

On the side in which I am equivalent to a brick, a piece of wood, a tree and a stone, in that general direction God's all-pervading Law does not in the least allow me to be different from the ordinary entity. Again in that direction where I am uniquely "I", in no way does God's unique bliss allow me to unite with all. The Lawgiver has made me belong to all and the Friend has made me His own – the thing that belongs to all is my nature, and the thing that is His own is my individual atman.

5 January 1909
(21 *Pauṣ* 1315 BE)

Three

Towards nature there is rule and towards our atman there is bliss. It is only through rules that we can unite with rules and it is only through bliss that we can unite with bliss.

Hence, where I belong to the common man, to the universal nature and to the human nature, if I do not conform myself to the rules there, I only become unsuccessful and create unrest. I cannot cajole even a particle of dust into doing something for me; if I observe its rules, only then does it observe mine.

For this reason, our first lesson is to learn the rules of nature and also to learn to follow the rules ourselves. It is through this education that we get acquainted with Truth.

He who is the culmination of this knowledge is Himself 'Śāntam'.[85] Wherever there is deviation from rules, wherever there is no union of one rule with another, there itself is unrest, wherever there is complete union, there itself is complete realization of He who is *Śāntam*.

Which form of God do we see in nature? We see His *śānta*[86] form. There, those that see this form narrowly see the effort and those that see it extensively see only peace. If the rules were fragmented, if the rules were not eternal and accurate then within a moment this vast universal peace would have been destroyed and would have given rise to a violent dance of meaningless and endless destruction; then in the whole world, contradiction would have emerged triumphant and would have torn apart everything fiercely with all its might. But take a look, amid the powerful excitation in the realm of the sun and the stars, Supreme Peace exists in the unwavering seat of rule. This very form of Truth is *Śāntam*.

It is because Truth is *Śāntam*, It is *Śivam*.[87] It is because He is *Śāntam* that He accepts all, protects all and everyone has taken eternal refuge in Him. Wherever we too have not been able to restrain ourselves, where we have not known the Truth and have not remained true to It, there we are bound to have unrest within and without, and it is that unrest which is ominous – the separation of one rule from another is, in fact, inauspicious.[88]

Advaitam[89] is manifested in the One who is *Śivam*. Where Truth is in the form of *śivam*, He is full of bliss, full of love; there lies His union with all. There is no union except in welfare;[90] evil itself is the demon of contradiction and separation.

At one end there is Truth and at the other there is bliss, there is welfare in between. So, it is through this welfare that we have to go to the abode of bliss.

The three stages of life that we had in our country – *brahmacharya*,[91] *gārhasthya*[92] and *vāṇaprastha*,[93] are established on these three forms of God – the forms of *śānta*, *śiva*[94] and *advaita*.[95]

If the form of *śānta* is attained through the practice of *brahmacharya* only then it becomes possible to realize the form of *śiva* within household dharma; or else, *gārhasthya* becomes the source of misfortune. To establish that welfare in the world, all self-interests get completely defeated and we understand to what extent the nature of true union is established by pure self-sacrifice. When we understand that completely, only then does it become possible to attain unimpeded union in love in every way with *Advaitam* who is that Supreme Atman in the form of Oneness.[96] In the beginning there is acquaintance with Truth, in the middle with welfare and at the end with bliss. First we gain knowledge, then we take action and finally we obtain love.

Just as our mantra of dhyana is 'śāntaṁ śivaṁ advaitam',[97] the mantra of our prayer is: *Asato mā sadgamaya, tamaso mā jyotirgamaya, mṛtyormamṛtam gamaya.*[98] Take me from untruth to Truth, from vice to virtue and from attachment to love. Only then, O Manifestation, You will be my manifestation; only then, O Rudra, You will become favourable in my life.

The culmination is neither in truth nor in welfare, but surely in *advaita*. The culmination is neither in universal nature nor in social order, but surely in the

Supreme Atman. This is the message of our *Bhāratavarṣa* – may we be able to make this message fruitful in our lives, may this be our only prayer.

6 January 1909
(22 *Pauṣ* 1315 BE)

The Whole

The One who has awakened us this morning has done so from every aspect. The rays of this light which has been emitted is also providing light in the sphere of our action, in the sphere of our knowledge, as well as in the sphere of our beauty. He has not sent separate messengers for all these different paths we tread; it is the same messenger sent by Him who has appeared smilingly before us as the only one representing all the paths.

But, the very nature of our understanding is such that we cannot see Truth as a whole in an instant. At first, we see It in parts and then we connect the parts to see It as a whole. In this manner when we try to see Truth in terms of Its fragments, we undoubtedly make the mistake to see It as a whole. In a picture there is the theory of perspective; according to that, the one which is far away is drawn smaller and that which is nearer is drawn bigger. If we do not do that then the picture does not appear true to us. But, in the case of the whole Truth there is nothing like far and near, all is of equal nearness. That is why after we see the nearer as bigger and the one that is far away as smaller, we need to rectify that on the basis of the whole Truth.

When man attempts to see the whole all at once, he sees it hazily, hence he first sees it in parts and then he unites the parts into the whole. For this reason, if he sees only the parts and completely denies the whole, then he has to be seriously answerable for that; again, if he only aims at the whole and completely ignores the parts then that emptiness[99] becomes totally futile for him.

For the past few days we had been observing the physical and the spiritual realms independent of each other. If it is not done in this manner, their clear pictures cannot be seen directly by us. But, when we get to know each one very clearly then there comes a time to rectify a great mistake. Again, there is a danger if we do not see these two unitedly.

Where these physical and spiritual realms have attained a complete harmony, may our aim not deviate from there at all. Where both have an established relation with each other amidst Truth, there may we not cause any internal discord between them by untruth. May we not build a wall merely through speech, reason and delusion and make the mistake of regarding that to be the only matter of Truth.

Just as the east and the west are held firmly together in an unbroken sphere, so the physical and the spiritual realms are firmly held together in an undivided whole. Amidst this, the moment we try to reject any one of them we would be found guilty before the whole, and the punishment for that offence is inevitable.

The extent to which *Bhāratvarṣa* has become excessively inclined towards spirituality and has lost its gravity towards physicality, it has to count and pay the fine to the same proportion even today, so much so that it is about to give away whatever possession it has. *Bhāratvarṣa* has lost its prosperity today and the reason for this is like that of a single-eyed deer which was not aware that the hunter's deadly arrow would strike it on the very side it had lost its sight. On the physical side it was carelessly blind; the physical realm has shot a death-arrow to it.

If it be true that the Western race is totally mad to attain complete success just in the physical sphere, then certainly it is to be known that one day the deadly divine missile[100] will strike the core of its heart from the other side.

Those that have unity at the root, when disunited from that, they not only get alienated, but also become opposed to each other. Those who remain as kin due to the inherent attraction, get tempted to indulge in annihilating clash through estrangement.

Arjuna[101] and Karṇa[102] were brothers born of the same mother. Meanwhile, if they had not lost the mutual bond with Kuntī[103] then being united with each other they would have been extremely powerful. Due to that inherent bond which they had forgotten, they went on saying, 'Either I would die or else you would'.

Similarly, if we direct our sadhana either primarily towards the physical realm or towards the atman then that results in a conflict between our inner nature[104] and the atman. Then the physical realm says, 'Let the atman die and I continue to live'. The atman says, 'Let the physical realm be utterly ruined, let me claim sovereignty'. Then those that belong to the group of the physical realm try to establish action as powerful and all the paraphernalia needed for it as enormous; there is no further room for compassion and affection, cessation and rest. On the other hand, those that belong to the group of the atman, completely stop the provision for the physical realm, completely put a stop to the role of action and completely try to uproot the physical realm by devising various odd tricks. They do not know that the well-being of their atman also rests upon one and the same root.

In this manner, it is mankind who creates a separation between those two realms that are the most intimate and the supreme support for each other, and turns them into formidable enemies. There is no such terrible enmity like this – because, both these sides are extremely powerful.

Hence, when we have seen the physical and the spiritual aspects of man independently, then as soon as possible it is necessary to see these two as perfectly united within absolute wholeness. May we not wrongfully attempt to tug at the bond of friendship of these two eternal friends so as not to enrage them both.

10 January 1909
(26 *Pauṣ* 1315 BE)

Power

Wherever the three streams of knowledge, love and power are united, there itself lies the holy place of bliss. The extent to which there is complete union of knowledge, love and action within us, our complete bliss lies to that very extent itself. The moment there is separation, there is suffering as well.

So, being tempted to use short cuts whenever we deceive someone, we would simply happen to deceive ourselves. If we think that we would ignore the door-keeper to pay a visit to the king, then we would be so disgraced at the main entrance that to pay a visit to the king would itself become difficult. If we think that by disregarding rules we will go beyond it, then we would have to undergo immense sorrow in the hands of irate rules.

When we accept a law completely only then do we obtain authority over it. The person who wants to become the head of a household has to conform to rules and regulations of the household more than all the others – it is through that acceptance alone he attains the right to authority.

That is why I said, while staying in the world itself we can go beyond the world, while staying within work itself we can go beyond work. That is in no way possible through renunciation or by running away.

This is because, the mukti attained by us becomes true only when obtained by our innate nature, not by the lack of it. If it is obtained only through completeness it attains fulfilment, through emptiness it results only in fruitlessness.

Hence, aim towards Brahman who is by nature liberated. He is not at all liberated in the form of "No", He is liberated only in the form of "Yes". He is Om; that is, He is "Yes".

That is the reason why the knowers of Brahman did not term Him inactive, they have very clearly called Him active. They said –

Parāsya śaktirvividhaiva śrūyate svābhāvikī jñānabalakriyā ca.[105]

I have heard that His supreme power and His diverse power, also His action of knowledge and His action of power are all innate.

For Brahman, action is innate, that is, the root of all His actions is within His nature itself and not without. He Himself is engaged in action, no one is making Him act.

In this way He is liberated only through His action because this action is innate in Him. There is also the innateness of action within us. Our power wants to get liberated within action – not only for external necessities, but for internal revelation as well.

It is for that reason, our innate mukti lies in our action itself. It is in action alone that we get liberated, get manifested. But, whatever causes mukti can also cause bondage. The tow rope by which a boat is towed away, it is that very tow rope which can be used to tie it. When the tow rope pulls the boat outwards only then it moves, when that rope pulls it towards itself, it remains immobile.

When our action also remains confined within the narrowness of our self-interest then that action becomes a terrible bondage. At that instant our power moves against that supreme power and against that diverse power. Then it does not move towards the Omnipresent, it does not move towards the many, it becomes confined within its own smallness. Then this power does not give us mukti, does not give us bliss, it only turns us in the opposite direction. The person who is devoid of action and is lazy, it is only he who is confined. The person who is engaged in trivial action and is selfish, undergoes rigorous imprisonment in the whole world. Day and night, in the prison of self-interest, he continues to go round in circles about a fixed point within a limited periphery, just as in a grinding mill and does not even have the capability to retain the fruit of this labour forever; he has to give it up, it is only toil that he is left with.

Hence, only to direct the action from self-interest to the Supreme Truth is mukti, to renounce action is not mukti. Whatever action we do, whether big or small, if we connect that with the innate universal action of the Supreme Atman, then that action cannot confine us to anything anymore – that action will turn into the action of Truth, the action of welfare and the action of bliss.

12 January 1909
(28 *Pauṣ* 1315 BE)

Prana

Ātmakrīḍa ātmaratiḥ kriyāvān eṣa brahmavidāṁ variṣṭhaḥ.[106] Those that are the greatest among the knowers of Brahman, their sport lies in the Supreme Atman, their bliss lies in the Supreme Atman, and they are always active.

Not only do they have bliss, they have action as well. By referring only to the first half of this sloka, the meaning of this utterance will be clearer.

Prāṇahyeṣa yaḥ sarvabhūtairvibhāti vijānan vidvān bhabate nātivādī.[107] He who manifests Himself as Prana within all, he who knows Him does not make any utterance beyond Him.

In prana, both bliss and action remain united together. In the effort of prana itself lies its bliss, and in the bliss of prana itself lies its effort.

Hence, if Brahman Himself is the form of Prana of the entire creation, if amidst the creation He Himself is infusing bliss through motion and motion through bliss, then he who is the knower of Brahman will not merely rejoice with Brahman, but will also perform action with Him.

He indeed is the knower of Brahman. It is not that he knows only Brahman, but he also speaks of Brahman. How would his bliss restrain itself if he does not speak of Brahman? He takes Brahman, the manifestation of Prana of the universe, within his prana and is 'bhabate nātivādī'.[108] That means, he does not want to speak of anything else but Brahman, he wants to speak only of Brahman.

How does man speak of Brahman? It is just in the manner the string of a sitar speaks to a song. It is through all its motion, vibration and action that it speaks – by manifesting the song in every respect it attains its own fulfilment.

How does Brahman speak of Himself? He speaks through His own action by pervading the infinite space with light and form, with rhythm and resonance! *Ānanda rūpamṛtaṁ yadvibhāti.*[109] Within action itself He utters His own message of bliss, sings[110] His own song of immortality. His very bliss and action have completely mingled together and have pervaded the realms of heaven and earth.

Even when the knower of Brahman speaks of Brahman, how else will he speak of Him? He has to speak of Him through action alone. He has to be always active.

What kind of action is that? Well,[111] it is that action through which he gets manifested as 'Ātmakrīḍa ātmaratiḥ',[112] that his sport is in the Supreme Atman, that his bliss lies in the Supreme Atman. It is that action which manifests that his bliss is not in fulfilling his own self-interest, not in spreading his own glory. He is truly 'nātivādī'[113] – in his action he does not want to manifest anyone else other than the Supreme Atman.

That is why that 'brahmavidāṁ variṣṭhaḥ'[114] in every action of his life echoes this music of *śāntaṁ śivamadvaitam*[115] through different languages and forms. The universal action sings in the same rhythm and in the same *rāgiṇī*[116] with his individual action.

The sport of the atman within is the sport with the Supreme Atman as well and that indeed is the action of life without. The bliss which is within is surging into the action which is without, that action which is without is repeatedly returning to that bliss which is within. In this way within and without there continues a wonderfully graceful cycle of bliss and action and due to the speed of that rotation newer realms of welfare are being created. Due to that cyclic motion, light is illuminated and love is overflowing.

In this way He who is manifested in the whole universe in the form of Prana, manifested at the same time in the forms of bliss and action, is that very Prana which the knower of Brahman manifests through his own prana itself.

So my prayer is this, 'Ye manifestation of Prana, may the string of my sitar not get rusted, may it not collect dust – may it keep playing day and night with the rhythm struck by the Universal Prana – may it keep playing in the music of action – may it keep playing in Your very name. Even if the string gets torn at times due to the powerful stroke, that too is acceptable, but may it not be slackened, may it not be unclean, may it not become futile. May its tune gradually rise in pitch, become grave, may it dispense with all obscurity and become True – may it pervade through nature and echo within the human atman – Ye *Āviḥ*, may it be blessed by Your manifestation!'

13 January 1909
(29 *Pauṣ* 1315 BE)

Place for Pilgrimage

Today I say once again: "meditate on He who resides within!" There is, in fact, a need to say this every day. When will the need to say, "we have the Eternal Refuge within us" come to an end?

Words get old and indistinct, their inner meanings gradually become obscure to us; at that time we avoid them as unnecessary. But, do the need to use them ever cease?

In this world, it is only the outside which is very familiar to us, that is why our mind considers the outside as our sole refuge. It seems that the infinite universe within us which always moves along with us, does not favour us at all. If our acquaintance with it were very clear then the sovereignty of the outside could not become so unbearable for us. Then the moment a harm had been done outside, we could not have considered that to be such a great loss, and by considering the rule of the outside as the ultimate one, we would not have decided to conform to that alone as our only goal.

Today our yardstick, beam balance and touchstone are all outside. On the basis of what people will say and do, we have already decided all that is right and wrong for us – that is why the words of people hurt us so deeply, the actions of people perturb us in an extreme manner, fear of public opinion is such a great fear, public disgrace is such an overwhelming disgrace. So, when people abandon us, we feel that we have no one else in the world. At that time, we do not have the confidence to say –

The one who is deserted by all, who has none to call his own,
It is You who are with him, there lies Your love –
Shelterless one who has the road as his home
He too dwells in Your abode.

The one who has been abandoned by all is not forsaken within his atman even for a moment; the inner shelter of the person, whose home is the road, cannot be snatched away for a moment even by the most powerful tyrant. The man who has not erred against the Indweller, in no way can people of the outside world punish him by putting him in a prison and by sending him to the gallows.

We exist in this world like subjects of an anarchical kingdom, no one protects us, we remain outside, many of our powers are being snatched away from diverse directions. There is no trace as to how much is being unnecessarily robbed of us; he whose weapon is sharp is piercing our inmost conviction, the person whose power is more is keeping us under his feet. We move from door to door to seek refuge from various people for the sake of happiness, prosperity and self-protection. Even for once we do not have any knowledge that our King is seated in the unwavering throne of our inner atman.

Simply because we do not have the knowledge of that, we have given outsiders all the responsibility to judge, and I too judge others externally. I am unable to forgive anybody truly and to love someone eternally, the wish to do welfare constantly becomes narrow and gets obstructed.

Until I achieve that Truth, that welfare and that love with complete ease, every day I have to say: "meditate upon He who is within". If I do not truly realize the Truth within my inner atman then I would not be able to see that Truth within others as well and will not be able to establish a true relationship with them. When I know that I am within the Supreme Atman and that the Supreme Atman is within me, then as I see another person I will surely be able to see that he too is within the Supreme Atman and the Supreme Atman is within him – then it would be easy for me to show forgiveness, love and tolerance towards him, then self-restraint would not merely be an external observance of rule. Until that happens, the outside remains everything to us and puts a veil completely across everything obstructing all recesses – we only have to say –

Meditate upon the One who remains within –
Leave out every other thing.
In worldly crisis there's no relief at all
Except in performing His sadhana.

This is because, if one only knows the world to be the sole entity then it becomes full of crisis – it is only at that point anarchy takes advantage of the helpless being and utterly ruins him.

Come every day, come to the innermost core of the heart. May all uproar cease and no harm reach over there, may no defilement touch that place. Do not let anger harbour there, do not give indulgence to distress, do not fan the desires into flame – because, that is the very place for your pilgrimage, for your temple of God. If you do not obtain a little solitude at that place then there is no place on earth where you can obtain any solitude, if you harbour any defilement there then the gates of all holy places on earth will be closed to you for ever. Come into that unperturbed pure heart, come to the shore of the ocean of that Infinite, come to that mountain peak of the very high One. Stand there with hands folded together. Bow there and make namaskar. Every day, after worship, carry the holy water from that vast mass of ocean-water, from that water which is perennially flowing from the waterfall of the mountain peak and sprinkle that over your outside world; all sins will be cleansed, all afflictions will cease.

16 February 1909
(4 *Phālgun* 1315)

Observer

Save your inner realm from the attacks of the external one. Do not combine the two and see them as one. Do not consider everything to be solely intrinsic to the world. If you do so, you will not find any way out of the worldly crisis.

Time and again, in the midst of violent clashes of actions, realize your heart to be detached. Every now and then realization has to be made repeatedly in this manner. Amidst immense uproar it has to be instantly seen once that no such noise reaches the inner atman. There all is peaceful, calm and pure. In no way would we allow any external turmoil to enter there. Amid this huge crowd of coming and going, social formalities, fun and frolic, delve deep into the innermost core of your heart with lightning speed – go there and see the lamp burning steadily, the sea devoid of high waves is still in its own bottomless depth, the cry of sorrow does not reach there, the roar of anger is silent over there.

In this whole world there is nothing at all, not even a grain, which the Supreme Atman has not pervaded; but in spite of that, He is an Observer, He is under the control of none. This universe is no doubt His. Though He is undoubtedly Omnipresent, He is beyond it.

We should know our inner atman in a similar manner – the world is His, the human body is His, the intellect is His and the heart is His. He indeed pervades the world, the body, the intellect and the heart, yet our inner atman transcends this world, this body, this intellect and this heart. He is the Observer. This very "I" that has been born into this world, has assumed a particular name and has experienced various pleasures and sorrows, He continues to see this external aspect of Himself solely as a Witness. When we become the knower of the atman, when we have perfect realization of our inner atman, only then do we realize our eternal form with full conviction and despite being in the midst of all joys and sorrows, we go beyond them, we observe our own life and the world as an observer.

In this way when we know the atman in its purest form as detached from all actions, from the world, from all grievances, then we can see that it is not a void; then we see the pure, calm Supreme Space, that Supreme Being within us, where there is 'Satyaṁ jñānamantaṁ Brahma nihitaṁ guhāyām'.[117] We come to know of that wonderful luminous Supreme Sheath within us, where there is existence of that extremely bright Light of lights.

This is the very reason why the Upanishads have repeatedly said, "Know your inner atman, only then you would know the Immortal, only then would you know the Supreme One. Only then, in spite of being in the midst of everything, by entering into all, you would attain mukti without renouncing anything at all". *Nānyaḥ panthā vidyate ayanāya.*[118]

18 February 1909
(6 *Phālgun* 1315 BE)

The Eternal Abode

The Upanishads say: *Ānandaṁ brahmaṇo vidvān na bibheti kadācana.*[119] The person who has known the bliss of Brahman never fears.

Where will we look for that bliss of Brahman? Where will we know it? We will know it within the inner atman.

For once, see the atman in the inner abode, in its eternal abode – where the atman is beyond external pleasure and sorrow, beyond all the restlessness of the world. Enter that secret innermost cave and see – you will see that the bliss of the Supreme Atman is manifested day and night within the atman, it has no rest even for a moment. The Supreme Atman is full of bliss in this individual atman. Where there is the never-ending union of that love, enter there and look at that place. Only then would you realize within the very depth of your heart what the bliss of Brahman is and only then would you never have any fear from anything else any more.

Where lies your fear? It is at that place where anxiety and ailment, infirmity and death, separation and union prevail; it is where arrival and departure, pleasure and pain exist. If you see the atman only in the outer world – if you realize it solely from one activity to another, from one subject to another – if you know it as completely entwined and intermingled as one with variety and flux – only then would you see the atman as extremely poor and soiled, would you see it encompassed by death and would continue to mourn for it. You would then connect that which is not true and not permanent with the atman, and would mistake it to be true and permanent. In the end when all those would continue to perish due to the rule of the world, you would then think that the atman itself is undergoing decay and destruction. Time and again, in this way you will get scorched in mourning and despair. Since you have wilfully given a superior position to the world alone, the world in turn will overwhelm and defeat your atman at every step with that power given to it by you. But, see the atman in the inner abode, in the midst of the Eternal, in the midst of Brahman; only then will the entire power of pleasure and grief go away. Why then is there any fear of harm, criticism, sickness, death or anything else at all? The atman is ever triumphant. The atman is not a slave of any other slave of the transient world, the atman is established in the Infinite and in immortality. The bliss of Brahman is manifested in the atman. For this reason, those that know the atman as the form of Truth, know the bliss of Brahman and those that know the bliss of Brahman are 'na bibheti kadācana'.[120]

Parame Brahmaṇi yojitachittaḥ
Nandati nandatyeva.[121]

Those that have seen themselves as liberated in the Supreme Brahman, they become happy, happy, truly happy! And in the world those that know themselves as attached, 'lament, lament, truly lament!'[122]

19 February 1909
(7 *Phālgun* 1315 BE)

Three Levels

We observe three phases in our lives. Human life is being shaped into three broad levels – the physical, the religious and the spiritual.

In the first phase, the physical world is everything to us. Then we simply remain outside. At that time the physical world becomes the only realm of all our perceptions. At that stage, all our inclinations, thoughts and efforts are directed towards the outside. Even whatever takes shape in our mind, we cannot do without establishing that externally; even the matters cherished in our mind assume external form in our imagination. We regard Truth to be only that which can be seen and touched by us. That is why also by confining our God to an external object or by giving Him an external form, we equate Him with the physical matter itself. We try to appease this external God by external means. We conduct sacrifices before it, make offerings of food to it and dress it. Then the injunctions put forth by that God are also external by nature. The injunction that to take a dip in which river is holy, to take which kind of food is a sin, in which direction the head has to be laid down while sleeping, which mantra, in which manner, in which lunar day and in which measure of time ought to be chanted – are all then considered religious rituals.

In this manner through the senses of sight, smell and touch; through mind, imagination, fear and bhakti, we explore the outside. By causing injury to it in a variety of ways and in turn getting injured by it, we reach the limit of our acquaintance with the outside. Then we no longer consider the outside as the sole entity. So we no longer regard the outside as our sole refuge, our only hope and wealth. Just because one day it had awakened our complete hope and had attracted our entire mind, we developed utter disrespect for it when we saw its limitations. Then we started to abuse the physical world as an enchantress, there arose a feeling of revolt to completely deny the world in every possible way. Then we continued to say, "It is this in which there exist only physical and mental ailments, death and unceasing movement like that of an ox yoked to a grinding mill, that we regarded as the Truth and had completely surrendered ourselves to it – shame on this ignorance of ours!"

Then we totally abandoned the outside and tried to set up our home on the inside. That outside which we one day honoured as a sovereign, we defeated that in a fierce battle and proclaimed only the inside to be victorious. Those desires which drove us like a bailiff for so long in the pursuit of all that was external, we engaged ourselves in an effort to uproot them completely by throwing them into jail, by impaling them and by sending them to the gallows. We had completely ignored the threat of those sufferings and wants with which the outside had kept us in fetters of slavery. After performing the *rājasūya yajña*,[123] by defeating all the sovereigns of mighty power outside, in the north, the south, the east and the west, we hoisted the victory flag at the pinnacle of the highest palace of the capital of our inside. We put shackles on our feet of desire. We kept a strict guard on our happiness and sorrow. We only stopped after overturning the previous kingdom all over.

In this way when we have already established ourselves on the inside by curbing the extreme sovereignty of the outside, what really do we then see in the innermost cave? It is not at all the pride of victory. It is not just a fully detailed and an effective means of imposing self-control. It is not just the bondage of the outside in place of the bondage of rules of the inside. In the tranquil, restrained, engrossed, pure sky of consciousness we have seen such an effulgent light of bliss, which has illuminated both the inside and the outside. It is radiating rays of goodness from the innermost core towards the entire universe.

Then all the conflicts between the inside and the outside become resolved. Then there is no victory but joy; no struggle but sport; no separation but union; not "I" but all; neither outside nor inside, then It is Brahman: *Tacchubhraṁ jyotiṣāṁ jyotiḥ*.[124] Then in the supreme union of the atman with the Supreme Atman, the whole universe is united. Then there is compassion devoid of self-interest, forgiveness devoid of arrogance, love devoid of ego; then there prevails uninterrupted fulfilment of knowledge, bhakti and action.

22 February 1909
(10 *Phālgun* 1315 BE)

Philosopher's Stone

His name is the Philosopher's Stone,
His grace in the form of peace awakens in the devotee's heart!
He alleviates the anguish of sinners.

Do we attain that Philosopher's Stone during this *upāsanā* at dawn? If we attain only a grain of it then may we not confine that only within a pleasurable sensation of our mind. It should be made to touch us, its touch should turn our entire day into gold.

During the day, every now and then that Philosopher's Stone should be made to touch the words that I utter, should be made to touch the thoughts of my mind and should be made to touch my actions in the world.

If that be so, what was trivial will be glorified within a moment, what was dull will become bright, and what was valueless will become priceless.

We will allow that Philosopher's Stone to touch our morning *upāsanā*, to touch everything throughout the day, to touch His name and His dhyana – to touch this 'śāntaṁ śivaṁ advaitam'[125] mantra. We will not let *upāsanā* be the prized possession of our heart, we will make it the refuge of our nature; we will not attain only tenderness through it, but will also establish ourselves.

There is a saying that morning clouds are futile, they do not rain. Likewise, may our *upāsanā* at dawn never be blown away by the morning wind itself just after being manifested for a moment.

This is because, when the sun is blazing hot only then is there a need for tenderness, when thirst is intense only then is there a need for rainfall. It is only in the midst of a more arduous worldly task that there is dryness which causes burning. When it is immensely crowded, when the uproar is great, only then do we lose ourselves; at that time itself if we cannot use what we have accumulated at dawn, if like an endowed property it is solely engaged in the act of performing puja at the temple, if there is no opportunity to make it work for the needs of the world – then it becomes useless.

There are certain moments in a day which appear extremely dull and intensely intolerable. At the time when the Omnipresent remains hidden more than anyone else, when we are either completely engaged in office work or when the radiance of our inner atman becomes extremely dull due to the inaction caused by digestion of food, during the obsession of that dullness and inaction, may we not indulge ourselves with triviality – may we directly perceive the glory of the atman even then. May we remember at once that we stand in the realm of 'bhūrbhuvaḥsvaḥ',[126] may we remember that the form of the Infinite Consciousness is emanating consciousness within us at this moment, may we remember that this very 'śuddhaṁ apāpaviddham'[127] dwells in our hearts at this moment. At the root of all witty conversations, in all activities and in all restlessness, may the unshaken realization of fulfilment never be completely concealed from us.

Yet, let no one think that sadhana really implies completely giving up all laughter and gossip, and all rejoicings in this world altogether. If we really fail to maintain the little natural relationship we have with someone, it takes advantage over us unnaturally – in the very effort to renounce that artificially, the noose becomes even tighter. An object which is transitory and external by nature, in an effort to renounce it, many a time that itself turns into an object of dhyana within our heart.

I will not renounce, I will preserve it; but, I will preserve it at the right place. I will not regard the trivial to be great, will not allow the desired to take the place of the beneficial,[128] and at all times, in all actions, I will let the *upāsanā* go on in the immovable court of that secret chamber within my heart. I will never, by no means allow the mind to understand that He is not there – because that is an utter lie.

At dawn, with extreme bhakti, collect the dust of His feet in your heart – that is our Philosopher's Stone. Allow that bhakti to touch our fun and frolic, our activities, our property and everything we have. Everything will spontaneously become great, will become pure and will become worthy of oblation to Him.

24 February 1909
(12 *Phālgun* 1315 BE)

Prayer

O Truth! Within my inner atman, You are the endless Truth – You are there. There is simply no limit to the fact that You are in this atman at this time and place with such profundity and closeness. Since time immemorial this atman has been uttering this very mantra: "Satyam". You are there, truly You are there. May this very mantra which emanates from the unfathomable depths of the atman fill my mind and pervade all other sounds of the world and rise above them all and say: *satyaṁ satyaṁ satyam.*[129] Take me to that Truth, to that most secret eternal Truth of my inner atman, where there is no utterance at all except 'You are there'.

O the Refulgent Light! In my mind's space You are 'jyotiṣāṁ jyotiḥ'[130] – that light cannot be contained in the light of crores of solar realms of Your infinite space – in that light the consciousness of my inner atman is illuminated. Place me in the midst of my inner space and cleanse me thoroughly with a deluge of purity and sacredness. Make me radiant. May I completely forget all my other surroundings and attain an unblemished, immaculate, sinless, illuminated body.

O the manifestation of Immortality! In the secret abode of my inner atman, You are 'ānandaṁ paramānandam'.[131] At no time indeed, is there any end to Your union at that place. Not only are You present there, but are also united; not only is Your Truth manifest there, but also is Your bliss. You have scattered that very infinite bliss over Your whole world. Whether in motion, in life, or in beauty, it never exhausts itself in anything else. It is uncontainable anywhere else in the infinite space. It is Your limitless bliss itself that I have fixed in my inner atman. You have not allowed anyone from Your creation to enter there. In that place there is no light, no form, no movement, except Your calm intimate bliss. By standing amidst the abode of bliss give me a call once, O Lord! I am scattered in all directions, may your call of immortality be rung and echoed everywhere in my world, may it go far away, and enter everywhere very secretly. May I respond from all directions and say, 'Here I come, here I come!' Call me, 'Come dear, come! Come back dear, come back!' Within the abode of eternal bliss of this inner atman, may all that I have remain at one place with oneness and calmness, with profound depth and utmost secrecy.

O Manifestation! By Your manifestation annihilate my "I" completely, do not spare anything else of mine, nothing at all, not a trace of my ego should be left behind. Make me become full of You. Let me be only You, only full of You. Let there be light only full of You and bliss only full of You.

O Rudra! Let sins be burnt and turned to ashes! Radiate your terrible heat. Let nothing be hidden anywhere, let everything from the root to the fruit full of seeds get scorched. This, in fact, is the fruit of numerous wicked attempts made over a long period of time, grown in every node of the tree, hidden behind the leaves. The roots of sins have gone down into the abyss of the heart. There is no such fuel to match Your terrible wrath. When the sins will burn, only then will this "I" attain fulfilment. Then it will culminate in light.

After that, O the most gracious One, may Your graciousness continue to diffuse through all my thoughts, words and actions. May Your delightful graciousness penetrate into every pore of my body and make it a form of divinity. May my body remain as the holy receptacle of Your grace of immortality in the world. Let that graciousness of Yours perfectly calm my intellect, purify my heart and direct my power towards welfare. May Your grace protect me for ever from the danger of separation from You. May Your graciousness remain as an eternal wealth of my heart to serve as the refuge on the path of my whole life. When, by virtue of Your gracefulness, I shall realize Your Truth, Your effulgent light, Your immortality and Your manifestation that dwell in my inner Atman itself, only then would I be redeemed.

26 February 1909
(14 *Phālgun* 1315 BE)

Detachment

Yājñavalkya says –

Na vā are putrasya kāmāya putraḥ priyo bhavati
ātmanastu kāmāya putraḥ priyo bhavati.[132]

This means, not because you desire your son that he becomes dear to you, but because you yearn for the Atman alone that your son becomes dear to you.

The significance of this is, just because the atman realizes its own self in the son, the son becomes its own and that is why its joy lies in the son.

When the atman continues to be alone within the bounds of self-interest and ego, it becomes very dull indeed, then its truth does not get exhilarated. That is why the atman realizes itself within the son, within the friend, within different people and continues to be full of joy because its truth continues to attain completeness.

During childhood, while learning each letter *ka, kha, ga,*[133] independently in the *Varna parichay,*[134] I derived no joy from them. That is because I could not get any meaning in those independent letters. After that when the letters were joined together to form words such as 'kara', 'khala' and the like, then as the letters revealed their significance, my mind started to experience joy[135] to some extent. But, such disjointed words cannot provide sufficient interest[136] to the mind; they bring about pain and weariness. Then, even today I clearly remember the day when I read the words 'water drips', 'leaves quiver'.[137] I derived immense joy on that day; because the words then became replete with deeper meanings. Now, my mind does not derive any pleasure in merely reciting 'water drips', 'leaves quiver', it rather gives me a feeling of displeasure. Now I wish to realize the syntaxes which have significance only in sentences with deeper meanings.

Similarly, the alienated atman is like an alienated part of speech. Its significance cannot be completely obtained in isolation. For this very reason the atman tries to realize its truth within the many. When it gets united with its friends and relatives it sees a form of its own fulfilment; when it knows its relatives, strangers and many more people as its own, then it no longer remains a small atman, it becomes a great atman.

The only reason for this is that the complete truth of the atman lies within the Supreme Atman. My "I" attains fulfilment only in that great "I". That is why knowingly or unknowingly it is in the quest of that Supreme "I". What happens when my "I" unites with the "I" of my son? Then I attain joy by realizing that Supreme "I" who is within my own "I" as well as within the "I" of my son.

But, then the problem is that my "I", on this pretext, cannot understand clearly that it moves a little towards that great "I". He thinks that he has attained the son only and that it is owing to some special quality itself that the son gives joy. Therefore, it gets obstructed due to the bondage of this attachment. At that moment it only wants to embrace its son and friends. Then due to the pull of this attachment, it gets involved in a number of sins as well.

Hence only to evoke detachment through true knowledge Yājñavalkya says, "We do not truly want the son, we yearn for the Atman alone". If we understand this message properly, only then does the blind attachment towards our son gets severed. Then the pretext alone cannot become the goal to obstruct our path.

When we continue to derive joy by comprehending the vast significance of literature, then every word with its independent identity does not obstruct our minds any more. Every word reveals just the meaning and not merely the word itself. Then it is as if the very word loses its own independence.

Similarly, when we know the Truth then it is within that undivided Truth itself that we know all the fragments. By being independent they do not obstruct our knowledge any more. This condition itself is the condition of detachment. In this condition the world does not consider itself to be the ultimate and does not go on to take hold of our entire mind and action.

When the realization of the significance of a poem becomes deep, becomes illuminating to us, only then the fruition of each of its words becomes particularly beautiful to us due to the sweetness of that entire emotion. At that time, when we look back, we see that no word is meaningless, the essence of the whole is being revealed in every word itself. Then, every word of that poem becomes the cause of particular joy and amazement to us. Then as its words help us in the realization of the whole instead of obstructing us, they become immensely valuable to us.

Similarly, when detachment overcomes the delusion of independence and makes us acquainted with the great Truth within the Omnipresent, then on returning from that great acquaintance, each independent entity becomes fulfilled through the essence of the Omnipresent. One day, those words that had to be read by spelling them, those words that were obstructing our path at every step, each of them carries us only towards that Omnipresent and do not obstruct us.

Then the joy that is felt, is love itself. That love does not bind; that love pulls us along. That love is pure and unopposed. It is that very love which is mukti – the death of all attachments. The funeral-mantra of this death itself is –

> *Madhuvātā ṛtāyate madhu kṣaranti sindhavaḥ*
> *Madhvīrnah santvoshadhīḥ.*[138]
> *Madhu naktam utoshaso madhumat pārthivaṁ rajaḥ*[139]
> *Madhumānno vanaspatirmadhumāṁ astu sūryaḥ.*[140]

The wind carries nectar, the river and the ocean exude nectar. May all the herbs and the trees be filled with nectar, may the night be filled with nectar, may the dawn be filled with nectar, may the sand particles of this world be filled with nectar, may the sun be full of nectar.

When the bond of attachment has been severed then water, land and sky, inanimate objects, animals and human beings, are all filled with immortality – then there is no limit to joy.

Attachment binds our minds to worldly possessions. When within those worldly possessions the mind attains the Truth beyond them, then in the manner a butterfly cuts open its cocoon and comes out of it, in the same manner, through detachment the mind severs the bond of attachment. As soon as the bond of attachment is severed, complete and beautiful love manifests itself everywhere in the form of bliss. Then we can understand the meaning of this mantra 'ānandarūpamṛtaṁ yadbibhāti'.[141] All that is being manifested is that form of bliss, that form of immortality. No entity then prides itself and says, 'I am being manifested': only bliss is being manifested, nothing but bliss. That manifestation is deathless. There is death for all others, but that manifestation itself is immortal.

27 February 1909
(15 *Phālgun* 1315 BE)

Collectedness

The second great obstacle to our sadhana is the lack of practice of sadhana itself. Maybe we have not had practice of any kind of sadhana at all. Whenever something appears before us, we probably get attracted towards that. By drifting and dashing ourselves repeatedly against all places, we proceed. We move because the current of the world flows without any effort made by us; we have neither oar, nor helm, nor even a sail.

We never practised accumulating our power and inclination together from all directions under strict control to serve a certain purpose. It is due to this that power and inclination have the tendency to go out of hand. There is no trace as to where they really are; there is no possibility that they would come running whenever they are summoned. When they are tempted by food items they are used to and find appetizing, only then do they come together on their own or else by no other means.

It has become a practice only to scatter oneself in a wasteful manner. Even thoughts get scattered, action becomes disorderly, nothing remains rooted in one place.

In such a situation it is not only true that there is no attainment, but no true happiness as well. In this there is only the lethargic obsession with ignorance and vice.

This is because when we associate our power and inclination with a certain purpose, then that purpose itself carries them along. Then their burden does not fall upon our own shoulders any more. Otherwise, we have to carry them and shift them from one place to another and in this way we always have to pull them in opposite directions. When we do not find any means to unburden them, we continue to create some artificial means to do that. So much for the worthless sports, worthless amusements and worthless paraphernalia! Ultimately, those artificial arrangements also become an additional burden that presses us from all directions. This is how the burden of life goes on accumulating and we never get any mukti from that till death.

So I was saying that only in the state of sadhana there is a kind of joy, not to speak of attainment. In the pursuit of a noble aim if one's diversion is concentrated and is directed towards a particular path then that itself seems to sustain oneself. Even if the little effort needed to consider our sadhana as joy and to proceed with determination and pride diminishes within us then there lies a great danger. At any cost, in spite of facing repeated failures, the efforts needed to concentrate all those powers have to be strengthened. Just as a baby learns to walk by tumbling over and getting hurt repeatedly, it has to be taught to walk. This is because in the path of attainment, there is a need to awaken this very faith in the first place that the goal is true; then it has to be known whether the goal is within or without, whether it is at the periphery or at the centre; then there is need to learn to follow the right path. There is need for both stability and motion. The mind will become calm through faith, and effort will gain momentum through sadhana.

28 February 1909
(16 *Phālgun* 1315 BE)

Dedication

When the image of attainment is visible to some extent then the sheer joy of it spontaneously pulls us along – who would dare to stop us then! Then no weariness, no weakness remain there.

But, in the very beginning of sadhana, the image of attainment does not manifest itself in this manner even from a distance. Yet the path is also not an easy one. What force makes us move forward?

At this point of time, it is Dedication which undertakes the charge to guide us. When bhakti awakens, when our heart is full, then there is really no worry, then the path, in fact, is no longer felt to be a path to tread; then we seem as though we are flying. But, when bhakti is afar and the heart is empty, who is our support during those trying times?

Then our only support is Dedication. It is the only one that can carry the dead weight of our withered heart.

The camel is the vehicle for those that have to travel across the desert path. It is an extremely tough and strong vehicle – it does not have even a little luxuriousness. It does not get food, still it walks. It does not get any drink, still it walks. Even when the dessert sand becomes hot, still it walks, it walks silently. Even when it appears that the desert ahead is unending, perhaps there is no other option but death, its walk does not stop even then.

Similarly, it is only Dedication which can drive us along the desert path of dryness and emptiness, without taking any food or even without getting anything – its prana is so tough that even in the midst of criticism and weariness, amid thorns and shrubs, it can find its food. When the desert storm comes thrashing at it with a deadly vehemence, it bows its head and allows the storm to pass over it. Who else is there so steady, so patient and so persevering like it?

In this monotonous and incessant wilderness, at times the vision of a mirage comes to us to mislead the path. Diverse forms of success are not seen every now and then. It seems, we are at the same place as we were the day before. We try to concentrate, yet our mind wanders about; we call out to our heart but it does not respond to our call. We always feel, we are being distressed by the efforts of futile *upāsanā*. But by carrying the terrible load of that futile *upāsanā*, Dedication has the ability to keep on walking day after day.

The progress is continuous. There is no trace of doubt that little by little it is getting closer to its destination. See over there, from somewhere all of a sudden there appears an oasis of bhakti – within this vast expanse of parched paleness, there lies the pleasant greenness of the date palm bower filled with the cluster of nectarous fruit. A fountain of cold water is flowing under that lone shade. By drinking that water, by bathing in that water, by resting under the shade, we proceed with our journey once again. But that sweetness and soothing freshness of bhakti does not move all along with us. Then again there is that tough, parched, untiring Dedication. It has a quality – someday if by any chance it is able to drink the water of bhakti then it can save that up in a secret chamber within itself for many days. Even on a day of severe dryness that is its only resource to quench the thirst.

The very bhakti towards the One who can be attained through sadhana is what we truly call bhakti, but dedication is the bhakti towards sadhana itself. It is this very austere, difficult and dry sadhana which is the highly valued treasure of Dedication. It has a deeper sense of joy in sadhana. This joy is pure and causeless. In this unwavering joy it drives despair away and does not even fear death. The day this Dedication, our only companion in the path of the desert, reaches its destination, it completely surrenders us in the hands of bhakti and hides itself in its servant's chamber; it does not take pride in anything, it does not make any demand – on the day of success its happiness lies in keeping itself hidden from the view.

1 March 1909
(17 *Phālgun* 1315 BE)

The Function of Dedication

Not only does Dedication direct us along a dry and difficult path with tireless perseverance, but it also cautions us continuously. By proceeding in the same manner daily we tend to become fatigued and unmindful. Dedication never wants to forget; it gives us a push and says, 'What is happening? What are you doing?' It reminds us, 'If you do not proceed during cold, you would surely suffer when it is hot'. It shows us, 'Water is leaking from the slit of your water-vessel. What will happen when you are thirsty?'

There is no limit to the manner in which we continue to misuse our energy throughout the day – in so much of idle talk and in so many useless activities. All of a sudden, Dedication reminds us, 'This very thing which you are misusing in such a way is very necessary indeed – be quiet for a while, be a bit calm, do not exaggerate so much, do not cross your limits like that, do not dip your legs unnecessarily in that water which should be stored carefully for drinking'. When we are up to the neck in triviality, being extremely self-oblivious, even then it does not forget us; it says, 'Fie! What is this?' It remains seated very close to our heart, nothing escapes its sight.

When we come closer to gaining attainment, we obtain the natural wisdom of love, then the sense of proportion develops of its own. Just the manner in which an inborn poet naturally maintains his rhythm, we too can naturally regularize our life from beginning to end amidst beauty in its pure form. Then deviation itself becomes difficult. But during the days of destitution when that natural power of joy is no longer there, then at every step there is a break in rhythm; where we are not supposed to stop we become lazy, where we ought to stop we cannot control our speed. Then it is this firm Dedication which is our only support. It never sleeps, it is wide awake. It says, 'What is that? Oh, there appears a crimson hue of anger! Look, there you are trying to flaunt yourself! Well, remember that very thorn of enmity that still remains pierced in your memory! Why do I suddenly see you in so much unexpressed distress? Now that you are going to sleep at night, where lies that peace within your heart to enter this pure, serene chamber of sleep'?

During the days of sadhana, this very eternal touch of caution of Dedication is our prime joy. The more we know that this Dedication is awake, the more we feel assured within our heart. If on any day due to the misfortune of self-oblivion we fail to see it, only then do we apprehend danger. When we are unable to find our ultimate friend, it is Dedication which remains as our supreme friend. Every day its firm image is invested before us with pure beauty. This calm, detached and holy hermitess makes our poverty pleasant by radiating power, peace and light amidst our emptiness.

When Columbus' faith regarding his destination became very firm, it was Dedication alone which gave him confidence daily in the voyage through the unknown sea route devoid of any sign. His sailors did not have that firm faith in their hearts, they did not also have that dedication during their voyage at sea. Every day they were busy to see some visible form of success; when they did not obtain anything at all, their energy got used up; that is why as they passed their days, as the sea did not end, their impatience too started to build up accordingly. They were about to revolt, they wanted to get back. Yet, without observing any sign of certainty from outside, Columbus' dedication continued to proceed silently. But the case was such that there was no way to stop the sailors any longer, they were about to reverse the course of the ship. Just then a sign was seen, there was no doubt that there was a shore. Then everyone was full of joy, all wanted to proceed enthusiastically. Then all considered Columbus as their friend and thanked him.

During the first stage of sadhana no one extends support to us – all express their doubts, all create obstruction. Even externally I do not see any clear sign which I can show as the clear proof of my true conviction to everyone and to myself. Then in that mid-sea, amidst doubts and oppositions, may Dedication never leave us even for a moment. When the coast will come closer, when the coastal birds will fly and perch on your mast, when the flowers of the coast will dance upon the sea waves, then there will be no dearth of praise and favour. But till then only Dedication, the Dedication that overcomes hopelessness, the Dedication which has the capacity to withstand shock, the Dedication indifferent to external encouragement and the Dedication unmoved by criticism – at no cost, for no reason should that Dedication renounce us. May it continue to gaze at the compass, may it continue to firmly hold on to the oar.

1 March 1909
(17 *Phālgun* 1315 BE)

The Obverse

Viśvakarmā, that great Atman who works by dwelling in the hearts of the people,[142] indeed works in great secrecy. There is no doubt that His work is truly progressing; there is unhappiness only because we do not know that the work is really going on. Just because we did not take part in the little we were supposed to do for that work, our lives seemed to have become insignificant. In spite of that every day, at every moment, Viśvakarmā is working out of the joy of His innate knowledge, power and action. He strings a sunbeamed day of my life with a moon-and-star-studded night, and again He continues to string that night with another luminous day. His joy is profound in the making of my life like a gem-studded necklace. If I had joined Him, this joy would have been mine as well. In this wonderful creation of art, so many holes are being drilled, so many bores are being made, so much is being burnt, so many blows are being struck – it is amidst these blows that I lay my claim to Viśvakarmā's joy of creation.

But, I did not even give a look towards that cave within me, where the blissful Viśvakarmā is engaged in working day and night; all my life I went on gaping only at the outside. I mingle with many, laugh and gossip with them and think that the day is being spent somehow – it is as if the sole aim of spending the day is merely to pass it. It is as though the day has no meaning.

It seems on entering the theatre of human life we sit like fools turning our back towards the direction in which the dramatic performance is taking place. We see only the columns, the cots and the crowd of the theatre. Later on when the lights have gone out, the curtain has dropped, we cannot see anything anymore, there is deep darkness – then perhaps I ask myself, 'What did I come here to do, why did I pay for the ticket at all, what is the meaning of these columns and cots, why at all have so many people gathered here?' Everything is a deception indeed, everything is, in fact, a meaningless child's play. Alas, no detail at all was available regarding the act of joy that is being performed on stage.

The One who is performing the sport of joy of life is, in fact, doing so just being seated within – those columns and cots are merely external forms, they are not really the main things. For once, turn your gaze within; only then would you be able to understand all the meanings.

Whatever is happening is, in fact, taking place within. Is it only outside you that this darkness is getting dispelled and that the sun is rising gradually? If it were only outside you then from which direction would you have entered there? At this moment Viśvakarmā indeed has flooded your sky of consciousness completely with the colour of the rising sun. Observe within you that an emerging sun is raising its head like the bud of a golden lotus, is about to spread its luminous petals gradually everywhere – it is within you indeed. This itself is the joy of Viśvakarmā. It is in the field of your life that He is incessantly weaving such a vast, wonderful cloth, with so many gold, silver and multi-coloured threads, it is truly within you – that which is completely outside is not at all yours.

So see it right now. See this dawn as the dawn of your inner self, see it as His creation of joy within your consciousness alone. This does not belong to anyone else, this is not there anywhere else – this dawn of yours is only there within you and it is only He who alone dwells there. Amidst your profound solitude, within this infinite space of your mind, lies His wonderful, vast sport – it goes on day and night without rest. If you turn your back against this wonderful dawn, if you want to see it only externally, you will not derive joy from it, you will not obtain any meaning in it.

When I was in England I was a mere boy. I had an invitation at a place a little away from London. I boarded a train in the evening. It was winter then. On that day everything was covered by fog. It was snowing. The stations that came after London were on the left. Whenever the train stopped, I opened the window, stuck out my head to the left and amidst that haze of fog I called someone to know the name of the station. My destined station was the last one. When the train stopped there I looked only to the left – when I saw no light, no platform on that side, I sat back at my seat without any worry. After a short while the train started back towards London again. I said, "What's this!" In the next station when the train stopped, I asked, 'Where is such and such station?' The reply I heard was, 'It is exactly from where you are coming right now'. I got down from the train quickly and asked, "When will the next train arrive?" "At midnight", was the reply I received. My destined station was on the right side.

In the journey of our life we always seek those stations that are on the left. We are rest assured that there is nothing on the right. One after the other we went on passing through them. The place where I had to get down, even there too I looked towards the world, looked only to the left. I saw that there was total darkness, everything was hazy due to the fog. The opportunity I had obtained was lost; the train was going back. At the place where there was the invitation, the merriment and joy started to become a thing of the past. When will the train be available again? The very opportunity that I had obtained, when will I be able to obtain that again – at which midnight?

The ultimate place is one such station which we can reach through the passage of human life. If I do not get down there, if I do not look at the side where its platform is, then the whole journey seems to be an extremely foggy meaningless matter to me, there is no doubt about it at all! I did not understand why I paid the fare for the ticket, why I boarded the train, why at all I travelled in the dark night and what really happened. "Where was my invitation, where was the arrangement for the feast made, where would my hunger be appeased, and where would I obtain shelter"? Without obtaining any answers to these questions, I had to end the journey by being utterly confounded.

O Truth, I want nothing else, turn my face towards that direction where You are, where the Truth is – in fact, I only look towards untruth! On the stage of Your sport-of-joy You have lighted lamps in rows; I stare at the darkness opposite to that and think hard, what do all these mean? Turn me towards Your light. All I see is death – I cannot make any meaning out of that, I am being overwhelmed with fear. Just on the other side of it is immortality, within it lies all meaning, who will make me understand that? O *Āviḥ*! I am unfortunate that my vision is totally absent in that very direction where you are eternally manifested. For that reason I see You only as Rudra, I am simply unable to know that Your graciousness has continuously enveloped my atman for ever and ever. When an infant turns its back towards its mother, it cries hard on seeing darkness; once it turns around it comes to know that its mother is, in fact, there embracing it. O Mother, turn us around in the direction of Your graciousness, only then would I be able to know in a moment that I have already been protected, my protection is for eternity – or else the wails of the fear of defencelessness will never cease by any means.

2 March 1909
(18 *Phālgun* 1315 BE)

To See the Truth

Through the mantra of our dhyana, we practice dhyana on the Creator in the midst of His creation. *Bhurbhubaḥsvaḥ*[143] are continuously being created by Him; at every moment the sun, the moon, the planets and the stars are being manifested through Him; at every instant our consciousness emanates from Him; it is He who is ceaselessly manifesting all – this itself is our dhyana.

To see this itself is said "to see the Truth". We see all events as external events only. We do not derive any joy from them. They become old and appear to take the shape of a wound up machine to us; just as the current of water flows over the pebbles, the flow of worldly events incessantly passes through our mind in that way. The mind does not respond to that, all the sights appear to be trivial and the days seem to be insignificant. That is why we derive joy while keeping our consciousness awake by merely engaging ourselves in artificial excitements and by the creation of futile activities.

This is precisely what happens when we look towards the events alone. It neither gives us any essence, nor any food. To a certain extent, it only occupies our senses, our mind, our heart, but does not reach up to the end. So, whatever essence it has, that tends to get dried up on the surface itself and does not awaken our deeper consciousness. The daily activity occurs in its unfailing regularity – the sun continues to rise, the river continues to flow, the plants and the trees continue to grow, everyday work continues regularly. That is why we wish to see such a sight that we do not see every day, we are curious to know about such events that do not match with our regular happenings.

But, when we know the Truth, our atman becomes completely fulfilled. Truth is for ever new, its essence is inexhaustible. The sight attains fruition when the innermost Truth is seen amidst the entire array of events. Then all attain fulfilment in greatness, awe and bliss.

It is for this very reason, amid all the matters of the universe, at least once daily with the mantra of our dhyana we try to practise dhyana upon He who is the Supreme Truth of the universe. Amidst the entire array of events we direct our gaze inwards to behold the One who is the fundamental power of the universe. Then the veil of inertness gets dispelled from our sight; then the world, like a machine, no longer remains within the usual orbit of all our attention. This vast manifestation pervading the infinite space is emanating, is dispersing at every moment from the Truth consisting of Knowledge – it is by realizing this itself that our consciousness attains fulfilment. Then being in the midst of fire, water, herbs and trees, we can proclaim that everywhere in the Infinite Truth, in the Infinite Knowledge and in the Infinite Brahman, His manifestation is in the form of bliss and immortality.

We will not merely see the countless number of events simply as innumerable forms of events; amidst them we will see the Infinite Truth steadily and calmly, it is for this reason that our mantra of dhyana is the Gāyatrī[144] – *Om bhūrbhubaḥ svaḥ tat saviturvareṇyam bhargo devasya dhīmahi dhiyo yo naḥ prachodayāt.*[145] Let us practise dhyana upon the venerable power of that God who is ceaselessly creating all these realms of *bhūrbhubaḥsvaḥ*[146] – He is incessantly activating our power of intellect as well.

16 March 1909
(3 *Caitra* 1315 BE)

Creation

This very fact that some of us sit here early in the morning for *upāsanā*, even this is a creation. That Creator is in the midst of this creation too.

We usually say this is how the things have turned out. A handful of us conferred on this matter, then we sat together and since then it has been continuing in this manner on a regular basis.

Though this is no doubt an event, but it is not the Truth. If seen from the point of view of an event it is a trivial matter, but to see it from the point of view of Truth it is simply amazing, every day itself it is amazing. While remaining at the centre the Truth is drawing several unfamiliar souls from various directions and is continuously creating this very congregation. We think we would sit here for some time, finish our activity here and then would proceed for some other work elsewhere, that settles it – but that is not such a small matter. When we study, teach, eat, wander about, even then the Creator of this assembly is engaged in its very creation. Viśvakarmā, who is 'janānāṁ hṛdaye sanniviṣṭaḥ',[147] has been doing his work while dwelling among us, He is arranging the articles of worship within the minds of each one of us in different ways. It is as if He has no other work to do. As His creation of the universe is a great work, the creation of this appears to be equally a great work too. The realm of our *upāsanā* is continuously in the process of being created – day in and day out. The process still continues when we are asleep and even when we have forgotten all about it. When Truth prevails, it can never be possible that nothing happens or that there is cessation of it even for a moment.

In the centre of the universe there is the all-pervading 'Truth' and it is for that very reason we observe the universe every day in its proper position and according to rule. It is because 'Truth' is performing Its work among the few of us that we come and sit here daily every morning. The whole universe goes round that one Truth and offers *praṇām* to It. The place where our telescope is beyond the range of vision, the place where it is beyond the reach of our minds, even there so many luminous realms continuously surround It and say: 'Namo namah'.[148] In a similar manner we too have sat down by surrounding this Truth in our realm of *upāsanā*. He who is seated amidst this world and beyond, is seated in this courtyard. Not only does He manifest consciousness amongst us, but also radiates the power needed to propagate this particular creation in which we select few are participants. In this particular process of ongoing creation, He is directing the minds of the few of us in a number of ways on this particular matter. He is unifying the diversities of nature, of stock notions and of learning of the few of us at this very moment. And when we get up from this place and go elsewhere, even then He will not give rest to His work.

We will directly behold that Truth, that Creator of our realm of *upāsanā* among us here, we will walk all the way round Him and offer our *praṇām* to Him together. We will know every day that just as the sun, the moon, the planets and the stars are His eternal creation, that He has made the few of us to sit over here is His similar creation too. His incessant bliss is being manifested in this very action, we will see that Revealer before we depart.

16 March 1909
(3 *Caitra* 1315 BE)

Loaded Boat

I composed a poem titled 'The Golden Boat',[149] an interpretation of it can be rendered on this occasion.

Man has been cultivating crops throughout his life. The little field of his life is like an island surrounded by the unmanifested from all directions, only that little part has been manifested in him. That is why the Gītā says:

Avyaktadīni bhūtāni vyakta-madhyāni bhārata
Avyaktanidhanānyeva tatra kā paridevanā.[150]

When the time is up, when the level of water rises from all directions, when it is the time again for that very piece of land to get submerged into the unmanifested, then he can load up the boat of the world with whatever eternal fruit he has of the work of his entire life. The world will accept all, and will not reject even a grain of it. But when man says, 'Take me along with those, keep me as well' the world then says, 'Where is the space left for you? What will I do with you? Whatever is to be kept from the harvest of your life, I shall keep them all, but you are not really worth keeping'.

Every man contributes something or the other to this world through the work of his life; the world accepts and preserves them all, it does not allow anything to get wasted – but, along with that, when man wants to make his ego eternal then his effort becomes futile. We have to surrender our ego in the form of tax unto the clutches of Death to settle up accounts for the life that has already been enjoyed by us. It is not something which should be saved at any cost.

17 March 1909
(4 *Caitra* 1315 BE)

Attainment of Nature

Irrespective of the nature of our atman, may we make that nature free from obstacles – this is the only sadhana in our lives.

What is the nature of the atman? Whatever be the nature of the Supreme Atman it is the same for the atman as well. What is the nature of the Supreme Atman? He does not accept, He bestows.

He engages Himself in creation. The very purpose of creation is renunciation. There is no obligation, no compulsion attached to this renunciation that He makes. The sole dharma of bliss is to bestow of its own accord and to renounce by itself. We know that too. Without being bound by any condition our joy and our love attain fulfilment only through self-renunciation. It is for this reason that the Upanishads say: *Ānandāddhyeva khalvimāni bhūtāni jāyante.*[151] This is the very nature of the Blissful One.

The atman has a likeness to the Supreme Atman. Our atman too is not joyful while receiving, it is joyful while giving. If this very surge that we will grasp, grab and save appears like the deformity caused by a disease, then there would be no limit to resentment and anger. When we say with all our heart 'We will give', only then it is the day of our rejoicing. At that very moment all resentment gets dispelled, all anguish becomes pacified.

We have to practise sadhana to realize this blissful form of the Atman. How would we do that?

The fact that there is a hungry ego, that poor one who wants to hold everything in its grip, that miser who gives nothing without the aim of taking anything, does nothing without the aim of gaining anything, it is that very ego which has to be kept outside. It should not be given a warm reception as given to one's closest relative and should not be granted entry into the inner chamber. The ego, in fact, is not the atman's kin; because the ego is mortal, whereas the atman is immortal.

The atman is 'Na jāyate mṛyate',[152] neither does it take birth nor does it die. But, that ego has been born, it has been given a name; if it is unable to do anything else it at least does everything to establish its name at any cost.

This ego that I have, I should see it as an outsider. When it would be sorrowful, I would say then that it is filled with sorrow. Not only in its sorrow, I would not partake of any of its property, riches, fame and honour.

I will not say I am getting and taking all these. Every day I will try to make this effort that I should not accept anything my ego tries to grasp. I will say repeatedly that it is not mine, that is outside me.

As I am unwilling to keep the external thing that should be kept outside, I have become fully loaded with waste. It has become difficult to get on with that burden. Due to the variation of that death-pervading-paraphernalia, every day I undergo death. By intertwining the Atman with this very mortal ego, I become wearied in its grief, sorrow and burden.

The nature of the ego is to pull inward and the nature of the Atman is to push outwards – that is why if these two get intertwined, a great whirlpool is created. One force continuously moves outward while another force continues to attract inwards – a great danger becomes imminent. The atman being attracted against its nature goes on whirling; it does not move toward the Infinite, it revolves round a fixed point like an ox yoked to a grinding mill. It moves but does not progress – so, in this movement it only feels pain, it does not find fulfilment.

That is why I said, we would have to be saved from this danger. We will not be identical with our ego, we will keep our distance from it. We will bestow, we will do work, but when our ego will come dancing while licking and biting the fruit of that work gripped in its hand then we will never ever accept that fruit soiled by eating. *Karmaṇyevādhikāraste mā phaleṣu kadācana.*[153]

18 March 1909
(5 *Caitra* 1315 BE)

Commandment

The scriptures have specifically prescribed which ones of the evil deeds should not be committed and have proclaimed them to be specifically forbidden by God.

If proclamations are made in such a manner, it makes us think as if God has decreed certain laws according to His own will and if a person breaks those laws he will incur the wrath of the Lord of the universe. I cannot accept this matter in such a narrow and hollow manner. He has not given any particular commandment, He has only proclaimed a single decree – that decree is prevalent across the entire universe. That is the only commandment.

He has only said, "Be manifest". He has said the same to the sun, to the universe and to mankind as well. So, the sun has become luminous, the earth has become the mother of life and man also has to manifest the atman.

In any corner of this universe wherever this commandment given by Him gets obstructed, there itself the bud gets withered, the river becomes stagnant and gets obstructed due to a net of moss – there itself lie bondage, distortion and annihilation.

When Lord Buddha, overcome with grief, sat in dhyana to seek the answer to this question as to why there is bondage, deviation and destruction; sorrow, sickness and death in man, what was the answer he received then that made him blissful? The answer he obtained then was that man would attain mukti only by realizing the atman, only by manifesting the atman. The obstacle towards this manifestation would lead to sorrow, there itself would lie his sin.

That is why initially he made man to accept some restrictions and then instructed him to follow the precepts. He said to him, 'Do not have greed, do not be jealous, do not get addicted to luxury'. He instructed man that by means of regular practice, he should set himself free from all those veils that have kept him enclosed. The moment those veils are removed, the atman would attain its true form.

What is that form? Neither is that emptiness, nor aversion to work, that is friendship, compassion and love towards the whole universe. Buddha did not tell us to renounce worldly desires only, he told us to propagate love. Just the way the sun attains its true nature only by radiating light, it is through the propagation of this love alone that the atman attains its true form.

The dharma of the atman is to pervade all the realms – the same is the dharma of the Supreme Atman. His dharma is perfect as He is 'Śuddhaṁ apāpaviddham'.[154] He is immutable, there is no obstacle of sin in Him. That is why He is all-pervading.

If the bond of sin is severed, our access too would be unhindered. What form shall we then attain? Like the Supreme Atman we will attain that form in which He is the Poet, the Sage, the Lord and the Self-born. We too will become the poet full of bliss, be the sovereign ruler of the mind, be free from bondage, manifest ourselves in our own holy light. Then the atman in all its thoughts, words and actions will manifest itself in the form of 'śāntaṁ śivaṁ advaitaṁ'[155] – it will not reveal itself in its agitated, tempted and fragmented form.

Maitreyī's prayer too is the prayer of that manifestation. The prayer which is inherent in all the buds and tender leaves of the universe, the prayer which is continuously emanating from the unfulfilled depths of time and space, the prayer which is there in every atom and molecule of the universe, the eternal cry of that prayer has pervaded the space which in the Vedas has been termed as 'krāndasī'[156] and 'rodasī',[157] that very eternal prayer of the human atman is Maitreyī's prayer. "Manifest me, manifest me! I am engulfed in untruth, manifest me in Truth. I am covered in darkness, manifest me in Light. I am obsessed with death, manifest me in Immortality. Ye *Āviḥ*! O fulfilled Manifestation! May my manifestation be only in You, may Your manifestation in me not meet with any obstruction – as soon as that manifestation is fully revealed, I would be saved eternally by the radiance of Your graceful countenance. In the obstruction of that manifestation lies Your displeasure, in that manifestation itself lies Your gracefulness".

In his own life, Buddha said this very prayer of complete manifestation on behalf of all mankind – that apart, man has no other prayer indeed.

22 March 1909
(9 *Caitra* 1315 BE)

Completeness

Another great man who came into this world to proclaim his Father's glory said, 'Just as your father is complete, you too should be complete'.

Even this utterance is not at all trivial. He has established the ideal of completeness of the human atman within the Supreme Atman and has instructed us to keep our aim fixed in that very direction. We have our *Brahmavihārā*[158] not within any limited space but amid that completeness. Just in the manner the Father is complete, the son too should always strive for that very completeness. Otherwise, how would there be a true union between the Father and the son?

It is also no small matter that he has given instructions regarding each one of the indications of completeness. As he said, "Love your neighbour as yourself", he did not in the least belittle those words. He did not simply say, "Love your neighbour"; what he said was, "Love your neighbour just as you love yourself". The person who aspires for *Brahmavihārā* has to attain this level of love – he must tread this very path.

Lord Jesus said, "Love even your enemy". He did not stop fearfully midway by saying, "Forgive your enemy". As he said, "Love your enemy", he has extended our aim up to *Brahmavihārā*. He said, "He who snatches away the dress you wear, give away even your *uttariya*[159] to him".

To a worldly person, all these instructions are nothing but exaggerations. This is because, he has no faith in any aim greater than the material world. He is prepared to give away not only the dress he wears but even his *uttariya* to the material world if that fulfils the purpose of his worldly necessities. But, if he considers *Brahmavihārā* to be a mere trifle compared to his needs then it becomes difficult for him to give away even his dress.

But, those who have come to mankind to proclaim that Brahman, the greatest of all, did not really intend to belittle Brahman from the point of view of the weak desires of worldly people. They have made the greatest utterance of all unhesitatingly till the very end.

By proclaiming such a great message in such a magnificent manner, they have instilled great faith in us. Through this they have revealed that the ultimate goal of humanity goes up to such an extent, its love is so profound, its renunciation is so great indeed.

Hence, in this great aim and in this great path, instead of driving us to despair, it will give us courage. It will enhance our reverence for our innermost greatness. It will completely awaken all our efforts.

If we constrict our goal by making it insignificant by untruth, if we limit our means with a fence of weakness, they diminish our faith – we do not get what we deserve and are unable to do what we have the ability to do.

But when great men have set great goals before us, they have shown respect for us. Buddha never felt any disrespect for anyone of us when he said, 'mānasaṁ bhāvaye aparimāṇam'.[160] Jesus too never expressed any disrespect even for the most wretched amongst us when he said, 'Just as your Father is perfect you too be perfect'.

Due to their reverence for us, we develop respect for ourselves. Then we no longer regard the difficult path of attaining the Omnipresent as an impossible path. At that time we pay attention to their voices and follow their message of fearlessness and proceed with joy towards this great journey to the Infinite. The message of Jesus is not an exaggeration. Buddha's message is not an exaggeration. If you aspire for the beneficial then accept the completeness of this Absolute Truth with respect.

For once, observe carefully within – see where it obstructs every day! Even when I want to unite with a single person there are so many obstacles that stand in the way. Union with that person is not becoming complete. It is being obstructed by ego, self-interest, anger and greed – due to indiscretion I hurt others and due to my own insolence I get hurt in turn. By no means am I able to cherish that humility by which self-surrender becomes extremely easy and pleasant. When I can see that this obstacle clearly exists, then is there any doubt that in my nature there are innumerable obstacles to my union with Brahman? That which will not allow me to unite with even a single person completely, will truly obstruct my union with Brahman. That which will make my neighbour distant from me, will also make Brahman distant from me. The manner in which I will hurt my enemy is the same manner in which I would also hurt Him. For this reason when one talks of the *Brahmavihārā* there is no chance to hold back anything of the world at all. Those great men have not shied away from anything, have not concealed anything while speaking. They say, one has to completely lay down one's life in order to be reborn in Him. By following their very path every day we have to completely give up our ego and self-interest, and have to live infinitely towards the path of friendship, love and the Supreme Atman. To those great souls that have given faith to man to journey on this great path, we offer our praṇāms to them with extreme bhakti and seek refuge in them.

25 March 1909
(12 *Caitra* 1315 BE)

Om

The meaning of the word "Om" is "Yes". It is an acknowledgement that It is there and It has been obtained. Yesterday while discussing the Chāndogya Upanishad we got an idea of the significance of the word "Om".

Wherever our atman finds 'Yes', there itself it utters "Om"!

When the gods went in search of this "Yes", where did they start looking for it and where did they ultimately find it? At first, they had searched the senses thoroughly. They said they would find this "Yes" through the sense of sight. But, they saw that there was no completeness in seeing with the eyes – it is fragmented into "Yes" and "No". There is no complete purity in it – it sees both good and evil; it sees some, but does not see others; it sees but does not hear.

In this way they searched everywhere: the ear, the nose, the speech, the mind – but there were fragmentation and conflict everywhere.

At last when they arrived at the heart of the Prana, they found one 'Yes' within this body. It is because, this Prana itself has the hold over all the prana of the body. It is in this Prana that all the powers of all the sense organs are united. As long as this great Prana exists, the eye sees, the ear hears, the nose also smells. It is not that within the Prana only one remains as 'Yes' and the other remains as 'No'; in it the senses of sight, hearing and smell all remain as 'Yes' in one place. Hence, it is in this very place of our body that we have found Om. Thereupon, our prayers with folded palms were fully answered.

The Chāndogya says, midway between the couple, that is, at the point of union between the two, there itself lies this Om. The place where at one end the Ṛk[161] and at the other the Sāma,[162] on one side the speech and on the other the music, on one side the Truth and on the other the Prana have become one, there itself is this music of completeness – Om.

The One in whom nothing has been excluded, within whom all the fragments have become a whole, all contradictions have become resolved, it is only to Him that our atman wants to accept as "Yes" with folded palms. It is unable to acknowledge its own supreme fulfilment prior to that; it has to face obstacles and meet with deception – it thinks that this "Yes" is only in sense organs, in wealth and in fame. In the end, it sees that in all of them there is sin, there is conflict and 'No' is merged with them.

It is because the Upanishad has seen the supreme fulfilment in the resolution of all conflicts, it did not lean towards only one aspect of Truth and try to completely uproot the other. That is the reason why it says –

Etaj jñeyaṁ nityamevātmasaṁsthaṁ
Nātahparaṁ veditavyaṁ hi kiñcit[163]

That means, He who is eternally located in the atman He alone is worth knowing, there is nothing else worth knowing beyond Him. Similarly, it says again –

Te sarvagaṁ sarvataḥ prāpya dhīrā
Yuktātmānaḥ sarvamevāviśanti.[164]

That means, those calm beings by becoming one with the Atman, by attaining the Omnipresent from all directions, verily pervade everywhere.

It is not 'ātmanyevātmanaṁ pasyati',[165] it is not only to see the Atman within the atman – it is also to see the Atman everywhere[166].

At one end of our mantra of dhyana there is *bhūrbhubaḥsvaḥ*,[167] and at the other end is our *dhī*,[168] our consciousness. By binding these very two into one in the middle, there is that revered God who on one end is creating *bhūrbhubaḥsvaḥ*[169] and on the other end is also sending out our power of *dhī* as well. He is not there exclusive of the either – that is why He is verily Om.

It is for this reason that the Upanishad says, those that know ignorance, those that know the world as the only truth, fall into darkness, again those that have Knowledge, those that know the Knowledge of Brahman as supreme and as alienated, fall into greater darkness. On one side there is Knowledge and on the other there is ignorance, on one side there is the Knowledge of Brahman and on the other there is the world. At that point where these two meet, there itself dwells our atman.

By remoteness nearness is discarded, by nearness remoteness is discarded; by motion pause is discarded, by pause motion is discarded; by the inside the outside is discarded, by the outside the inside is discarded; but –

Tadejati tannaijati taddūre tadvantike
Tadantarasya sarvasya tadu sarvasyāsya bāhyataḥ.[170]

He moves yet He moves not, He is far away yet near, He is within everyone yet He is also without. It means, He is in the midst of all, of motion-pause, far-near, inside-outside – He is all inclusive. He does not leave out anyone – that is why He is verily Om.

He is between the manifested and the unmanifested. On the one hand, He is manifesting all, on the other no one is able to manifest Him. For this reason the Upanishad says –

Na tatra sūrya bhāti na candratārakā
Nemā vidyuta bhānti kutahayamagniḥ.
Tameva bhāntamanubhāti sarvaṁ
Tasya bhāsā sarvamidaṁ vibhāti.[171]

There the sun does not give light, neither the moon nor the stars, nor even all these flashes of lightning give radiance. Where then does one find this fire? He is manifested, so everything is in the state of being manifested, it is due to His very radiance that everything else is illuminated.

He is *śāntaṁ śivaṁ advaitam.*[172] Here *śāntam* does not imply that there is no connection with motion. In fact, all the opposing forces have united there peacefully. The centrifugal and the centripetal forces, the forces of attraction and repulsion want to cancel each other out; but it is because these two opposing forces are truly unopposed in Him that He is *Śāntam*. My self-interest does not want to accept your self-interest, your self-interest does not want to accept mine; but in the middle where there is welfare, there your interest is truly my interest, and my interest is also your interest. He is Śiva, in Him the interest of all inheres in welfare. He is Non-dual, He is One. That does not mean that all these are not there at all. It means that all these are one in Him. I say I am not you, you say you are not I; He is that *Advaitam* who has united such opposition of you and I.

Where the couple has united, there itself He exists, where no one has been forsaken there itself is He. This very completeness which is all inclusive, yet not supported by any fragment – that which is not in the moon, the sun and mankind, yet within the entire moon, sun and all mankind – that which is not in the ear, the eye, the speech or the mind, yet within all the ear, eye, speech or mind – to that very One, to that very "Yes", to acknowledge that very completeness with whole heart and soul is the sound "Om".

28 March 1909
(15 *Caitra* 1315 BE)

Supreme Obtainment

We have to obtain Brahman. But, what does obtainment mean?

We have so far obtained food, clothing and various other articles in our worldly life. When we hear 'we have to obtain' then it seems as though it has to be obtained in a similar manner. If we fail to obtain Him in that very manner, we think that we have not attained Him at all. Then we hurriedly make efforts to obtain God in the manner similar to our obtaining all other wants. That means in the inventory of our goods and chattels, in which there are entries like I have a horse, a cart, a pot, a bowl, it should also include – I have a God.

But, we need to think deeply as our atman has a profound yearning to obtain God, what is the nature of that yearning? Is it the yearning to add another big article to our other articles?

It is certainly not so. This is because we feel totally lost by our repeated act of merely adding and accumulating things. Do we not long for God because we want to escape from the endless suffering of regularly adding up the articles in that manner? Would we count Him again as a third article and add to our inventory of goods and chattels? Should we increase the garbage further?

But, that our atman yearns for Brahman simply means, it is pained by plurality and so it yearns for One, it is disturbed by the transient and so it longs for the Eternal – it does not aspire for anything new, anything particular. He who is 'Nityahanityānām',[173] is the Infinite within the finite, our atman aspires to realize that Infinite. It wants the One who is 'rasānāṁ rasatamaḥ',[174] He who is the Supreme Essence – it does not want any other newer essence.

That is why the instruction of this sadhana given to us is: *Īśāvāsyamidaṁ sarvaṁ yatkiñca jagatyāṁ jagat*.[175] Whatever exists in this universe, see them all as being pervaded by God – do not seek or create any other additional thing to be seen. Only then will our atman obtain refuge and bliss.

This is how indeed you will know Him within the entire universe. And what else shall you enjoy? It is *tena tyaktena bhuñjīthā*.[176] You will enjoy that which He has bestowed. *Mā gṛdhaḥ kasyasvidhanam*.[177] Do not have greed for others' wealth.

This means it has to be realized that whatever there is in the universe He pervades them all, it has to be known that whatever you have attained have been bestowed upon you by Him. What will happen due to that? Well, you will obtain your fulfilment out of whatever you have obtained. 'Add something more' is not the subject of our prayer – because, where is the end to such manner of adding? But, may I only be able to realize that whatever I have obtained has been given to me by Him. Only then few would become many, only then would I find the Infinite within the finite. Otherwise, it is never possible to gradually add up the finite to obtain the Infinite – and even on performing crores of *upāsanā* it is impossible to arrive at the *upāsanā* of that very One. All the finite manifestations of the world have achieved fulfilment in His Infinite manifestation and all those innumerable objects of our enjoyment have attained fulfilment just because of His bestowal. If this very fact is known properly, there is no need to move from door to door to seek God at any particular place or in any particular form. And in order to quench our insatiable desire for enjoyments, we do not have to be particularly tempted for any specific object of enjoyment.

30 March 1909
(17 *Caitra* 1315 BE)

Self-surrender[178]

That is the reason why I was saying that the remark about attaining Brahman could not be regarded as proper. This is because He has already surrendered[179] Himself to us, He has no lack in any respect – one cannot just say that in this place He is absent and we have to seek Him elsewhere.

Hence it is not fitting to say that we have to obtain Brahman – instead, we should say, 'I have to surrender myself to Him'. Something is lacking there itself, so no union is taking place. He has surrendered Himself to us, but we have not surrendered ourselves to Him. We have widely separated ourselves from Him by imposing barriers of our numerous self-interests, pride and narrow-mindedness, so much so that we have even kept ourselves opposed to Him.

It is for this reason that Lord Buddha has instructed us to gradually erode this strong barrier of self-identity through various efforts. If really there is no entity greater than this, no joy beyond this, then there is no reason why we should destroy this self-identity with rigorous discipline. This is because if nothing ever exists, then this very ego that remains within us, this individual particularity itself, becomes entirely the supreme gain – then why should we not hold it in a tight grip instead of destroying it to such a great extent?

But the fact is that the One who has completely surrendered Himself to us, if we, in turn, do not surrender ourselves completely to Him then it would mean He has not been accepted by us at all. It is only on our part that the commitment is overdue.

This *upāsanā* is not the *upāsanā* to attain Him – it is the *upāsanā* to surrender oneself to Him. Day after day through bhakti, forgiveness, contentment and service, one has to completely surrender[180] oneself to Him in welfare and in love devoid of any obstacles – that is our *upāsanā* to Him.

Hence, may we not say, 'Why are we not able to attain Him?', instead may we be able to say, 'Why are we not surrendering ourselves to Him?' Our daily lamentation is that –

Whatever I have, couldn't give You
All, O Lord!
My modesty, fear, honour, dishonour,
Happiness, sorrow and contemplation!

May you continue to surrender, erode all, exhaust everything – only then would you be fulfilled in your attainment.

All manners of veils are drawn between You and me –
So I wail and weep, I realize You not,
Anguish so great thus sticks in my heart.

All our sorrows and pains are only due to our inability to get rid of our ego; the moment that would cease to exist, we would immediately be able to see I have already obtained all my attainments since time immemorial.

The Upanishads say: *Brahma tallakṣyamucyate.*[181] Brahman is, in fact, said to be the goal. What is this goal[182] for? It is not for procuring something and drawing it towards oneself, but to lose oneself completely. *Śaravat tanmayo bhavet.*[183] Just as an arrow totally enters into its target and remains absorbed in it, we have to be completely absorbed in Him.

I do not regard this act of being absorbed in Him solely as a matter of dhyana. In fact, it is the matter that involves the entire life. In every situation, thought and action, may there be this realization in me that I am truly within Him and there is no separation from Him anywhere. May this knowledge become absolutely clear in the mind every day: *ko hyevānyāt kaḥ prānyāt yadeṣa ākāśa ānanda na syāt.*[184] There would not be even the minutest effort in my mind and body if there were no bliss pervading the space; it is only His bliss which in the form of power provides efforts to all our actions, either big or small. This very knowledge that I belong to Him, I function with His power and I enjoy myself by His bestowal – has to be made as simple as breathing – this is the ultimate goal of our sadhana. If this happens, our existence, action, enjoyment, truth, welfare and happiness in this universe – all will become natural – this is because, within our consciousness we will unite with the One who is Self-created, the One whose knowledge, power and action are innate. Our entire yearning is for the sake of attaining this.

31 March 1909
(18 *Caitra* 1315 BE)

Self-confidence

With my body, prana, consciousness, intellect and heart – all taken together, I am the only one. This very totality, this completeness, knows itself as a single entity and loves itself.

Not only that, for this reason it seeks the one everywhere and the moment it obtains the one, it is filled with joy. Separation causes pain to it, it wants completeness.

In fact, whatever it wants, its quest is to achieve this completeness in some form or the other. It aspires to unite its own one with those of the many around it and to transform this small one into the greater One.

The fact that each one of us has attained completeness of unity within ourselves, with the power of this attainment itself we can realize all other unities of the universe. We can understand the society as one, mankind as one and the whole universe as one – so much so that whatever we cannot understand as one, we do not realize its significance at all, only our intellect continues to grope around for it.

Hence, the reason that we seek the Supreme One is solely for the yearning of our own "one". This "one" can never pause midway without taking its own oneness up to the level of the Supreme One.

The fact that we know the society as one, the basis of that knowledge is our atman; that we know mankind as one, the basis of that knowledge is this atman; that we know the universe as one, the basis of that too is this atman and that we know the Supreme Atman as *advaitam*, the basis of that is this atman as well. It is for this very reason that the Upanishads say: 'ātmanyevātmānaṁ pasyati'[185] – *Sādhaka*[186] sees the Supreme Atman within his own atman. This is because, the oneness which is there in the atman is that oneness which seeks and attains the Supreme Oneness. The knowledge that attains Self Knowledge through its own oneness, gets ultimate refuge within the Absolute Knowledge of the Supreme Atman. It is for this reason that the Supreme Atman has been called 'Ekātmapratyasāram'.[187] This means the innate confidence that an individual atman has towards itself, it is He who forms the essence of that innate confidence. The fact that our atman, by nature, knows itself as one, the essence of knowing that very one is to know the Supreme One. Similarly, the fact that we have a self-love, the bliss of the atman within the Atman, it is this bliss itself which is the foundation of love towards the human atman, towards the Universal Atman and towards the Supreme Atman. It means the complete and the truest manifestation of this self-love itself marks the love towards the Supreme Atman – the outcome of bliss of the Atman is in that Supreme Bliss Itself. The ultimate stage of our self-love is bliss in the Supreme Atman. *Tadetat preyaḥ putrāt preya vittāt preyahanyasmāt sarvasmāt antaratara yadayamātmā.*[188]

3 April 1909
(21 *Caitra* 1315 BE)

The Bonds of the Mantra

Some strings of a veena may either be of copper or of steel, may be thick or thin, may be tuned[189] up to play the middle note or the fifth. Yet, we have to tune them up so as to awaken a pure note in it – or else, everything would be spoiled.

We have to establish some special kind of intimate relationship with God. We have to play some unique tune.

The sun, the moon, the star, the herb and the large tree – all have contributed their individual strains to this great universal music. Will man not have to take part in the eternal resounding music as well?

But, even now I have not tuned up my life like a string – there has not been any manifestation of music in it yet. This life has become futile due to unconnected array of trivialities. In whatever manner possible, I have to establish a certain eternal tune amid this.

How will I tune up the string?

There are many ways in which God's veena can be attuned, one has to decide something to one's own liking regarding this.

The mantra is a means of attunement. With the support of a mantra we tune up the mind with the object of thought. It is like the tuning peg of the veena – it tightens the string and does not allow it to slacken.

At the time of marriage ritual, it is not that a knot is simply tied with a portion of the attire worn by the man and the woman,[190] a mantra is also chanted along with it – that mantra continues to tie a knot within the mind as well.

The mantra will help us in establishing the need to tie a knot between God and us. With the support of this mantra we will firmly establish some special relationship with Him.

Pitā nohasi:[191] is one such mantra.

If I attune my life to this tune, then in all my thoughts and actions a special *rāgiṇī* will be awakened. This very image that I am His child will take shape through my whole being. Within my entire being I will only manifest this fact that I am His child.

I am not manifesting anything at all today. I am taking my meal, doing my work, taking rest – it is just that. But, the fact that my Father dwells in infinite time and space is in no way manifested in me. I have not been able to secure any bond anywhere with the Infinite even today.

May the string of life be tuned up with that very mantra today. In eating, in sport, in sleep and in dream, may the mantra: *Pitā nohasi*[192] keep on playing repeatedly in my mind. May this fact be known to all that I have a Father in this world, may it be concealed to none.

Lord Jesus played that very tune in the world. The string of his life was tied in such a manner that in spite of undergoing severe suffering of unbearable pain, that string never sounded out of tune even for a moment, it went on playing the tune: *Pitā nohasi.*[193]

Along with the pure ideal of the tune which he has revealed to us, we have to tie the string with utmost care so that we no longer have to think about it ever again, so that in joy, in sorrow and in temptation, it spontaneously chants: *Pitā nohasi*.[194]

O dear Father! It is no mean task to properly manifest myself as Your child. This is because, *ātmā vai jāyate putraḥ*.[195] The child is without doubt the manifestation of the father. It is within the child that the father himself becomes eternal indeed. If I am unable to manifest Your untainted blissful fullness, then this tune of 'Pitā nohasi'[196] will not play anymore.

For this very reason, may my daily earnest prayer be: *Pitā nobodhi. Namastehastu*.[197]

9 April 1909
(27 *Caitra* 1315 BE)

The End of the Year

The world is a union of arrivals and departures. There is no separation between the two. We imagine the separation in our mind. Creation, preservation and annihilation have all become completely one. They are always merged into one. To remain merged into one is itself said to be the phenomenon of the whole world.

There is no separation between the end of the year today and the beginning of the year tomorrow – this end enters into that beginning with complete silence and with utmost ease.

But, it is necessary for us to pause once between this beginning and this end. For once we have to know arrivals and departures separately or else we will not be able to know these two unitedly.

It is for this reason that today, on the last day of the year, we have turned our face only towards departure. By keeping the setting sun before us, today our worship is by facing the west. *Yat prayantyabhisaṁviśanti*[198] – He into whom all the departures enter, to whose feet everyone prostrates silently at the last moment of the day, it is to Him that we shall make namaskar this evening.

Today we will know end or departure or death deeply with bhakti – we will not do injustice to it. We will know it only as His shadow, 'Yasya chayamṛtaṁ yasya mṛtyuḥ'.[199]

Death is exceedingly beautiful and extremely pleasant. It is death which has kept life very pleasant. Life is extremely difficult; it wants everything, it grabs everything. Like a miser, it does not want to let anything slip from its firm grip. It is only death which has made the difficultly of life full of essence, has relaxed the attraction of life; it is only death which brings tears to its unfeeling eyes, gives mobility to its immobile existence.

There is nothing as mercilessly difficult as attachment; it knows only itself, it shows mercy to none, it does not want to make even a little way for anyone at all. This attachment itself is the dharma of life; it only fights with everyone because it wants to take hold of everything.

Renunciation is very beautiful and extremely tender. It opens the door. It does not permit savings to be piled up only at one place and become overbearing.

It disperses and gives away. It is only death which has that generosity. It is death which serves and gives away. Whatever tends to get amassed at one place is dispersed all over by death itself.

We can forgive all only because death prevails over the world. Otherwise, our heart would not have softened by anything. All pass away, all depart, we too depart. This shadow of sadness has layered all places with compassion. By playing the soft tunes of *Pūravī*[200] *rāgiṇī* all around, it has made our heart to cry. When this tune of departure reaches our ears, forgiveness becomes very easy. Then detachment comes silently to transform our urge for accepting slowly into that of bestowing.

When we come to know that nothing remains then we do not regard sin, sorrow and loss as overwhelming any more. Adversity would have become a terrible threat if we had known that it would never move from where it is. But we know that everything drifts and even that too drifts away hence, we need not feel dejected about it. Amidst the endless journey, sin is a vice only at a particular point, but it moves on from there. It moves even though we are not always able to see that. Its path does not end there itself – it stands on the verge of change and rectification. If the sin of a sinner remained immobile in him then Rudra's infinite sceptre of rule would have become a terrible burden upon that immobility and would have totally annihilated it. But God's sceptre is not just suppressing it at one point, that sceptre is forcing it to move. This movement itself is His forgiveness. The death granted by Him always pardons, always carries that into forgiveness.

Will not the end of the year bring our lives to His doorstep of forgiveness today? That upon which there is a seal of death, that which is destined to depart, will we not allow it to depart even today? If there is anger, should that anger be dragged over to the new year again? Throughout the year whatever garbage of sin we have accumulated, when we bid farewell to the year today, will we not be able to part with even a little of that? Shall we not be able to step into the new year by forgiving, by being forgiven and by being pure?

May my grip be loosened today. I have not attained any comfort or success only by snatching and by fighting. Today, when I come before He who accepts all, may my heart be able to say to Him, 'I shall renounce and merge into You'. Today I shall not be able to completely renounce and completely merge in Him in a moment; yet, may my mind bow down in that very direction, may its folded palms be extended as a mark of offering to Him, may the flute continue to play in the very tune of the setting sun, may the heart wail in the very enchanted *rāgiṇī* of death. This evening, before accepting the responsibilities of the new year, let me offload all the burden onto the seashore where all responsibilities are released, let me immerse myself in self-surrender; let me be soothed, be free from filth in the waveless blue mass of water; let me accept the end of the year completely within my heart and be calm, be peaceful and be pure.

13 April 1909
(31 *Caitra* 1315[201] BE)

Mukti

The very morning that is revealed to us every day provides us with very little joy. This morning has become worn out due to our habit.

Habit belittles all great things due to the smallness of our minds. As it thinks itself to be bound so it binds everything as well.

When we travel abroad we do not go to see any new world. We go to see this very earth, water and sky completely free from our habit. By dispelling that veil and by observing this world with our eyes wide open, we can see that Inconceivable One who is never old in this eternal world. It is only then that we derive bliss.

Habit cannot easily envelop the one who is dear to us. For this very reason a dear one can eternally reveal to us the Inconceivable, the Infinite. The fact that we see our dear one, this very act of seeing does not end there – he remains beyond our seeing, hearing and all our understanding. Our joy is only because of that.

So the Upanishads said, 'ānandarūpamṛtam'[202] – the manifestation of bliss of God is immortality. We find no joy in that which is dead to us, which ceases to exist. Wherever we see the Infinite within the finite, we see the Immortal, there itself lies our bliss.

This Infinite itself is the Truth; to see It is to see the Truth. Wherever we fail to see that, there itself we have to understand that due to our own lethargy, ignorance, habit and stock notions we have obstructed the Truth, that is why we do not obtain any joy in that.

Be he a scientist, a philosopher or a poet, it is indeed his job to dispel all these veils of ignorance and the habit of man, in order to show the infinite form of Truth in this world, and to show whatever we see as Truth – it is neither to create, nor to imagine anything new. To show this Truth as liberated only means to enhance man's claim to joy.

As in the manner to leave home and to go to a faraway country is not said to be mukti from darkness, to open the door of the house itself is considered to dispel darkness. So to renounce the whole world alone is not mukti – whatever we see beyond the bondage of sin, self-interest, ego, lethargy, ignorance and stock notions, to see this truly, whatever we do to do this truly, wherever we stay to stay there truly, is indeed mukti.

If this utterance alone were true that Brahman is blissful only in His own unmanifested form, then if we had not merged into His unmanifested form, there would have been no escape for us from the grip of unhappiness. But that is not so, in manifestation itself lies His bliss. Why else did He manifest this world? Has any great external suffering forced Him to manifest Himself? Has any entity called Maya[203] completely overwhelmed Brahman to manifest itself?

That, in fact, is never possible. So the Upanishads say: *Ānandarūpamṛtaṁ yadvibhāti.*[204] This very manifested world is nothing but His eternal bliss itself which assumes form and gets manifested. Bliss itself is His manifestation, in manifestation itself lies His bliss.

If He is blissful in getting manifested only, then for obtaining bliss should I seek out the unmanifested? If His will itself is manifestation then how shall I possibly avoid that influence of His manifestation by this humble will of mine?

Without taking part in His bliss I can never be blissful. Wherever my union with it will be complete, there itself will I attain mukti, there itself will I attain bliss. Only by freely realizing His manifestation in this universe will I be liberated – only by making His manifestation in me freely revealed will I be liberated. By severing the worldly bondage, that is to say the bondage of existence, is not mukti – it is not by making existence merely a form of bondage but a form free from bondage itself is mukti. Only to renounce work is not mukti, to do work derived out of joy itself is mukti. To accept that bliss in which He is manifesting, to accept the work with the bliss in which He is doing work – is what we call mukti. Not to renounce anything, but to accept everything itself in a truthful manner is mukti.

When will this habitual world of every day that appears worn out to me and this habitual dawn that appears dull to me become new and bright to me? It is on that day when my consciousness gets awakened by love with renewed strength. All that was devoid of beauty yesterday becomes beautiful today whenever it strikes me that today I will meet the One I love. The complete power that consciousness attains through love, it is through that very completeness it sees the Infinite within the finite, the Formless within the form – it does not have to go to any new place. It is only due to that lack the Infinite Truth remained confined within the finite.

The universe is His form of bliss; but we only see the form, we do not see bliss. That is the reason why form only hurts us at every step. The moment we see bliss, no one will be able to obstruct us any more in any way. That itself is mukti.

That mukti is not the mukti of detachment, that is the mukti of love. It is not the mukti of renunciation, it is the mukti of union. It is not the mukti of dissolution, it is the mukti of manifestation.

20 April 1909
(7 *Baiśākh* 1316 BE)

After the Holidays

At Śāntiniketan *Brahmavidyālaẏ*[205]

After the holidays we have assembled here again. It is not to alienate ourselves from work that at times we take a break from it like this. This is the means to renew our relation with work.

At times, if we do not go far away from our place of work like this, we cannot understand the true significance of our work. To become continuously absorbed in work is to give too much priority to work itself. Then like the cobwebs, work overwhelms us from all directions in such a way that we lose even the ability to understand its true purpose. That is why to gain an opportunity to see our regular work anew, we at times distance ourselves from it. Its aim is not solely to provide rest to the spent energy.

We will not see work alone. We also have to see the master. We will not spend our days like the labourers of this world-factory by smearing soot all over the body amidst the intense heat of fire and terrible noise of the engine. If we happen to see the master of the factory for once at the close of the day after taking a bath and changing our clothes, then we can establish a link between him and our work, we can do away with the supremacy of the machine; only then do we derive joy from our work. Otherwise, we only become identical to the machine by continuously operating the wheel of the machine.

Today at the end of the holidays we have returned to our place of work again. Do we not see work in a new light this time again? The inherent truth of this work had become dull to us by constant practice; do we not feel joy when we see it bright again?

What is this joy all about? Is it in having seen the image of success directly? Is it because we think that we have done what we wanted to do? Is it the joy of feeling proud of our self-achievement?

No, that is not so. Man takes pride in his own power when he considers work itself to be the ultimate and steeps himself in it. But when we see the inner truth of work, we see that entity which is much greater than work. Then just as our pride fades away and our heads bow down in reverence, our chest swells with joy. At that moment we not only see the movement of the machine made of iron, we are able to see our blissful Lord as well.

Within this school here, there is an effort to do welfare. But, is it only a machine to do welfare? Is it merely to make rules and to enforce them? Is it only to teach a language, to teach how to solve sums, to toil and to set others to toil? Is it only to build a huge school and to think 'I have obtained a great result'? No, it is not so.

It is extremely deceptive to see this effort as great, to feel proud of the very fruit of this effort as great. There is no doubt that good result is obtained from the celebration of welfare, but that is only a secondary result. The fact is, amidst the work of welfare, the manifestation of the benevolent One becomes clear to us. If we look at the right place we can see the universal benevolent One beyond the work of welfare. That is the ultimate success of the celebration of welfare. The work of welfare is a sadhana to see Viśvakarmā in the light of Truth. The person who is lazy cannot see Him. His manifestation is hidden in the heart of the person who is slothful. That is the reason why we do work, or else there cannot be any glory of work while doing work itself.

If we feel at heart that our work is a sadhana to attain that benevolent Viśvakarmā, then whatever obstacle, lack and opposition that exist in our work cannot disappoint us. This is because to overcome the obstacle itself is a part of our sadhana. In fact, our sadhana remains incomplete unless we encounter obstacles. At the time when we face opposition we do not become anxious for the fear of spoiling the work; this is because there is a result even much greater than the result of work. It would not do to make a firm resolve that if we struggle against opposition we would surely succeed; in fact, we do not know whether we would succeed or not – but by struggling continuously against opposition, the obstacles of our minds erode; due to that our flame becomes unblemished, and gradually becomes radiant and in that very radiance the universal Manifestation starts to get revealed within our minds. Rejoice that there is obstacle in work. Rejoice that you have to endure several blows from different directions as long as you do your work and that which you contemplate would repeatedly be defeated. Rejoice that people will misunderstand you and will insult you. Rejoice that you will repeatedly be deprived of that pay you greedily awaited. This is because that itself is sadhana. The person who wants to light a fire, how would it do if he mourns for the burning of wood? Forget about the miser who only wants to pile up dry wood. So after the holidays, we resume our work today with joy in the midst of all its obstacles, wants and imperfections. How do we do it? It is by observing the One who is seated beyond work.

To take a look at Him enhances the power of work, yet there is no trace of insolence; we no longer see the form of effort while making an effort, only its peaceful image is revealed; the work continues yet there is stillness like the water at high tide, everything continues to be dreadfully still. All calling and shouting, proclamation and rumour, completely cease. There is no superfluity of thoughts, words and action. Then power veils itself and becomes beautiful – as beautiful as the constellation in today's evening sky. Extending a complete image of peace with its immense power, intense speed and tremendous enthusiasm what a lovely smile it smiles! In order to see that peaceful, extremely beautiful form of the Supreme Power from the seat of our action, we too will calm our insolent efforts, we will adorn the extreme pain of work with beauty and overwhelm it. Our work – *Madhu dhauḥ, madhu naktam, madhumat pārthivaṁ rajaḥ,*[206] will unite with all these and will become nectarous.

1909
(1316 BE)

End

In a song there is the terminal point of a measure, in prosody there is a caesura, and even in this very writing, the authority of the full stop is in no way inferior to the other parts of this writing. These very full stops have steered this writing – they are not allowing this writing to meander constantly into aimlessness.

In fact, when a poem comes to an end, even that ending itself is a major part of the poem. This is because a good poem never ends in a void. Even where it ends, it speaks; these unspoken words must be given the scope to express themselves.

If, where a poem ends, all its strains and words run out, then the poem becomes ashamed of its poverty. When a person turns completely bankrupt celebrating a particular occasion with utmost pomp, the pomp ends up revealing not his wealth but his conspicuous poverty.

A river stops where it does because the sea begins there – so, there is no harm in its stopping. In fact, this is a stop only from one direction, not from the other.

There are many such stops in people's lives as well. But it is often seen that a person feels ashamed to stop. That is why we often hear from the English that to die in harness by falling flat on one's face while running at full speed is a glorious death indeed. Nowadays we too have started to use this expression.

Whenever a person denies that there is fullness somewhere, he thinks there is dignity only in movement. A person who knows neither enjoyment nor charity, knows only how to save.

But, in enjoyment or charity, when one's savings go on diminishing, the savings come to an end in one form but come to fruition in another. Where there is no fruitful end to this saving, there is shamefaced miserliness.

Those who see life as a miser do not want to stop anywhere by any means; they go on saying, 'Let's go, let's go, let's go'. In stopping, their movement achieves neither completion nor profundity. They accept only the whip and the bridle; they do not accept a great and beautiful end.

Even after having passed their youth, they drag that youth along with them – and there is no end to their toil and trouble in carrying out that burdensome task. Apart from that, what shame, what anxiety, what fear!

When a fruit ripens, its dignity lies in departing from the branch. But if it thinks that renouncing the branch is a sign of poverty, then there is nothing more pitiful than that fruit!

As soon as one accepts a position, one should think to oneself, "Once I fulfil the obligations of this position, I will renounce it". 'This position must be protected at any cost by dragging it to the end – this is my honour and my achievement' – those that have learned this lesson from their childhood, grasp their positions, until some accidental death drags them by force like a bailiff.

In our country, end is acknowledged, so no disgrace is found in it. And hence, for it, to renounce is not to beat a retreat.

This is because renunciation does not really imply emptiness. We cannot truly deem it a failure when a ripened fruit falls from its branch to the ground. On the ground, the nature and field of its efforts become transformed; it is not a retreat into inactivity. There the stage of preparation for a greater birth is taking place. There lies the period of living in concealment – there is the entry from the outside into the inside.

> In our country they say: *Pañcāśordhvaṁ vanaṁ vrajet.*[207]

But that forest is not the forest of leisure; it is rather a forest for the practice of austerities. There man's prolonged effort for saving enters into the field of bestowing.

The ideal to do is not man's only ideal; the ideal to become is also of immense importance. As the paddy plant was growing by struggling against sunlight and rain, it was beautiful. But with the production of grain at harvest, when its days in the field are over and its days in storage begin, it is beautiful too. Is there any disgrace that the entire history of sun and rain of the paddy field is deeply silent within that harvest?

If we make such a resolve that we will see man's life only in his field and not in its harvest, we only spoil that life. So I say, there comes a time in man's life when it is time to stop. The thing we demand from a man at work, if we demand the same when he stops working, it is not only to do him injustice – but to deprive ourselves as well.

The claim that we may make on a person in repose, is not the ideal to do, but the ideal to become. When everything is in motion, always in the state of making and breaking, of rising and falling, then we cannot identify ourselves completely and calmly with the ideal to become. When all motions cease, then we are able to see the ideal to become. There is also the need for man to see this state of fulfilment, this form of calmness. We want both – the seedlings in the field and the paddy in the granary.

Men of action consider work to be the only thing of value. That is why they seek only to extract work from people until their last moment.

The worth of a person depends solely on the demands of a society. In a society which demands war, the soldier is highly valued. Therefore, everyone gives up all other efforts and tries his level best only to become a soldier.

Where the demand for work is great, utmost effort of man is to proclaim himself active till the last moment. It can be said that man is almost without a full stop and only unceasing action[208] prevails there. At that point where man stops, he gets nothing there, he only feels ashamed. There, work is like alcohol which when consumed, brings fatigue. Amidst the stillness there, man does not show any significant expression. At that place the image of death is the ultimate void and full of horror. And there life is constantly churned, perturbed, afflicted and gains momentum by artificial impulse of hundreds and thousands of machines.

September/October 1910
(*Āśvin* 1317 BE)[209]

Awakening

May our minds be awakened on this special day of our ashram. In our lives, the day of festival is different from any other day, it does not match the tune of every day. But, there is a connection between this day of our festival and all the other days; it is like a diamond pendant in the middle of a pearl necklace. There is a connection, there is uniqueness as well. This is because man has a little aspiration for that uniqueness. On certain days man wants to come away a little from his daily life and wants to have the taste of its joy. For the same reason we go out for a picnic to have our food at a distance. We try to get the very item of our everyday use in a newer way, different from its regular habit. It is for this reason that we have made the preparation to enjoy the food of our ashram by moving a little away in a special manner today.

But, in the preparation for a picnic when the food items are kept quite far away from the picnic spot and have to be carried there in huge amounts, then the stock of our storehouse comes to our notice in a moment. If there has been wastage every day, we will see a shortage on that day.

In our preparation for an extremely delicious meal[210] in this picnic today perhaps we will find something lacking. If that be so, how else would we then externally cover that lack which is within? Those who live in the city do not have any lack of equipment, it is only by means of those they can save the honour of their festival. At our place over here, the path to all such accomplishments is blocked. But, there is no fear. The demand has been placed for the festival of our ashram on a daily basis. Here in the nest of the birds of the sal forest, under the sky over the vast expanse of land as the playground of the wind, every day the tune of our festival has been gathered at least to some extent. But due to forgetfulness of every day, the symphony has not reached our heart properly. Today we need to do away with the lethargy of habit and pay attention to it just once, we do not have to procure anything else from outside. Let us calm our mind and sit; let us extend our folded palms in prayer, then from the forest of nectar, the nectarous fruits will fall of their own upon our palms. To enjoy that preparation which prevails everywhere on its own is indeed our festival. We did not see Him just because we did not call Him every day, today we would indeed see Him the moment we call Him from the bottom of our hearts. We have no need to stimulate our minds by the impact of any external excitement. This is because there is no gain in that, rather there is loss of power in it. When the sap inside a tree gets the touch of spring, only then the flower blooms, that flower itself is Truth. The external excitement which evokes a momentary delusion is only a mirage; we should take care not to be deceived by that. Let us awaken the power which is within us. If we get its response even for a moment then its fulfilment lasts for ever. Even if we can be true for a moment, then that Truth will never perish; that seed of immortality will be sown for ever in the field of our eternal life. If we can properly bring the wick of the lamp of our mind to touch the holy sacrificial fire which is eternally burning at the place of the sacrifice of this universe then at that moment itself our wick could be enkindled.

May our awakening be fulfilled amidst Truth today, may the light of this dawn not veil us today, may the eternal Light be manifested today, may the green canopy of the earth not conceal anything today – may the eternally Beautiful Being reveal Himself today! Just in the manner an infant embraces its mother completely, may our consciousness unite with the Supreme Consciousness. While reciting poetry, as our mind attains the poet's joy through his rhythm and language, today within this dew-drenched calm and holy universal beauty, may we directly perceive that universal joy with all our hearts and minds.

22 December 1913
(7 *Pauṣ* 1320 BE)

The Day of the Initiation

That day when we have to see the ashram in its true light, the music of joy will begin to play, garland of flowers will swing and rays of the sun will become brighter – because, it is only through joy that it is possible to see the Truth, not by any other means. Through our extreme attachment we grasp everything externally. It is for this very reason that a certain day comes for us to see the inner form of joy by getting rid of that attachment.

Which day did Maharṣi,[211] the founder of this ashram, choose as the day of festival to see this true form? It was the day of his[212] initiation. The day of initiation is the very day when man accepts that which is great within him, the Eternal Life within him. No effort is put by man for his being born into the world; the preparation has been made long before his coming here. But, when man goes beyond himself on his own and accepts initiation from the light of the sun; from the entire sky, from the holy air, from the supreme refuge of this vast universe – the day when he says, "I belong to mankind for all eternity and have an immortal life, it is within me that the Infinite, the Omnipresent, the Supreme God is manifested" – that is the day of the festival of entire mankind. Very similar was the day of initiation, the day Maharṣi offered *praṇāms* to the Infinite within the universe, the day he realized the Immortal Life within himself and presented himself to Him as an offering, he realized that the very day was truly a day of festival and he has bestowed that upon us. It is by taking refuge in Maharṣi's initiation that we are here. This ashram is the external form of that day of his initiation. This is because here the initiation is in action, in learning and in teaching – initiation into that eternal life. That supreme mantra of initiation prevails in this ashram. Even if we forget that fact every day, at least today in the light of joy of the festival, be prepared to clearly realize that form of immortality of the ashram. Be awakened today, behold the Truth. Listen to that mantra of initiation which prevails in the air today –

Īśāvāsyamidaṁ sarvaṁ yatkiñca jagatyāṁ jagat;
Tena tyaktena bhuñjīthā mā gṛdhaḥ kasyasviddhanam.[213]

'The Supreme Will through which the whole universe is preserved and governed, the Supreme Will through which the sun, the moon and the stars are regulated and the Infinite *ārti*[214] lamps all over the sky are never extinguished, realize this that the entire universe is pervaded by that Supreme Will!' All pulsate with the rhythm of His will, with the spark of His bliss. Realize that bliss. As He renounces, we enjoy ourselves. As He renounces, the fountain of life flows in every direction, the river of bliss flows through various branches and sub-branches, there is no end to the flow of sweetness in the pure love between husband and wife in every house – in the deep love of parents towards their children That life, that joy and that love moves in an endless flow! Enjoy yourself, enjoy yourself with joy! In the blueness of the sky, in the greenness of the forest, in knowledge, in love and in joy – enjoy it, enjoy it to the fullest extent! *Mā gṛdhaḥ*.[215] May there be no filth, no greed in the mind – let there be freedom from all bondage of sin and greed. This is the mantra of his[216] initiation.

This mantra has created this ashram, this mantra has protected this ashram. Today's festival under the sky of this ashram, in its holy air, in its pure light, in the vast expanse, is to see, to listen, to accept this mantra in our closely associated lives. May the mind be awakened, may the God of this ashram be manifested, may He open the door of His temple. May His love and blessing be bestowed upon these young lives who are as tender as flowers, may they bloom in holiness, love and purity; may they remember this auspicious day, may they accept this mantra – this viaticum for life. The whole path of life lies before them – may they accept the blessing of immortality and proceed with their journey, may they progress by attaining the initiation for their whole life. May this mantra of initiation help them to overcome all the dangers, obstacles and troubles in their paths. Be awakened, awaken your life!

Morning
22 December 1913
(7 *Pauṣ* 1321 BE)

More[217]

We want more, we want more – this song is the song of festival. We have come to that storehouse where we will obtain more. The earth is full of food and wealth, man's home is full of love and affection, he is born on the lap of Lakṣmī.[218] There we spend our days meeting our needs. At times man's festival lies in coming out of that to the courtyard of the storehouse of "more".

At one time man greatly feared the gods on earth. Man could by no means decide as to whom to appease to lead a life of happiness and ease, who if displeased would bring about trying times. The terror-struck men had then assembled with the sacrificial animal to appease that power which had no connection with the atman. The puja performed out of fear is certainly not a festival. Just as a coward who falls in the clutches of a dacoit says, 'Whatever I have I give you all, but do not kill me', to appease the unseen power of the world, that day man said, 'I will give you all, do not put me in danger'. But that is surely not a gift of joy. There is nothing to fear once the God of joy is realized. That is because this God of joy is, in fact, 'More' – it is He who transcends all – whatever I have obtained and known, He is more than that; what I have not obtained, what I have lost, He is much more than that too; He is more than wealth; more than fame; more than comfort. That is why in the puja of that More, in the festival of that More, man says with joy, 'Take my wealth, my life and my fame'. Man's knowledge of this very "more", within himself and without, is not at all a knowledge that offers much comfort. The day man discovers that he is not a beast, his God is not a beast, he is great and his God is great, on that very day he accepts supreme sorrow. On that day man is truly victorious, he is truly brave – so a celebration of victory will not take place on that day. Just in the manner a bird begins to sing with causeless joy at the very touch of light at the edge of darkness, man too begins to sing on that day at the touch of the Supreme Light. That day he says, 'I am the child of the Immortal'. He says, 'Vedāḥ metam.[219] I have attained the One'. With that power of attainment he realizes that Immortal Being within himself, he is not afraid any more, he pays no heed to death; in the face of danger he says, 'My path is before me, I will not step back, I know no defeat – O Rudra, Your grace is endless'.

Give this a thought just once; at this very moment when we are celebrating the festival of joy here, what a terrible battle is being fought among men overseas! What does this light of Dawn see there today – what a horror of destruction! There, amidst this horror, man is preaching humanity – there a summons has come from history, all have come out when they have heard that summons. Those that have erred, those that have not erred – in this war which side is responsible to what extent – these are matters of distant future. But, there is a summons from history – that summons has been heard by the German, the English, the French, the Belgian, the Austrian and the Russian. It is through history that the God of history will accept His puja; His festival is in the midst of this battle. This is the commandment of the God of history that it will not do for any race to amass its national interest in order to make its nationalism narrow. Man has arranged to offer human sacrifice at the feet of that demon of national interest for such a long time, that is why an order has been given to demolish the temple of that demon today. The God of history said, 'Well![220] The walls of the temple of this demon of national interest should be crushed and knocked down to the ground by all of you, this human sacrifice cannot continue any longer'. As soon as this order has been received, the cannon-balls from both sides dashed against that wall. The group of brave men has been carrying its offering of blood-red lotus[221] for the puja of the God of history. Those that were leading the life of comfort shunned that comfort and said, 'We will not keep a tight grip on our lives, there is much more within man than just life'. In the roaring of the cannon that victory song of humanity has rung. Mother is wailing, wife and child have become widowed and orphaned respectively, and are beating their breasts. Amid that wailing the festival is going on. When business and trade were going on, money was being amassed at home, power was being pervaded throughout the royal kingdom – there was a summons to come out. When Śiva[222] drew in the scorching breath into His conch,[223] mother had to weep and say, 'Go ahead!' With her own hands the weeping wife had to dress her husband with a coat of mail. Today in the oblation of death overseas, there is that great festival of life.

Has the sound of that festival not yet reached our festival here today? Who has uttered this mantra, 'Leave everything – come out', into the ear of the man who is a coward, who yearns for comfort, who scrambles and scuffles every day for some petty self-interests! He who has the storehouse of "more" said, 'Go! Disregard death and do come out!' Would we not be able to know that great man of valour today, the man who has become ecstatic by drinking the amrita of "more"? Did we not erect the temple of an ignorant god, a lesser-god in this country to perform his puja with all the necessary sixteen articles?[224] Did we not offer sacrifices of human intellect and power to him? Should we not destroy that temple of delusion and ignorance due to which one man hates another and keeps him at a distance? Do we not have that fight before us? We have to receive ill treatment from our friends and relatives. We will accept sorrow and will have to put up with insult, criticism and ridicule – we will not be afraid of those.

In our Śāntiniketan, the God of history has pointed out that very mantra of immortality through which we would obtain that power. *Īśāvāsyamidaṁ sarvam.*[225] There is nothing to fear, everything is pervaded by fulfilment. That very immortality is beyond death. See it as being pervaded by God – that abode of bliss will be revealed everywhere. There will be no fear! Discard all that is useless and come out.

The joy of worldly pleasure and guilt of delusion have entangled us at every step. Never fear, leave aside everything, purify yourself in the ablution of valour and come out. The wail that has sounded throughout the universe today has no tune of fear in it; history is being created through that – it is within this that the God of history derives His bliss. That wail is quiet within Him. Within that 'śāntaṁ śivaṁ advaitam'[226] death has ceased to exist. With His own hands He has applied the tilak of victory on the forehead of man. He has stood amidst separation and opposition. The place where the travellers have journeyed, where a sharp and loud noise of death has echoed, there see that 'śāntaṁ śivaṁ advaitam'.[227] Today accept the blessings of Rudra who is the supreme refuge. The gracious smile of Rudra is seen only when He sees that His valorous children have defied sorrow. Only then does that smile of His gracious countenance radiate and get immersed in the light of Truth. May that graciousness of Rudra be radiated all over our lives in today's festival.

In the morning.
22 December 1914
(7 *Pauṣ* 1321 BE)

Innermost Peace

Your gaze indeed pervades the entire sky.
You see me with steadfast gaze day and night.

Will I realize this here, within the core of my heart – that He continues to gaze at my face? Should all these words be uttered amidst this uproar[228]? In the starlight, in the soothing darkness, when the steadfast gaze of an eye falls from the infinite sky upon the realm of silence within a *bhakta*'s heart, then in the midst of that very silent solitude this profound message of supreme bliss can be awakened – this is what it appears to be. But, that is not so. It is certainly not true that in the midst of that very solitude a *sādhaka*'s festival becomes complete. It is in this noisy fair of man, amidst this wonderful sport of buying and selling, it is within this very uproar itself that the hymn of His puja is chanted – to move far away from this is never to partake in His festival. The music which is produced from every star in the sky, keeps repeating itself throughout the ages. There is no noise, no crowd, no pushing and shoving – it is as if in the galaxy, the *Bāul*[229] in His universal form,[230] is repeatedly playing a particular tune on His *ektārā*. But, is the music that is played in the human world produced from a single string? So many varieties of strings, that of hostility and warfare, of opposition and struggle are being clattered – there is no limit to their diversity. But, amid these diversities and conflicts, the tune of peace is being played. The six cardinal passions[231] are attacking mankind from all directions, the sport of frantic dance[232] is going on, but even so many discordant notes could not, in fact, wipe out this single tune! This very tune: *śāntaṁ śivaṁ advaitam*[233] has started playing in the midst of all these conflicts, revolutions and hostilities.

Do we not see in today's mela an image of this very festival which continues in the history of mankind? Here, some are engaged in shopping, some are playing games while others are listening to the yatra.[234] But no prohibition has been imposed on anything – it has not been said, 'Upāsanā is being performed here, all of you sit quietly and be good'.[235] May the tremendous uproar that continues within the human race throughout the world defile the quiet peace of Śāntiniketan. Only man causes uproar, no other creature does that. But, has man's uproar ever been able to stop his music till today? God wills to extract the gem from the ore of the mine, He will really reclaim His puja from within this very uproar of disharmony – because when man, the creature of this uproar, attains peace then what else can ever be compared to that supreme peace? That peace is not there in the unpeopled ocean, not in the stillness of the dessert, nor at the inaccessible mountain peak – that profound peace is within the atman. The noise from all directions gets defeated while trying to attack that peace which is kept well-guarded within the depths of this uproar. The market[236] has already been set up, there is noise of buying and selling – amidst that itself every man is carrying a yogic asana[237] within his own atman. Ye yogi, wake up, your asana for yoga is ready, take your own asana – sit where there is uninterrupted peace in the midst of this uproar, amidst distress, agitation and conflict of the inherent six cardinal sins. Light the lamp of your festival there, no untamed gust of wind will be able to put it out. Do not be scared of uproar – as the kernel is protected by remaining inside the bitter covering of the shell within the ovary of a fruit, peace sought by man has always been protected likewise by being surrounded by this uproar. Man has indeed always placed his personal God above his earthly possessions. Where his attachment has entangled all the threads of life, it is in the midst of that itself that the pinnacle of his temple looks up to the abode of God.

There is no harm in the fact that our mind has not become propitious today. However, let the mind of one wander wherever it wants to – there is no prohibition. In spite of this limitless independence, man's place of puja has always been carefully protected. We have come to realize that utterance in the midst of this uproar. Irrespective of one who has bhakti, one who is devoid of bhakti, the worldly person, the businessman and the sinner – His puja is being performed within all of them. It is in this mela itself that His puja has taken place, it is amidst this very uproar that His hymn has been chanted. It is at this very place we hear that sound of footsteps of 'śāntaṁ śivaṁ advaitam',[238] It is on the path of this marketplace that His footprints have been left. He frequents Himself in this very fair of man's coming and going – it is here itself that He reveals Himself.

Night
22 December 1914
(7 *Pauṣ* 1321 BE)

Notes

Arise! Awake!

1 Kaṭha Upanishad, 1.3.14. 'Uttiṣṭhata jāgrata' translated into English as 'Arise! Awake!' are two words taken from a sloka of the said Upanishad.
2 The word 'karma' has been translated in these essays to mean 'acts', 'activities', 'actions' and 'work' depending on the context. The word 'karma' though present in *COD* has been defined as 'the sum of a person's own actions in this and previous states of existence, viewed as affecting their future fate' is not applicable in the *Śāntiniketan* essays. But even then I cannot retain the word 'karma' and provide the deduced meanings in the first endnote and continue employing the word as in the Bengali Source Text; Tagore has employed another word which is synonymous to the meaning of 'karma' as is applicable in the *Śāntiniketan* essays. The word is 'kāj', which also means 'work', 'action', 'activities' among others. There are essays where 'karma' and 'kāj' occur close to each other having similar meanings. Hence, I have decided to translate 'karma' into English. Only on two occasions have I retained the word 'karma' due to culture-specificity of the terms, 'Karma Yoga' and 'karma yogi'.
3 *Ektārā* is a folk single-stringed musical instrument of India. It is used by the *bauls* or wandering minstrels as an accompaniment to their songs.

Lack

4 The Bengali title of this essay is 'abhāb', a word that has been translated as 'lack', 'loss' and 'wants' depending on the context.
5 The Bengali word in the text is 'saṁsāric'. Tagore uses the noun form 'saṁsāra' primarily in one sense – either to refer to the 'phenomenal world', or to the 'world' or 'worldliness' or 'lifestyle'. The translation of the word in any given place depends on the context.
6 The Bengali word 'kṣati' has been translated either as 'loss' or as 'harm' depending on the context.
7 A *pie* is a quarter of a *pice*. A *pice* is one-fourth part of an anna and one sixty-fourth part of a rupee.
8 It is a sign of paying respect or showing honour to a deity, an elderly person or a person worthy of respect by touching the feet of that deity or person. During Tagore's time, it was a common practice for the younger ones in the household to offer *praṇām* to senior members of the family.
9 The Bengali phrase 'daś bār' literally means 'ten times' and in colloquial Bengali usage it denotes 'many times'.

Sin

10 I have translated the Bengali word 'pāp' either as 'sin' or as 'vice' depending on the context.
11 White [Śukla] Yajur Veda, 30.3. 'Viśvāni duritāni deva savitar parāsuva' means 'O God, Savitar! Dispel all the sins far away and send us only that which is benevolent.' Tagore omitted 'deva savitar' from the above sloka. This sloka is also found in Ṛg Veda 5.82.5.
12 Īśa Upanishad, 8. 'Śuddhaṁ apāpaviddham' means 'pure and unaffected by sin'.
13 Muṇḍaka Upanishad, 3.2.5. The words 'sarvataḥ prāpya' mean 'attainable everywhere'.
14 The word 'mukti' has been retained in the essays to mean 'liberation', 'freedom' and 'ultimate liberation' (moksha) depending on the context.
15 Bṛhadāryaṇaka Upanishad, 2.4.3. 'Yenāhaṁ nāmṛtā syam kimahaṁ tena kuryām' is said by Maitreyī, the younger wife of Yājñavalkya, means 'What should I do with that by which I would not be immortal?'

Sorrow

16 White Yajur Saṁhitā, 16:41. 'Obeisance to the Bestower of Divine joy and of worldly pleasures'.
17 The act of bowing and folding the elbows at right angles and joining the palms of both hands together touching each other in front of the chest, parallel to the heart [*anāhata cakra*] (or sometimes in front of the forehead [*ājña cakra*] mostly while doing it to a deity) with finger tips pointing upward. It is a sign of reverence to those that are superior to oneself. It is also a sign of greeting in India which indicates reverence for the other being.
18 The Bengali word 'śakti' meaning 'power', 'force', 'energy' or 'strength' has been employed in keeping with the context.
19 In the Bengali text, Tagore had employed the word 'Śiva' which is the name of a Hindu God, but in this context it means 'benevolent'.
20 In the Bengali text, Tagore had employed the word 'śivatara' which is the superlative degree of the word 'śiva' to emphasize the attributes of 'Śiva' which means 'the most benevolent' in this context.

Renunciation

21 The word *upāsanā* means worship.
22 The original Bengali word is 'pāoẏā'. It has been translated either as 'obtain' or 'attain' in keeping with the context.
23 The Bengali word is 'mukta' which means 'liberated', or 'free'. Here it has been translated as 'free' depending on the context.
24 Karma Yoga is that union with God where a devotee attains Him through selfless work or action. See the entry of 'Karma-Yoga' from *A Dictionary of Advaita Vedanta.*
25 The Bengali word in the text was 'karmi'. I have interpreted it as 'karma yogi'. A karma yogi is a person who does selfless work, that is, he does not expect any result for the work he has performed and eventually realizes God through his selfless work or action.
26 See the Bible, Matthew 19:23-24. The parable of 'The Rich Young Man'.
27 The word 'amrita' is referred to as the Divine nectar of immortality obtained by the churning of the ocean. It is from the myth of the *Samudra Manthana* (Churning of the Ocean). Amrita had to be obtained by the Gods to regain their power lost by being continuously defeated by the demons. Tagore makes a pun on 'amrita'; at one instance he gives the literal meaning of the word and again he gives the mythical meaning. Whenever the literal meaning is applicable, it has been translated either as 'immortal',

or 'immortality' and whenever its mythical meaning is implied by Tagore, 'amrita' has been transliterated. Here the word 'amrita' has been retained as it connotes to the mythical drink of immortality. The translation of the word or its transliteration in any given place depends on the context.

The Prayer

28 The anglicized word for *Bhāratvarṣa* is India (Bharat).
29 The Bengali as well as Sanskrit word 'vanaspati' means the 'king of the woods'. Here I have translated it as the 'greatest tree'.
30 The word *tapasyā* means penance or religious austerities.
31 This alludes to Bṛhadāraṇyaka Upanishad, 2.4.2.
32 See 'The Prayer', note 31. This speech is by Yājñavalkya in reply to Maitreyī's query as mentioned in the previous note.
33 See 'Sin', note 15 .
34 See 'Sin', note 15.
35 See 'Sin', note 15.
36 Here Tagore interprets Matreyī's desire for 'immortality' as desire for 'love'. Also see 'Sin', note 15.
37 See 'Sin', note 15.
38 A *brahmavādinī* is a woman who knows and speaks about Brahman or the Vedas.
39 Bṛhadāryaṇaka Upanishad, 1.3.28. 'Lead me from untruth to Truth. Lead me from darkness to light. Lead me from mortality to immortality.'
40 Aitareya Upanishad, 'Invocation'. 'Āviravirma edhi' means 'O self-luminous Brahman, be manifest on to me'.
41 Rudra is the Vedic God of the storms. At later times he came to be considered as the manifestation of Śiva (the third God of the Hindu Trinity), as the destroyer.
42 Śvetāśvatara Upanishad, 4.21. 'Rudra yatte dakṣiṇaṁ mukhaṁ tena māṁ pāhi nityam' means 'O Rudra, may Your benignant face protect me eternally!'
43 See 'The Prayer', note 40.
44 The Sanskrit word 'Āviḥ' means 'Self-luminous'.
45 See 'The Prayer', note 42.
46 See 'The Prayer', note 42.

Dispersed Fair

47 The universal man here could mean man (human race) eternally existent in all ages (time) and throughout the universe (place).
48 Plates are made by sewing or attaching the sal leaves by either thread or twigs in single or double layers.
49 The Bengali phrase 'jatrā korā' literally means 'undertaking a journey'. It also means invoking the Gods for a fruitful and safe journey. Here the phrase suggests the latter interpretation.
50 The Bengali word is 'yūg', Sanskrit 'yūga'. There are four *yūgas* or ages: *Satya*, *Tretā*, *Dvāpara* and *Kali* (the present *yūga*). Possibly Tagore is making a pun on the word.
51 *Bhairavī* refers to a particular *rāgiṇī* in Indian classical music. This particular *rāgiṇī* is sung or played in the morning.

End of Festival

52 *Jajim* is a word of Persian origin. It is a fine bedding spread on the floor for people to sit on.
53 The Bengali word 'Kaḍī' refers to a small shell or a cowrie used previously as a coin.
54 Here 'fifteen annas' mean a major part of a share.

55 The Bengali word in the text is 'visarjan' which popularly means immersion of clay idols of deities after Hindu religious festivals. It also means 'giving up' or 'bidding farewell'. Here, Tagore seems to imply both the meanings of 'visarjan' especially since actual immersion is often involved in religious festivals.
56 The Bengali word was 'bideśi' which if literally translated into English would mean a 'foreigner.' But the sense implied in this context is that of 'stranger.'

Ferry Me Across

57 Originally the Bengali word was Hārī, another name for God. In the Bengali text, Tagore uses the word 'Hārī' which is another name for Kṛīṣṇa. In this context it refers to God.
58 A *sādhaka* is a spiritual aspirant.
59 In the Bengali text, Tagore uses the word 'Hari'.
60 In the Bengali text the word 'birahiṇī' is written which is used in case of a female who is estranged from her lover.

This Shore – the Other Shore

61 The Bengali word is 'ākāś' which generally means the 'sky', but it also means 'space'. So, the word 'space' is apt in this context.
62 Bṛhadāraṇyaka Upanishad, 4.3.32. 'This is its supreme goal, this is its supreme glory, this is its highest world, this is its supreme bliss.'
63 The word 'eṣaḥ' means 'this'. Here it is interpreted as 'He'. Also see 'This Shore – the Other Shore', note 62.
64 This 'it' refers to 'asya', that is 'its'.
65 Taittirīya Upanishad, 2.7.1. The words 'ko hyevānyāt kaḥ prāṇyāt. Yadesa ākāśa ānanda na syāt' mean 'Who could regulate the prāna [inspiration] and the apāna [expiration] if this Bliss [Brahman] never existed in the space [of the heart]?'

Day

66 The word *jñānī* in this context means a knowledgeable person, a person who possess *jñāna*. It also indicates a person who possesses spiritual knowledge.
67 Chāndogya Upanishad, 7.23.1. The actual quotation is 'nālpe sukhamasti bhūmaiva sukham' which means 'There is no bliss in the finite, there is bliss only in the Infinite.'
68 The word 'tapasyā' means penance or religious austerities.
69 In the Hindu mythology Viśvakarmā is considered to be the 'Divine Architect'. A parallel could be drawn with Vulcan. The name Viśvakarmā first featured during the Vedic times and was used as an epithet for Indra and Surya. There are several references in the Ṛg Veda regarding him: as Father and Generator (Ṛg Veda, 10.81–82) and as Creator (Ṛg Veda, 10.81.3).

Night

70 Śvetāśvatara Upanishad, 4.1. The words 'bahudhā śaktiyogād varṇānanekānnihitārthodadhāti' mean 'who by manifoldly applying His own powers creates much diversity for deeper purpose'.
71 Kaṭha Upanishad, 2.2.8. 'Ya eṣa supteṣu jāgarti kāmaṁ kāmaṁ puruṣo nimirmāṇaḥ' means 'When all persons are asleep, there is the One who remains awake and continues to create desires one after the other', here Yama begins to tell Naciketā about Brahman.

At Dawn

72 The three realms of *bhūḥ*, *bhuvaḥ* and *svaḥ* are mentioned in this essay by Tagore. *Bhūḥ loka* denotes the world of the common man, *Bhubaḥ loka* denotes the world of the scholar, while *Svaḥ loka* refers to the world of the saints. There are seven higher *lokas* or worlds – *Bhūḥ*, *Bhubaḥ*, *Svaḥ*, *Mahaḥ*, *Janaḥ*, *Tapaḥ* and *Satya*. These are the first three subtle planes of existence. This can also be interpreted in a different way. The words *bhūrbhuvaḥ svaḥ* form the first line of the *Gāyatrī* mantra following *Om* found in the Ṛg Veda, 3.62.10. The *Gāyatrī is, in fact, the name of a Sanskrit poetical metre that contains eight syllables in three lines each. But the following translated mantra is the one addressed to* Sāvitrī, the sun, and is whispered into the ear of a boy during his sacred-thread ceremony called *upanayana by his guru. Of course, now any one can chant it but previously there was scriptural prohibition against chanting it if not initiated by a guru to his disciple. It was considered esoteric, women and non-Brahmins were never allowed to chant this sacred mantra.*

The *Gāyatrī* mantra can also be found in the White [Śukla] Yajur Veda, 3.35 as follows:

'May we attain that excellent glory of

Savitar the God:

So May (sic.) he stimulate our prayers.'

73 *Brahmaloka* is the 'Abode of Brahma', which is above the seven *lokas* (worlds) as mentioned in the Vedic scriptures namely, *Bhūḥ*, *Bhubaḥ*, *Svaḥ*, *Mahaḥ*, *Janaḥ*, *Tapaḥ* and *Satya*.

74 Tilak is a vertical red mark worn on one's forehead made with one's finger dipped in sindoor. In this context it is the sign of victory.

Beauty

75 The Sanskrit word 'Satyam' means 'Truth'.

76 Muṇḍaka Upanishad 2.2.7. 'Ānandarūpamṛtam yadvibhāti' denotes 'The Atman which is full of bliss and is immortal is manifest in all things.'

77 The original Bengali word is 'śithil' which has been translated as 'relax', 'lessen', 'minimize' or 'ease off' depending on context.

78 The name of goddess Lakṣmī is used in different contexts. Here Lakṣmī is a metaphor for the abundance of good fortune and beauty of the universe.

Law

79 White Yajur Veda 32.10. 'Sa eva bandhurjanitā sa vidhātā' means 'That [Supreme Atman] is our Kinsman, Progenitor and Providence'.

80 See 'Law', note 79.

81 See 'Law', note 79.

82 Īśa Upanishad, 8. The words 'yathātathyatoharthān vyadadhāt śāśvatībhyaḥ samābhyaḥ' form the last portion of this sloka. It means 'He is proclaiming all His precepts of divine law accurately for all eternity'.

83 See 'Law', note 82.

84 See 'Law', note 79.

Three

85 The Sanskrit word 'śāntaṁ' means 'embodiment of peace'. See Māṇḍūkya Upanishad, 7.

86 The Sanskrit word 'śānta' is a variation of the Sanskrit word 'śāntam'. See 'Three', note 85.

87 The Sanskrit word 'Śivam' in this context means the 'embodiment of bliss'. See Māṇḍūkya Upanishad, 7.

88 The original Bengali word 'amangal' has been translated either as 'inauspicious' or as 'misfortune' depending on context.

89 The Sanskrit word 'Advaitam' means 'non-dual'. See Māṇḍūkya Upanishad, 7.

90 The original Bengali word 'mangal' has been translated as 'welfare' or as 'goodness' or as 'auspicious' depending on context.

91 According to the Hindu scriptures there are four stages of human life. The first stage is that of the student-life, *brahmachārya*, where a student leads a life of complete celibacy, devoting himself to the study of the scriptures and other books of knowledge. The second stage is that of the *gārhasthya*, the life of a householder. The third stage according to the scriptures is *vāṇaprastha* where a man leaves his home at the age of 50 and goes to the forest to spend the rest of the days of his life doing spiritual meditation. He could go to the forest with his wife. And the fourth is that of *sannyāsa*, a stage when man renounces the world and lives a life of an ascetic.

92 See 'Three', note 91.

93 See 'Three', note 91.

94 The word 'śiva' is the variation of the Sanskrit word 'śivam'. See 'Three', note 87.

95 The word 'advaita' is a variation of the Sanskrit word 'advaitam'. See 'Three', note 89.

96 'Oneness' here denotes the Supreme Being.

97 The Sanskrit words 'śāntaṁ śivaṁ advaitam' mean He is the 'embodiment of peace, bliss and is non-dual'. See Māṇḍūkya Upanishad, 7.

98 See 'The Prayer', note 39.

The Whole

99 The word is 'śūnyatā' which means 'zero', 'emptiness' or 'void'. The Buddhist philosopher Nāgārjuna provides the interpretation of *Śūnyavāda* in the following lines:

'Śūnyam iti na vaktavyam aśūnyam iti vā bhavet
Ubhayaṁ nobhayaṁ ceti prajñaptyarthaṁ tu kathyate'

which means 'It cannot be called void or not void, or both or neither, but in order to indicate it, it is called the void' (Radhakrishnan *Indian Philosophy* I: 663).

100 *Brahmāstra* is a divine missile of Brahma (one of the three Hindu trinities) which can never be averted once released. It is meant for mass destruction.

101 Arjuna is a famous character from the *Mahābhārata*. He is the son of the God Indra and Kuntī. As it was not possible for Pāndu to have children, Kuntī made use of her boon and was granted sons, Arjuna was the third of the Pāndavas. The Bhagavad Gītā which is considered to be a part of *Mahābhārata* is about Kr̥ṣṇa's instruction to Arjuna in the battlefield of Kurukṣetra. Kr̥ṣṇa instructs Arjuna to uphold the path of duty and forgo everything else.

102 Karṇa is also an important character of the mahā-kāvya *Mahābhārata*. He was born of Kuntī's union with the God Surya. He was born with armour ('Kavaca') and a pair of earrings ('Kundala') attached on his person. As Kuntī was a maiden she put her new born son in a basket and floated it in the river. That child was later found and brought up by Adhiratha, a charioteer and Rādha his wife. He was a great archer. He became a general in the war of Kurukṣetra.

103 Kuntī was the daughter of Śūrasena and her initial name was Pr̥thā. She belonged to the Yādav clan and was the aunt of Kr̥ṣṇa. As King Kuntībhoja was childless she was adopted by him and thus she was named Kuntī. She is an important character in the *Mahābhārata* and was the mother of Karṇa and the first three Pāṇḍavas. She was the first wife of King Pāṇḍu.

104 The Bengali word 'prakr̥ti' has been translated as 'physical realm' or 'nature' depending on context.

Power

105 Śvetāśvatara. Upanishad, 6.8. 'Parāsya śaktirvividhaiva śrūyate svābhāvikī jñānabalakriyā ca' means 'It is heard that He [Brahman] possesses divine powers and has diverse powers and His actions of Knowledge and powers are innate [in Him]'.

Prana

106 Muṇḍaka Upanishad, 3.1.4. These words mean 'Sporting with the Supreme Atman, rejoicing with the Supreme Atman, he is fully active, he is the greatest among all the knowers of Brahman'.
107 Muṇḍaka Upanishad, 3.1.4. These words mean 'He is truly Prana, He is in the heart of all livings beings; he who has Knowledge of Him does not discourse on anything else.'
108 See 'Prana', note 107.
109 See 'Beauty', note 76.
110 The Bengali word is 'bolchen' which means to 'say' or to 'utter' but in this context 'sing' is appropriate.
111 The Bengali word is 'nā' which literally means 'no' but here I use 'well' depending on context.
112 See 'Prana', note 106.
113 See 'Prana', note 107.
114 See Prana', note 106.
115 See 'Three', note 97.
116 The word 'rāgiṇī' refers to the feminine form of raga. In classical Indian music, it is said that each of the six basic ragas has six wives termed as *rāgiṇī*.

Observer

117 Taittirīya Upanishad, 2.1.3. *Satyaṁ jñānamantaṁ Brahma nihitaṁ guhāyām* means Brahman is 'Truth, Knowledge and Infinity, who resides secretly within the cave of the heart.' As in several of the Upanishadic quotations, Tagore alters this one too to suit his lecture.
118 Śvetāśvatara. Upanishad, 3.8. The words 'Nānyaḥ panthā vidyate ayanāya' mean 'there exists no other path to the ultimate Goal'. Some commentators have translated ayanāya as 'immortality.' Also see Swami Lokeswarananda trans., Śvetāśvatara. Upanishad.

The Eternal Abode

119 Taittirīya. Upanishad, 2.4.1. The sloka 'Ānandaṁ brahmaṇo vidvān; Na bibheti kadācaneti' means 'The knower of the Bliss of Brahman, never fears.'
120 See 'The Eternal Abode', note 119.
121 Bhaja Govindam (Moha Mudgara) is an eighth century devotional song composed by Ādi Śankarācharya. Tagore juxtaposed a few sections of Bhaja Govindam in his speech. The words 'Parame Brahmaṇi' means 'to the Supreme Brahman' taken from verse 7, 'yojitachittaḥ' means 'whose mind is given up' taken from verse 22, 'Nandati nandati nandatyeva' means 'He alone is happy, happy, verily happy', taken from verse 19. So, what Tagore said was the one whose mind is given up to the Supreme Brahman is 'happy, happy, verily happy'.
122 Tagore has written 'śocati śocati śocatyeva!' in the Bengali text. The Sanskrit word 'śocati' means 'lament' and is found in several places in the scriptures such as: Bhagavadgītā 12.17, 18.54; Śrīmad Bhāgavatam 1.17.27, 3.30.2, 4.14.35, 4.25.57-61, 4.28.47, 6.10.9, 10.85.48-49; Śrī Caitanya Caritamṛta, Madhya 8.65, 23.110, 24.132; Muṇḍaka Upanishad 3.1.2. See translations of Muṇḍaka Upanishad by Swami Nikhilananda and Swami Lokeswarananda.

123 *Rājasūya yajña* is a sacrifice performed by a monarch so as to establish his supremacy over other kings.
124 Muṇḍaka Upanishad, 2.2.9. *Tacchubhraṁ jyotiṣāṁ jyotiḥ*, 'That [Brahman] is pure, It is the Light brighter than any other lights'.

Philosopher's Stone

125 See 'Three', note 97.
126 See 'At Dawn', note 72.
127 See 'Sin', note 12.
128 In the Bengali text used for this translation, a footnote has been provided asking the following question: 'The desired to take the place of the beneficial?' in the Visvabharati edition in two volumes edited by Kanai Samanta. In the Bengali Source Text, the words 'desired' and 'beneficial' were interchanged. But that would not be in keeping with Tagore's line of thought in this sentence, and hence, they were changed.

Prayer

129 Uttering the word '*satyam*' three times in succession means to swear an oath or promise by three solemn affirmations.
130 See 'Three Levels', note 124.
131 The words "ānandaṁ paramānandam" are in Govindāstkam composed by Śankarāchārya. Each of the nine stanzas ends with 'paramānandam' which literally means '[He] who is supreme ananda' which means God, and 'ānandam' in stanza 8 means '[He] who gives happiness'.

Detachment

132 Bṛhadāraṇyaka Upanishad, 2.4.5. These words form part of the conversation Yājñavalkya has with Maitreyī regarding the nature of the Absolute Self: 'Truly, not because you desire the son, my dear, is the son loved, but the son is loved for the sake of the Atman'. In the Upanishadic śloka 'priyā bhavanti' is inscribed instead of Tagore's 'priyo bhavati' in both the cases. However, the meaning remains the same.
133 If written in Bengal script, they would be in single letters.
134 *Varna parichay* is the Bengali primer. Literally 'varna' means alphabet or letter, and 'parichaẏ' means introduction. In this context the phrase means specific knowledge of the alphabet.
135 I translated the Bengali word 'sukh' as 'joy' or 'pleasure' or 'happiness' depending on the context.
136 The original Bengali word 'ras' which comes from Sanskrit 'rasa', meaning 'juice' or 'essence'. Throughout these essays I have translated 'ras' as 'essence' or 'interest' depending on context.
137 'Jal pariteche. Pātā nariteche' is the eighth lesson of the first volume in *Varna parichay* written by Īśwarchandra Vidyasagar. In Bengali, Vidyasagar's sentences are in present continuous tense while Tagore's are in present simple tense.
138 Ṛg Veda 1.90.6.
'The winds trickle out nectar over the person who observes the Law:

The rivers exude nectar,
May all the medicinal herbs be nectarous'.

139 Ṛg Veda 1.90.7.
'May our night and dawn be nectarine, May a grain of terrestrial dust be imbued with nectar' – the first part of the seventh sloka has been quoted in the text.

140 Ṛg Veda 1.90.8.
May the king of the woods be nectary to us,
May the sun be nectarial as well' – the first part of the eighth sloka has been quoted in the text.
141 See 'Beauty', note 76.

The Obverse

142 Kaṭha Upanishad, 2.3.17. Here Tagore has alluded to the following words, *janānāṁ hṛdaye sanniviṣṭaḥ* which means 'always resides within everyone's heart'.

To See the Truth

143 See 'At Dawn', note 72.
144 This refers to the Gāyatrī mantra which is regarded as the essence of the Vedas, found in the Ṛg Veda, 3.62.10.
145 See 'At Dawn', note 72.
146 See 'At Dawn', note 72.

Creation

147 See 'The Obverse', note 142.
148 These words 'Namo namah' are uttered repeatedly as reverential salutation.

Loaded Boat

149 The poem 'Sonār Tarī' ('The Golden Boat'), (*Rabindra Rachanāvali* 2: 12) was composed by Tagore in February/March 1894 (*Phālgun* 1298 BE).
150 These slokas are from The Bhagavadgītā, 2.28. This means 'Living beings are unmanifested in their beginning, manifested in their middle and unmanifested again in their end, O Bharata [Arjuṇa]. What is there to lament in that?'

Attainment of Nature

151 Taittirīya Upanishad, 3.6.1. *Ānandāddhyeva khalvimāni bhūtāni jāyante* means 'from bliss indeed these beings are born'.
152 Kaṭha Upanishad, 1.2.18. 'Na jāyate mṛyate' means 'is neither born, nor dies'.
153 Bhagavadgītā, 2.47. This means 'You have a claim to work alone and never indeed to its fruits' – this is one of the essential messages of the Bhagavadgītā.

Commandment

154 See 'Sin', note 12.
155 See 'Three', note 97.
156 'Krāndasī', *Bangla Bhashar Abhidhan*. 1986 ed. Rabindranath Tagore was the first to introduce and use the words krāndasī and rodasī in Bengali. In the Ṛg Veda, 2.12.8, 'krāndasī' (noun) means 'cry'. In *Bangiya Sabdakosh* (695), *Krāndasī* means 'sky and earth' (own translation). The word rodasī comes from the Sanskrit word 'rodah' ('rodas'). 'Rodas' means 'sky, heaven and earth' (own translation). See *Bangiya Sabdakosh*. Rodasī

was found in the Ṛg Veda, 9.22.5. It means 'earth and heaven'. The word 'rodas' is of neuter gender while 'rodasī' is of feminine gender. In the *Chalantika* (631), 'rodasī' means 'heaven and earth' (own translation), in case of 'krāndasī' it has been mentioned that the '(root meaning is "That which rains") sky. Sky and earth' (own translation), see *Chalantika* (161). So 'krāndasī and rodasī' would mean 'The sky which rains upon the earth.'

Also see Chatterjee (142, Note 82), regarding rodasī, the following were inscribed, 'This word, *rodasi*, from *rud*, "to roar, cry",' is of the same meaning as the word 'Krandasi' occurring in the Ṛg Veda, 2.12.8; 6.25.4; 10.121.6.

157 See 'Commandment', note 156.

Completeness

158 The word 'Brahmavihārā' consists of two words 'Brahma' which means 'Noble' and 'vihārā' which means 'dwelling', 'abiding' or 'living'. So, 'Bhramavihārā' means 'Noble Living', or 'Living in the exercise of good-will' (Sayādaw 1). The 'expression "*Brahmavihārā*" includes loving-kindness (*mettā*), compassion (*karuṇā*), sympathetic-joy (*muditā*), or rejoicing in their happiness or prosperity of others, and equanimity (*upekkhā*), or indifference to pain and pleasure' (Sayādaw 1). It is a term found in Buddhism.

159 An *uttariya* is a cloth loosely wrapped around the upper portion of a person's body in India.

160 Metta Sutta, 7: The words *mānasaṁ bhābaye aparimāṇam* mean 'let him [one] cultivate a boundless heart' (Pesala 3).

Om

161 Ṛk and Sāma in the Chāndogya Upanishad have been interpreted in several ways. The speech is considered as Ṛk while the Sāma is considered as the prana but they are again considered as the same because while singing, a person holds his breath. So, they both merge into Om. Om is the 'udgītha'. See Chāndogya Upanishad, 1.3.4 and 1.7. Again the Sāma Veda is said to be 'ut' of the 'udgītha' which denotes heaven, the Ṛg Veda denotes the earth, that is the 'tha', the space between the two is the Yajur Veda, the gī'. This Sāma is derived from the Ṛk See Chāndogya Upanishad, 1.3.7. and 1.3.9. The Ṛk is the star while Sāma is the moon but they converge at one point. See Chāndogya Upanishad, 1.6.5. Again the Ṛg Veda is considered to be the eyes and Sāma Veda to be the self. See Chāndogya Upanishad, 1.7.3., etc. These show that the two meet at one point and become one. The Ṛk is one extreme and the Sāma is another, so, if the Ṛk is the root, the origin, the Sāma is the fruit, the derivative, the refined part (my interpretation).

162 See 'Om', note 161.

163 Śvetāśvatara Upanishad, 1.12. 'One [Brahman] who eternally dwells within the atman is only worth knowing, nothing else needs to be known beyond this'.

164 Muṇḍaka Upanishad, 3.2.5. 'Those self-realized beings by uniting themselves totally with the Omnipresent enter all.'

165 Bṛhadāryaṇaka Upanishad, 4.4.23. The words 'ātmanyevātmanaṁ pasyati' mean 'he sees the Atman in his own atman.'

166 Bṛhadāryaṇaka Upanishad, 4.4.23. Here Tagore refers to the quote 'sarvaṁ ātmanaṁ pasyati' which means 'he sees everything as the Atman'.

167 See 'At Dawn', note 72.

168 Here Tagore has used the word *dhī* to mean consciousness (*cetanā*), instead of intellect (for attaining Knowledge).

169 See 'At Dawn', note 72.

170 Īśa Upanishad, 5.
'That moves and does not move as well; That is far as well as near;
That is the innermost Being, as well as the outermost Being of all'.
171 Muṇḍaka Upanishad. 2.2.10. 'The sun does not emit light there. Neither the moon and the stars, nor the thunder bolts, nor even the fires [sacrificial] radiate light. When He shines, everything sparkles in His light; by His light everything is radiant.' The same sloka is also present in Kaṭha Upanishad, 2.2.15.
172 See 'Three', note 97.

Supreme Obtainment

173 Kaṭha Upanishad, 2.2.13. 'One who is the Eternal among the transient ones'.
174 Chāndogya Upanishad, 1.1.3. The words 'rasānāṁ rasatamaḥ' means 'the essence of all essences'.
175 Īśa Upanishad, 1.2. The sloka –

'Īśāvāsyamidaṁ sarvaṁ yatkiñca jagatyāṁ jagat
Tena tyaktena bhuñjīthā mā gṛdhaḥ kasya sviddhanam'
means 'In this world everything is perishable, yet pervaded by the Supreme Being. So, protect the Atman by renunciation. Never have greed for anyone's wealth'.

176 See 'Supreme Obtainment', note 175.
177 See 'Supreme Obtainment', note 175.

Self-surrender

178 The literal meaning of the Bengali word 'samarpaṇ' is 'surrender' and 'atma' here refers to the 'individual self'. But nowhere in this whole essay has Tagore used the word 'samarpaṇ' literally except in the title.
179 The Bengali word is 'diẏei' meaning 'by giving' which is a variation of the verb 'deoẏa' which literally means 'to give.' Here it has been translated as 'surrender' depending on the context.
180 The Bengali word is 'deoẏai' meaning 'to [surely] give' which is a variation of the word 'deoẏa'. See 'Self-surrender', note 179.
181 Muṇḍaka Upanishad. 2.2.4. The words mean 'Brahman is said to be the state of being an aim'.
182 The Bengali word 'lakṣa' has been translated either as 'goal' or as 'aim' depending on context.
183 These words are from Muṇḍaka Upanishad, 2.2.4. They mean 'Then the ātman becomes wholly absorbed in Brahman as the arrow is absorbed in the target'.
184 See 'This Shore – the Other Shore', note 65.

Self-confidence

185 See 'Om', note 165.
186 The word 'sādhaka' means spiritual aspirant.
187 Maṇḍukya Upanishad, 7. 'The essence of the consciousness of the Atman [is He]'.
188 Bṛhadaraṇyaka Upanishad, 1.4.8. 'This [Atman] is dearer than a child, dearer than wealth, dearer than all other things. It is inmost'.

The Bonds of the Mantra

189 The original Bengali word is 'bāँdhan' which means 'bond' here. Tagore plays on the meaning of the word. The root word 'bāँdha' could mean 'to tie', 'tune', 'attune', and 'bind'.

190 In the Hindu marriage ritual, the priest conducting the marriage ties a sacred knot using a corner of the *anchal* of the bride's saree and the corner of the groom's *uttariya*. This ties the bride and the groom in a sacred bond.
191 The White Yajur (Saṁhitā), 37.20. 'Pitā nohasi' means 'You are our Father'.
192 See 'The Bonds of the Mantra', note 191.
193 See 'The Bonds of the Mantra', note 191.
194 See 'The Bonds of the Mantra', note 191.
195 The words 'ātmā vai jāyate putraḥ' are taken from Śrī Caitanya Caritāmṛta, Madhya 12.56. It is indicated in the scriptures that 'his self appears as the son'. Here 'his' refers to the father. These words were uttered by Śrī Caitanya Mahāprabhu himself.
196 See 'The Bonds of the Mantra', note 191.
197 The White Yajur (Saṁhitā), 37.20. 'Pitā nobodhi. Namastehastu' means 'Awaken us like a father. Salutations to Thee!'

The End of the Year

198 Taittirīya Upanishad, 3.1.1. 'Yat prayantyabhisaṁviśanti' means 'That towards which they advance [at the time of dissolution], they enter into That'.
199 Mahānārāyaṇopanisad, Hiranyagarbha-sūkta, 1.3. 'Yasya chayamṛtaṁ yasya mṛtyuḥ' means 'to whom immortality and death remain subservient like shadow'.
200 *Pūravī rāgiṇī* is a mode of Hindustani (Indian) classical music. It is played or sung in the evening.
201 'On new year's day whatever was said' has not been written. The previous sentence is a translation of the Bengali footnote that was provided at the end of 'Barṣaśeṣ' ('The End of the Year') of the first volume.

Mukti

202 See 'Beauty', note 76.
203 It is 'maya' which makes one see Brahman as the phenomenal world, having name and form.
204 See 'Beauty', note 76.

After the Holidays

205 School of Brahminic learning.
206 See 'Detachment', note 139. Here Tagore rearranged the words in the slokas of the Ṛg Veda. 'Madhu dhauḥ' means 'Sweet be', 'Heaven to us'.

End

207 These words mean 'After crossing the age of fifty, a man should go to the forest'. Here Tagore alludes to ancient Indian scriptural injunctions. Also see 'Three', note 91.
208 Grammatically 'asamāpikā kriyā' in Bengali is an 'infinitive verb'. Tagore implies the metaphor of the Infinite verb in this context which denotes 'unceasing action'.
209 The talk 'End' ('Śeṣ') was printed in *Āśvin* issue of the Bengali journal 'Mānasī'. According to Prasanta Kumar Pal, the talk was probably delivered at the temple in Śāntiniketan in the Bengali month of August/Semptember 1909 (*Bhādra* 1317 BE).

Awakening

210 The original Bengali word is 'amrita'. It has been translated as 'extremely delicious meal' in this context.

The Day of Initiation

211 Here Maharṣi refers to Debendranath Tagore. The word 'Maharṣi' has been entered in the Concise Oxford English Dictionary, 11th edition, as 'Maharishi', a noun, meaning 'a great Hindu sage or spiritual leader'. See 'Maharishi' in *COD*, eleventh edition.

212 A moon dot (ঁ), was put over the pronoun 'tār', pronounced with a nasal accent, translated into English as 'his', as a mark or sign of respect.

213 See 'Supreme Obtainment', note 175.

214 *Ārti* lamps are lighted by dipping a wick in *ghee* (clarified butter) in an earthen or brass lamps to worship a deity.

215 See 'Supreme Obtainment', note 175.

216 A moon dot (ঁ) was put over the pronoun 'tār', pronounced with a nasal accent, translated into English as 'his', as a mark or sign of respect.

More

217 Tagore uses the Bengali word 'āro', which has been translated here as 'more' as an adjective, adverb, noun or pronoun depending on the context.

218 See 'Beauty', note 78. In this context Lakṣmī is a metaphor for riches.

219 Śvetāśvatara Upanishad, 3.8. 'Vedāḥ metam' means 'I have the sacred Knowledge of that Great Being'.

220 The original Bengali word is 'nā', literally meaning 'no'. But here the sense is not that of negation. In colloquial Bengali 'nā' is used for assertion as well.

221 Blood-red lotus here refers to the heart.

222 Śiva is the third God of the Hindu Trinity, Maheśwara, known as the destroyer.

223 It refers to 'Yogesha Nadam', the conch of Śiva.

224 The sixteen articles necessary for the ritualistic worship of Hindu Gods are: a seat [*Āsana*], welcome or auspicious arrival [*Svāgata*], water for washing the feet [*Pādya*], offerings [*Arghya*], water for purification [*Ācamanīya*], articles required for ceremonial ablution [*Snānīya*], dress [*Basana*], ornament [*Bhūṣaṇa*], scent or sandal-paste [*Gandha*], flower [*Puṣpa*], incense [*Dhupa*], lamp [*Dīpa*], an oblation of a mixture of honey, *ghee*, milk, curd and sugar [*Madhuparka*], betel-leaf [*Tāmbula*], the sacrament of offering drinking water to the manes or deities [*Tarpaṇa*] and bending down [*Nati*].

225 See 'Supreme Obtainment', note 175.

226 See 'Three', note 97.

227 See 'Three', note 97.

Innermost Peace

228 The Bengali word 'kolahal' has been translated as 'uproar' and 'noise' depending on context. It also has a derivative in this talk.

229 *Baul* is a class of devotees originally Hindu, especially of the Vaiṣṇava sect but later on went on to include sufis as well. The *bauls* are wandering minstrels singing and dressing in a specific manner to express their doctrine.

230 The Bengali word was 'viśvarūp'. Viśvarūpa is Lord Kṛṣṇa's universal form. One instance when the Lord revealed his universal form to Arjuna is in chapter XI of the Bhagavadgītā.

231 Six cardinal passions are lust, anger, avarice, delusion, pride and envy.

232 In the Bengali text Tagore had mentioned 'tāndav' which is a kind of dance having fierce gesticulations, mainly associated with Śiva and his followers.

233 See 'Three', note 97.

234 It is an open-air folk musical or dramatic performance or both, of rural origin devoid of any proscenium or background screen.

235 The Bengali word 'sādhu' as a noun means a pious or holy man or sage, but in this sentence Tagore has employed it as an adjective, meaning 'be good'.
236 The original Bengali word is 'hāt' which also means 'fair.' In this context 'market' is appropriate.
237 The word 'asana' here means a place for sitting. It could be made of either cloth, *kuśa* grass or wood.
238 See 'Three', note 97.

GLOSSARY

advaita: a variation of the Sanskrit word 'advaitam' having the same meaning 'non-dual', as in the context of *śāntam śivam advaitam*: 'embodiment of peace, bliss and is non-dual'. See Māṇḍūkya Upanishad, 7.

advaitam: 'non-dual', as in the context of śāntam śivam advaitam: 'embodiment of peace, bliss and is non-dual'. See Māṇḍūkya Upanishad, 7.

Agrahāẏaṇ: the eighth month of the Bengali Calendar, corresponding to the second half of November and first half of December.

amrita: divine nectar of immortality obtained by the churning of the ocean. It is from the myth of the *Samudra Manthana* ('Churning of the Ocean'). Amrita had to be obtained by the Gods to regain their power lost by being continuously defeated by the demons.

asana: the word in this context means a place for sitting. It could be made of either cloth, *kuśa* grass or wood.

Āṣāṛh: the third month of the Bengali Calendar, corresponding to the second half of June and first half of July.

Āśvin: the sixth month of the Bengali calendar, corresponding to the second half of September and first half of October.

āviḥ: self-luminous, as mentioned in the Mundaka Upanishad, 2.2.1.

Baiśākh: the first month of the Bengali calendar, lasting from the second half of April to the first half of May.

Bhādra: the fifth month of the Bengali calendar, lasting from the second half of August to the first half of September.

Bhāratvarṣa: anglicized word for *Bhāratvarsa* is India (Bharat).

bhavan: a residence or mansion in Bengali.

brahmacharya: the first stage of life is that of *brahmacharya* where a student leads a life of complete celibacy, devoting himself to the study of the scriptures and other books of knowledge. According to the Hindu scriptures there are four stages of human life.

Caitra: the last month of the Bengali year as per the Bengali Calender, it corresponds to the second half of March and the first half of April.

dhī: Tagore has used the word to mean intellect (for attaining Knowledge). It is a word in the Vedic Gāyatrī mantra.

ektārā: a folk single-stringed musical instrument of India. It is used by the bauls or wandering minstrels as an accompaniment to their songs.

eṣaḥ: this.

gārhasthya: the second stage of life is that of the *gārhasthya*, the life of a householder. The next two stages of life as per Hindu scriptures are *vānaprastha* and *sannyāsa*.

Jaiṣṭha: the second month of the Bengali calendar, starting from the second half of May and ending on the first half of June.

Kārtik: the seventh month of the Bengali calendar, lasting from the second half of October to the first half of November.

Lakṣmī: the Hindu goddess of fortune and the consort of Viṣṇu.

Māgh: the tenth month of the Bengali calendar, corresponding to the second half of January and first half of February.

Māghotsav: a festival celebrated by the Brāhmos in the month of *Māgh*.

maharṣi: entered in the *Concise Oxford English Dictionary* as 'Maharishi', a noun, meaning 'a great Hindu sage or spiritual leader'. In the context of these essays it refers to Debendranath Tagore, the father of Rabindranath Tagore.

mukti: it means freedom or liberation or ultimate liberation (moksha) depending on the context.

namaskar: the act of bowing and folding the elbows at right angles and joining the palms of both hands together touching each other in front of the chest, parallel to the heart [anāhata *cakra*] (or sometimes in front of the forehead [*ājña cakra*] mostly while doing it to a deity) with finger tips pointing upward. It is a sign of reverence to those that are superior to oneself. It is also a sign of greeting in India which indicates reverence for the other being.

Pauṣ: the ninth month of the Bengali Calendar, corresponding to the second half of December and first half of January.

Phālgun: the eleventh month of the Bengali Calendar, corresponding to the second half of February and first half of March of the English Calendar.

praṇām: a sign of paying respect or showing honour to a deity, an elderly person or to a person deserving respect by lying prostrate or bending and touching the feet of that deity or person.

prasād: the remnant of the food (or articles) spiritually tasted or accepted by a deity when offered to it (becomes prasād). Whatever is tasted or accepted by the deity becomes spiritually enhanced. It can also be the remnant of food (or other things) tasted or partaken of by a revered person.

Rudra: the Vedic God of the storms. At later times he came to be considered as the manifestation of Śiva (the third God of the Hindu Trinity), as the destroyer.

Sādhaka: a spiritual aspirant.

Śakābda: *Śakābda* or Śaka era is counted from the reign of Kaniska I in 78 A.D.

śānta: variation of the Sanskrit word 'śāntam' having the same meaning 'embodiment of peace', as in the context of *śāntam śivam advaitam*: 'embodiment of peace, bliss and is non-dual'. See Māṇḍūkya Upanishad, 7.

śāntam: 'embodiment of peace' as in the context of *śāntam śivam advaitam*: 'embodiment of peace, bliss and is non-dual'. See Māṇḍūkya Upanishad, 7.

Satyam: a Sanskrit word which means 'Truth'.

śiva: variation of the Sanskrit word 'śivam' having the same meaning 'embodiment of bliss'. It also means 'benevolent'. It could also mean 'the benevolent'. When not italicized yet capitalized, the word refers to the third God of the Hindu Trinity, known as the destroyer.

śivam: 'embodiment of bliss' as in the context of *śāntam śivam advaitam*: 'embodiment of peace, bliss and is non-dual'. See Māṇḍūkya Upanishad, 7.

Śrābaṇ: the fourth month of the Bengali year corresponding to the first half of July and the second half of August.

śrāddha: a Hindu rite held a few days after a person's death to pay respect to him or her. The number of days after which this ceremony would be held varies from caste to caste.

tapasyā: means penance or religious austerities.

tilak: as per the context here, 'tilak' is a vertical red mark worn on one's forehead made with one's finger dipped in sindoor. It is the sign of victory. According to the Hindu scriptures, it is the religious practice to apply sindoor or sandlepaste marks on eight parts of a person's body, they are head, forehead, ears, neck, arms, chest, the sides, the back and the navel, prior to performing puja.

upāsanā: means worship.

uttariya: a cloth loosely wrapped around the upper portion of a person's body in India.

vāṇaprastha: the third stage of life according to the scriptures is *vānaprastha* where a man leaves his home and goes to the forest to spend the rest of the days of his life doing spiritual meditation.

Viśvakarmā: in the Hindu mythology Viśvakarmā is considered to be the 'Divine Architect'. A parallel could be drawn with Vulcan. The name Viśvakarmā first featured during the Vedic times and was used as an epithet for Indra and Surya. There are several references in the R̥g Veda regarding him: as Father and Generator (R̥g Veda, 10.81–82), as Creator (R̥g Veda, 10.81.3).

WORKS CITED

Ashcroft, Bill, Gareth Griffiths, and Helen Tiffin. *The Empire Writes Back: Theory and Practice in Post-Colonial Literatures*. Gen. Ed. Terence Hawkes. 2nd ed. London: Routledge, 2002. Print.

Atmapriyananda, Swami. "Understanding Bhavamukha: Sri Ramakrishna's Unique State of Consciousness." *Prabuddha Bharata* 116.2 (Feb. 2011): 255–258. Print.

Bassnett-McGuire, Susan. *Translation Studies*. Rev. ed. London: Routledge, 1991. Print.

Bhabha, Homi. *The Location of Culture*. London: Routledge, 1994. Print.

"Bhajagovindam." *The Hymns of Śaṅkaṛa*. Trans. and Ed. T.M.P. Mahadevan. New Delhi: Banarsidass, 1980. 33–77. Print.

Bose, Buddhadeva. "Rabindranath Tagore and Bengali Prose." *A Centenary Volume: Rabindranath Tagore*. New Delhi: Sahitya Akademi, 1961. 102–113. Print.

Chakraborti, Basudeb. *Some Problems of Translation: A Study of Tagore's Red Oleanders*. Calcutta: Papyrus, 2005. Print.

Chāndogya Upaniṣad. Trans. Swami Gambhīrānanda. 1983. Kolkata: Advaita Ashrama, rep. 2018. Print.

Chatterjee, Jagadish C. *Wisdom of the Vedas*. Rev. ed. IL: Theosophical, 1992. Print.

Chaudhuri, Sukanta. *Translation and Understanding*. New Delhi: Oxford UP, 1999. Print.

Datta, Swati. *Exploration in Tagore Translation*. Kolkata: Bagchi, 2009. Print.

Gentzler, Edwin. *Contemporary Translation Theories*. 1993. London: Routledge, 2001. Print.

Ghose, Sisirkumar. *Makers of Indian Literature: Rabindranath Tagore*. New Delhi: Sahitya Akademi, 1986. Print.

Goswami, Krishna Das Kaviraj. *Śrī Caitanya Caritamrta*. Trans. His Divine Grace A.C. Bhaktivedanta Swami Prabhupada. 9 vols. Calcutta: Bhaktivedanta, 1974. Print.

Griffith, Ralph T.H., trans. *The Hymns of the Rigveda*. Ed. J.L. Shastri. 1973. New Rev. New Delhi: Banarsidass, 2004. Print.

———. *The Texts of the White Yajurveda*. Banaras: Lazarus, 1957. Print.

Hatim, Basil, and Jeremy Munday. *Translation: An Advanced Resource Book*. London: Routledge, 2004. Print.

His Eastern and Western Disciples. *The Life of Swami Vivekananda*. Vol. 1. 1914. Advaita Ashrama, 1979. Print.

The Holy Bible. New International Version. Michigan: Zondervan Bible, ed. 1984. Print.
"Kaladvani." *Bāṅglā Vishwakosh. 1886–1911*. Vol 3, 1988. Print.
"Karma." *Concise Oxford English Dictionary*. 11th ed. Rev. 2006. Print.
"Karma-Yoga." *A Dictionary of Advaita Vedanta*. Comp. Nirod Baran Chakraborty. Kolkata: Ramakrishna Mission Institute of Culture, 2003. Print.
Kenny, Dorothy. "Equivalence." *Routledge Encyclopedia of Translation Studies*. Ed. Mona Baker. London: Routledge, 2001. Print.
"Krāndasī." *Bangiya Sabdakosh*. 1966 ed. 2004. Print.
"Krāndasī." Entry 2. *Bangla Bhashar Abhidhan*. 2nd ed. Rev. and enlarged. 2006. Print.
"Krāndasī." Entry 3. *Chalantika*. Comp. Rajshekhar Basu. 13th ed. 1389 BE (1982 CE). Print.
Lal, Ananda, trans. *Rabindranath Tagore: Three Plays*. 1987. New Delhi: Oxford UP, 2001. Print.
"Maharishi." *Concise Oxford English Dictionary*. 11th ed. Rev. 2006. Print.
Mukhopadhyay, Prabhatkumar. *Ravindrajivana Katha*. 1959. Ananda: Calcutta, 1981. Print.
Muṇḍaka Upaniṣad. Trans. Swami Lokeswarananda. Calcutta: The Ramakrishna Mission Institute of Culture, 1994. Print.
"Muṇḍaka Upaniṣad." *Eight Upaniṣads*. Vol. 2. Trans. Swami Gambhīrānanda. 1958. Kolkata: Advaita Ashrama, rep. 2016. Print.
Naravane. *Rabindranath Tagore: A Philosophical Study*. Allahabad: Central Book Depot [194?]. Print.
Nikhilananda, Swami, trans. *The Gospel of Sri Ramakrishna*. By M. 1942. Madras: Sri Ramakrishna Math, 1996. Print.
Pal, Prasanta K. *Rabijibani*. Vol. 6. 1993. Calcutta: Ananda, Rep. 2004. Print.
———. *Rabijibani*. Vol. 7. 1997. Calcutta: Ananda, Rep. 2002. Print.
Pesala, Bhikkhu. *The Exposition of the Metta Sutta*. N.p.: Assn. for Insight Meditation, Latest ed. 2018. Print.
Purushasuktam. Trans. Swami Amritananda. Chennai: Sri Ramakrishna Math, 2004. Print.
Radhakrishnan, Sarvepalli. *Indian Philosophy*. Vol. 1. 1923. London: Allen & Unwin, 9th Imp. 1971. Print.
———. *The Philosophy of Rabindranath Tagore*. London: Macmillan, 1919. Print.
Ray, Benoy G. *The Philosophy of Rabindranath Tagore*. Calcutta: Progressive, 1970. Print.
"Rodosī." *Bangiya Sabdakosh*. 1966 ed. 2004. Print.
"Rodosī." Entry 2. *Bangla Bhashar Abhidhan*. 2nd ed. Rev. and enlarged. 2006. Print.
"Rodosī." Entry 3. *Chalantika*. Comp. Rajshekhar Basu. 13th ed. 1982 (1389 BE). Print.
"Sāl." *Bangiya Sabdakosh*. 1966 ed. 2004. Print.
Saradananda, Swami. *Sri Ramakrishna: The Great Master* [*Śrīśrīrāmakṛṣṇa Līlāprasanga*]. Vol. 1. Trans. Swami Jagadananda. Madras: Sri Ramakrishna Math, 2004. Print.
Sayādaw, The Venerable Mahāsi. *Brahmavihāra Dhamma*. Trans. U Min Swe (MinKyaw Thu). 1985. New ed. Burma: Buddha Sāsanānuggaha Organization, 2018. Print.
Spivak, Gayatri C. "The Politics of Translation." *The Translation Studies Reader*. 2nd ed. New York: Routledge, 2004. Print.
Śrīmacchaṁkarācharya. *Govindāṣṭkam*. Ed. and Trans. Amarnath Ray. Com. Śrīmadācārya Ānandagiri. Shrihatta: Deb, 1929 (1336 BE). Print.
Śrīmad Bhāgavatam. Trans. His Divine Grace A.C. Bhaktivedanta Swami Prabhupada. 8 Cans. New York: Bhaktivedanta, 1970–1976. Print.
Tagore, Rabindranath. "Chitra." *Collected Poems and Plays of Rabindranath Tagore*. Trans. Rabindranath Tagore. 1936. New Delhi: Macmillan, 2001. Print.
———. *Fruit-Gathering*. 1980. New Delhi: Macmillan, 1995. Print.
———. *Gitanjali*. 1913. New Delhi: Macmillan, 1977. Print.

———. *Gora*. 1909. New Delhi: Macmillan, 1995. Print.
———. *The Home and the World*. New Delhi: Macmillan, 1919. Print.
———. *Rabīndra Rachanāvalī*. Vol. 1. Calcutta: Visvabharati, 1986 (1393 BE). Print.
———. *Rabīndra Rachanāvalī*. Vol. 2. Calcutta: Visvabharati, 1986 (1393 BE). Print.
———. *Sādhanā: The Realisation of Life*. 1913. London: Macmillan, 1930. Print.
———. *Śāntiniketan*. 1949 (1356 BE). 2 vols. Kolkata: Visvabharati, 1984 (1391 BE). Print.
———. "Sanyasi, or the Ascetic." *Collected Poems and Plays of Rabindranath Tagore*. Trans. Rabindranath Tagore. 1936. New Delhi: Macmillan, 2001. Print.
"Taittirīya Upaniṣad." *Eight Upaniṣads*. Vol. 1. Trans. Swami Gambhīrānanda. 1957. Kolkata: Advaita Ashrama, rep. 2018. Print.
Tapasyānanda, Svāmī. *Bhakti Schools of Vedanta*. Madras: Sri Ramakrishna Math, 2003. Print.
———. *Śrīmad-Bhagavad-Gītā: The Scripture of Mankind*. 1984. Mylapore: Sri Ramakrishna Math, rep. 2008. Print.
Thompson, Edward J. *Rabindranath Tagore: His Life and Work*. Calcutta: YMCA, n.d. Print.
Vidyāsāgar, Īśwarchandra. *Vidyāsāgar Rachanāvalī*. Ed. Prafulla Kumar Patra. Complete ed. Kolkata: Patraj, 1987. Print.
Vivekananda, Swami. "The Open Secret." *The Complete Works of Swami Vivekananda*. Vol. 2. Ed. Mayavati Memorial. Kokata: Advaita Ashrama, 2003. Print.

FURTHER READING

Books

Aronson, Alex. *Rabindranath through Western Eyes.* Calcutta: Rddhi, 1978. Print.

Atkinson, David W. *Gandhi and Tagore: Visionaries of Modern India.* Hong Kong: Asian Research, 1989. Print.

Ayyub, Abu Sayeed. *Modernism and Tagore.* Trans. Amitav Ray. New Delhi: Sahitya Akad, 1995. Print.

Basak, Kakoli. *Rabindranath Tagore, a Humanist.* New Delhi: Classical, 1991. Print.

Bhattacharya, Asoke. *Education for the People: Concepts of Grundtvig, Tagore, Gandhi and Freire.* Rotterdam; Boston: Sense, 2010. Print.

Bhattacharya, Vivek Ranjan. *Tagore's Vision of a Global Family.* New Delhi: Enkay, 1987.

Biswas, Lakshmi and Rajendra Prasad Shrivastava. *Tagore and Iqbal: A Study in Philosophical Perspective.* New Delhi: Capital, 1991. Print.

Chakrabarti, Mohit. *Rabindranath Tagore: A Quest.* New Delhi: Gyan, 1995. Print.

Chakrabarti, Santosh. *Studies in Tagore Critical Essays.* New Delhi: Atlantic, 2004. Print.

Chakravarti, B.C. *Rabindranath Tagore, His Mind and Art.* New Delhi: Young India, 1971. Print.

Chakravarty, Amiya C. *Rabindranath Tagore and the Renaissance of India's Spiritual Religion.* Calcutta: Open Court, 1959. Print.

———, ed. *A Tagore Reader.* New York: Macmillan, 1961. Print.

Chatterjee, Bhabatosh. *Rabindranath Tagore and Modern Sensibility.* New Delhi: Oxford UP, 1996. Print.

Chatterjee, Suniti K. *World Literature and Tagore.* Santiniketan: Visva-Bharati, 1971. Print.

Chattopadhyaya, Debiprasad. *Tagore and Indian Philosophical Heritage.* Mysore: Prasaranga, U of Mysore, 1984. Print.

Chaudhury, Prabas J. *Tagore on Literature and Aesthetics.* Calcutta: Rabindra Bharati U, 1965. Print.

Chunkapura, Jose. *The God of Rabindranath Tagore.* 1st pub. 2002. Kolkata: Visva-Bharati, rep. 2008. Print.

Das, Chandra M. *The Philosophy of Rabindranath Tagore: His Social, Political, Religious And Educational Views.* New Delhi: Deep & Deep, 1996. Print.

Das, Saroj K. *Tagore and the Perennial Problems of Philosophy.* Calcutta: Rabindra Bharati U, 1971. Print.

Das, Taraknath. *Rabindranath Tagore, His Religious, Social and Political Ideals.* Calcutta: Saraswati, 1932. Print.

Dasgupta, Arun C. *Rabindranath: Poet Laureate of Humanity.* Calcutta: Khadi Pratisthan, 1948. Print.

Dasgupta, Surendranath. *Rabindranath: The Poet and the Philosopher.* Calcutta: Mitra & Ghosh, 1948. Print.

Das Gupta, Uma. *Rabindranath Tagore: A Biography.* New Delhi and Oxford: Oxford UP, 2004.

Dutta, Krishna, and Andrew Robinson. *Rabindranath Tagore an Anthology.* London: Picador, 1997. Print.

———, eds. *Rabindranath Tagore: The Myriad Minded Man.* London: Tauris Parke, 1995. Print.

———. *Selected Letters of Rabindranath Tagore.* Cambridge: Cambridge UP, 1997. Print.

Ganguly, Adwaita P. *Netaji Subhas Confronted the Indian Ethos (1900–1921): Yogi Sri Aurobindo's 'Terrorism', Poet Tagore's 'Universalism', and Mahatma Gandhi's 'Experimental Non-Violence'.* Dehra Dun: Vedantic, 2003. Print.

Ghose, Sisir K. *Life of Tagore.* New Delhi: Indian Book, 1975. Print.

———. *Rabindranath Tagore.* New Delhi: Sahitya Akad, 1998. Print.

———, ed. *Tagore for You.* Calcutta: Visva-Bharati, 1966. Print.

Ghosh, Nityapriya, ed. *The English Writings of Rabindranath Tagore.* New Delhi: Sahitya Akad, 2007. Print.

Hardy, Grant. *Great Minds of the Eastern Intellectual Tradition.* Chantilly, VA: Teaching, 2011. Print.

Hudson, Yeager. *Emerson and Tagore: The Poet as Philosopher.* Notre Dame, IN: Cross Cultural, Cross Roads, 1988. Print.

Iyengar, Srinivasa K.R. *Rabindranath Tagore.* Bombay: Popular Prakashan, 1965. Print.

———. *Rabindranath Tagore: A Critical Introduction.* New Delhi: Sterling, 1987. Print.

Khanolakara, Gangadhara D. *The Lute and the Plough: A Life of Rabindranath Tagore.* Bombay: Book Centre, 1963. Print.

Kripalani, Krishna. *Rabindranath Tagore: A Biography.* London: Oxford UP, 1962. Print.

Krishnamoorthy, Y. *Concept of God-Man Relationship in Tagore's Gitanjali.* Coimbatore: Rainbow, 1984. Print.

Lago, Mary. *Rabindranath Tagore.* Boston: Twayne, 1976. Print.

Mankuzhikary, Sebastian. *Metaphysical Vision of Tagore.* Ed. Joseph Therattil. Kochi: Grace J. Mankuzhikary, 2000. Print.

McDermott, Robert A., and Vishwanath S. Naravane, eds. *The Spirit of Modern India: Writings in Philosophy, Religion & Culture.* New York: Thomas Y. Crowell, 1974. Print.

Moores, D.J. *The Ecstatic Poetic Tradition: A Critical Study from the Ancients through Rumi, Wordsworth, Whitman, Dickinson, Tagore.* Jefferson, NC: McFarland, 2014. Print.

Mukherjee, Aparna. *The Social Philosophy of Rabindranath Tagore.* New Delhi: Classical, 2004. Print.

Mukherjee, Sujit. *Passage to America: The Reception of Rabindranath Tagore in the United States, 1912–1941.* Calcutta: Bookland, 1964. Print.

Mukherji, Bhabani C. *Vedanta and Tagore.* New Delhi: M.D. Pub., 1994. Print.

Napal, Dayachand, and Francis H. Kaumaya. *Rabindranath Tagore (1861–1941): A Short Appreciation.* Port-Louis, Mauritius: Neo, 1961. Print.

Naravane, Vishwanath S. *An Introduction to Rabindranath Tagore.* Madras: Macmillan, 1977. Print.

Nath, Bhupendra. *Rabindranath Tagore: His Mystico-Religious Philosophy*. New Delhi: Crown, 1985. Print.
Norman, Friedman. *Rabindranath Tagore: Glimpses of Bengal*. New Delhi: Oxford UP, 1986. Print.
Patyaiying, Paitoon. *Tagore and His Philosophy*. Dynamic: Meerut, 2005. Print.
Pradhan, Gaurav. *Rabindranath Tagore: (Literary Concepts)*. New Delhi: A.P.H., 2002. Print.
Radhakrishnan, Sarvepalli. *The Philosophy of Rabindranath Tagore*. London: Macmillan, 1919. Print.
Rabindranath Tagore in Perspective: A Bunch of Essays. Calcutta: Visva-Bharati, 1989. Print.
Ray, Benoy G. *Contemporary Indian Philosophers*. Allahabad: Kitabistan, 1947. Print.
Ray, Mohit K., ed. *Studies on Rabindranath Tagore*. Vol. 1. New Delhi: Atlantic, 2004. Print.
Ray, Sibnarayan. *Rabindranath Tagore: Three Essays*. Calcutta: Renaissance, 1987. Print.
Rhys, Ernest. *Rabindranath Tagore: A Biographical Study*. London: Macmillan, 1915. Print.
Roy, Pabitrakumar. *Rabindranath Tagore*. New Delhi: Munshiram Manoharlal and ICPR, 2002. Print.
Runes, Dagobert D. *Treasury of Philosophy*. New York: Philosophical Lib., 1955. Print.
Samantaray, Swati. *The Mystic Flights of Tagore*. New Delhi: B. R. Pub. Corp., 2010. Print.
Sastri, Ramaswami K.S. *Sir Rabindranath Tagore: His Life, Personality, and Genius*. New Delhi: Akashdeep, 1988. Print.
Sen, Sanat K. *Studies on the Nature of Love*. Kolkata: Suchetana, 2012. Print.
Sen Gupta, Kalyan. *The Philosophy of Rabindranath Tagore*. Aldershot: Ashgate, 2005. Print.
Sengupta, Subodh C. *The Great Sentinel: A Study of Rabindranath Tagore*. Calcutta: Mukherjee, 1948. Print.
Sharma, Arvind. *The Concept of Universal Religion in Modern Hindu Thought*. New York: St. Martin's, 1998. Print.
Shastri, K.S. Ramaswami. *Rabindranath Tagore: Poet, Partriot, Philosopher*. Srirangam: Sri Vani Vilas, 1924. Print.
Srivastava, Abhisek K. *God and Its Relation with the Finite Self in Tagore's Philosophy*. New Delhi: Oriental, 1976. Print.
Tagore, Saumyendranath. *The Poet's Philosophy of Life*. Calcutta: Tagore Research Institute, 1966. Print.
———. *Rabindranath Tagore: Philosophy of Life and Aesthetics*. Kolkata: Aparna, 2006. Print.

Book chapters

Bandyopadhyay, Asit. "Religion, Philosophy and Spiritualism." *Studies on Rabindranath Tagore*. Vol. 1. Ed. Mohit K. Ray. New Delhi: Atlantic, 2004. Print.
Chakravarty, Amiya. "Some Aspects of Tagore's Philosophy of Life." *On Tagore*. New York: Tagore Soc. of New York, 1984. Print.
Ghosh, Raghunath. "Some Philosophical Issues in Rabindranath Tagore." *Humanity, Truth and Freedom: Essays in Modern Indian Philosophy*. New Delhi: Northern, 2008. Print.
Kopf, David. "Rabindranath Tagore as Reformer: Hindu Brahmoism and Universal Humanism." *The Brahmo Samaj and the Shaping of the Modern Indian Mind*. Princeton, NJ: Princeton UP, 1979. Print.
Krishnamoorthy, K. "Tagore's Concept of Beauty." *Genius: Tagore Select*. Ed. Mahendra Kulshrestha. New Delhi: Lotus, 2006. Print.
Lesny, Vincent. *Rabindranath Tagore: His Personality and Work*. Trans. Guy McKeever Philips. London: George Allen and Unwin, 1939. Print.
Nussbaum, Martha C. "Religions of Humanity II: Rabindranath Tagore." *Political Emotions*. Cambridge, MA: Harvard UP, 2013. Print.

Sen, Sachin. "Tagore's Philosophy of Literature." *Genius: Tagore Select.* Ed. Mahendra Kulshreshtha. New Delhi: Lotus, 2006. Print.

Sengupta, Dilip. "Tagore and World Peace." *On Tagore.* New York: Tagore Soc. of New York, 1984. Print.

Sharma, Rajesh. "Exchange Value: Nobel Transactions and Rabindranath Tagore." *Relevance of Tagore in Contemporary India.* Ed. Krishan Chand. Chandigarh: Centre for Research in Rural and Industrial Development, 2013. Print.

Vajpeyi, Ananya. "Rabindranath Tagore: Viraha, the Self's Longing." *Righteous Republic: The Political Foundations of Modern India.* Cambridge, MA: Harvard UP, 2012. Print.

Articles

Basu, Manisha. "The Play of Living Creation: Time and Finitude in Tagore's Humanism." *Comparative Literature* 65.1 (2013): 46–61. Print.

Basu, Rajasri. "Holistic Development: A Tagorean Vision." *Forum for World Literature Studies* 2.3 (2010): 427–436. Print.

Catlin, George E.G. "Rabindranath Tagore: Catlin, George E.G. Rabindranath Tagore." *Journal of the Royal Society of Arts* 109.5060 (1961): 613–628. Print.

Chakrabarty, Dipesh. "Radical Histories and Question of Enlightenment Rationalism: Some Recent Critiques of 'Subaltern Studies'." *Economic and Political Weekly* 30.14 (1995): 751–759. Print.

Chatterjee, Kalyan K. "The Biblical Imagination of Rabindranath Tagore." *Renascence: Essays on Values in Literature* 66.1 (2014): 47–56. Print.

Chaudhuri, Haridas. "The Concept of Brahman in Hindu Philosophy." *Philosophy East and West* 4.1 (1954): 47–66. Print.

Chellappan, Kasiviswanathan. "Human Love Divine in Tagore and Subramaniya Bharathi." *Meerut Journal of Comparative Literature and Language* 1.1 (1988): 17–26. Print.

Dhar, Banshi. "The Humanism of Rabindranath Tagore." Indian Literature 16.1/2 (1973): 147–152. Print.

Dimock, Edward C., Jr. "Rabindranath Tagore: 'The Greatest of the Bauls of Bengal'." *Journal of Asian Studies* 19.1 (1959): 33–51. Print.

Dommergues, André. "Rabindranath Tagore's Aesthetics." *Commonwealth Essays and Studies* 7.2 (1985): 1–10. Print.

Hay, Stephen N. "Rabindranath Tagore in America." *American Quarterly* 14.3 (1962): 439–463. Print.

Jevons, Frank B. "Sir Rabindranath Tagore: Poet and Philosopher." *Proceedings of the Aristotelian Society,* New Series 19 (1918–1919): 30–45. Print.

Kampchen, Martin. "Rabindranath Tagore and Germany." *Indian Literature* 33.3 (1990): 109–140. Print.

Lewisohn, Leonard. "Rabindranath Tagore's Syncretistic Philosophy and the Persian Sufi Tradition." *International Journal of Persian Literature* 2.1 (2017): 2–41. Print.

Maitra, Susil K. "Reason in Hindu Philosophy: Classical and Contemporary." *Philosophy East and West* 11.3 (1961): 125–142. Print.

Mukherji, Prafulla C. "Rabindranath Tagore in America." *Modern Review* 110 (1961): 383–392. Print.

Naravane, Vishwanath S. "The Place of Aesthetics in Tagore's Thought." *Indian Literature* 4.1/2 (1960): 146–154. Print.

Pozza, Nicola. "Scope and Limits of 'Inclusivism' in Modern South Asia: Questioning Tagore's and Agyeya's 'Universalism'." *Politeja: The Journal of the Faculty of International and Political Studies of the Jagiellonian University in Krakow* 40 (2016): 197-214. Print.

Pratt, James B. "Tagore's Hibbert Lectures." *The Journal of Religion* 11.3 (1931): 465–466. Print.

Sattar, Arshia. "The Mirage of Indian Identity." *Indian Literature* 54.3 (2010): 257–259. Print.

Sen, Malcom. "Mythologising a 'Mystic': W.B. Yeats on the Poetry of Rabindranath Tagore." *History Ireland* 18.4 (2010): 20–23. Print.

Surie, Poonam. "A Living Legacy: The Relevance of Tagore in Today's World." *Forum for WorldLiterature Studies* 2.3 (2010): 396–426. Print.

Urquhart, William S. "The Philosophical Inheritance of Rabindranath Tagore." *International Journal of Ethics* 26.3 (1916): 398–413. Print.

Vallauri, Mario. "The Universal Faith of Rabindranath Tagore: The Work and Life of Rabindranath Tagore." *East and West* 12.2/3 (1961): 119–121. Print.

Webb, Adam K. "The Countermodern Moment: A World-Historical Perspective on the Thought of Rabindranath Tagore, Muhammad Iqbal, and Liang Shuming." *Journal of World History* 19.2 (2008): 189–212. Print.

Dissertations

Alston, Faustine. "Rabindranath Tagore: The Philosophy and Technique of His Works." Diss. M.A. Ohio State University, 1917. Print.

Arora, Rajat K. "Study in Contemporary Indian Aesthetics with Special Reference to Tagore and Aurobindo." Diss. University of Delhi, 1965. Print.

Babu, Shyam. "Samkaleen Bhartiya Darshan Mein Manvatavad Kee Avadharna: Ek Samnvyatmak Adhyayan, Rabindra Nath Tagore, Swami Vivekanand Evam Mahatma Gandhi Ke Vishesh Sandarbh Mein." Diss. Rani Durgavati Vishwavidyalaya, 2000. Print.

Bhanja, Nilendra N. "Das Wesen der Religion bei Rabīndranāth Tagore." Diss. Philipps-University Marburg, 1961. Gelnhausen: Heinrich Schwab, 1963. Print.

Bhattacharyya, Raghunath. "Introduction to the Philosophy of Tagore." Diss. Rabindra Bharati University, 1981. Print.

Chakraborty, Prakriti. "Influence of Buddhism on Tagore's Writing." Diss. Visva Bharati, 1985. Print.

Chattopadhyay, Santinath. "Religion of Man: A Critical and Comparative Study on Rabindranath Tagore." Diss. University of Calcutta, 1982. Print.

Dandapani, Saraswathy. "Study of Tagore's Literary and Philosophical Thought with Special Reference to His Humanism." Diss. University of Madras, 1989. Print.

Das, Chandra M. "Philosophy of Rabindra Nath Tagore and the Upanishads." Diss. Gauhati University, 1981. Print.

Das, Rama K. "Neo Vedantic Concept of Maya with Special Reference to the Philosophies of Swami Vivekanand, S Radha Krishnan and R Tagore." Diss. Magadh University, 1989. Print.

Das, Subhasish. "Wordsworth and Rabindranath Tagore: A Comparative Study." Diss. Rani Durgavati Vishwavidyalaya, 2001. Print.

Reddy, Vedre N.K. "Concept of Man in Rabindranath Tagore and Sarvepalli Radhakrishnan." Diss. Osmania University, 1965. Bangalore: IBH Prakashana, 1973. Print.

INDEX

acintya-bhedābheda 13, 17
advaita 17, 77
advaitam 33, 77, 82, 88, 102, 104, 108, 109, 112, 126, 127

b(B)āul 8, 127
Bhagavadgītā, The 8, 15–16, 58, 134n122, 136n150, 136n153, 140n230
bhakti 11, 12, 13, 16, 48, 87, 88, 89, 94, 95, 106, 111, 114, 127
bhāvamukha 14, 16
bhedābheda 13
Bible, The 8, 129n26
brahmajñāna 15
Brahman 12, 14, 15, 16, 17, 24, 25, 26, 28, 29, 34, 35, 38, 46, 59, 80, 81–82, 100, 105, 106, 108, 109, 110, 111, 116
Brahmavīhāra 105–106, 137n158
Brahmo 14, 15, 24, 26; Samaj 2, 4, 6, 8, 23, 24, 26
Buddhism 8

Chitra 1, 10
Christ 59, 105

darśana 8
'Devotee, The' 1, 10
dharma: as in duty, right practice and religion 7, 48, 58, 59, 69, 76, 77, 102, 104, 114; as a text (*Dharma*) 1, 2

finite 9–14, 16–17, 28, 29, 30, 32, 33, 34, 36, 38, 39, 40, 68, 109–110, 116, 117
Fruit-Gathering 1, 6, 11
'Fruit Seller from Kabul, The' 10

Gītā, The *see* Bhagavadgītā, The
Gitanjali: Song Offerings 1, 11
Gorā 1, 9

Hlādinī Śākti 8, 20
Home and the World, The 19

Infinite 9–14, 16–17, 28, 29, 30, 33, 34, 36, 38, 39, 41, 46, 53, 61, 64, 67–68, 72–73, 81, 86, 88, 89–90, 98, 109, 113, 115, 116, 117, 123, 126

Jesus *see* Christ
jñāna 15
jñānī 24, 25

Kṛṣṇa 12, 16, 17

Maya 17, 116
Metta Sutta, The 106n160
Mukti 5, 12, 18, 22, 26, 27, 28, 29, 34, 35, 39, 56, 59, 75, 76, 80, 81, 85

n(N)irguṇa 15, 16

philosophy: Bāul philosophy 8; philosophy of life 18; Sri Ramakrishna philosophy 16; Tagore's philosophy 8–18

Red Oleander 1, 11
religion 7–9; *see also* dharma

s(S)aguṇa 15, 16
Śāntiniketan 1, 2, 3, 6, 7, 8, 9, 10, 11, 12, 13, 17, 19–26, 27, 43, 45; ashram 5, 6;

essays 5, 7, 8, 9, 11, 14, 16, 17, 42, 43, 46, 47, 49; lectures 5, 6; part-1 20–21; part-2 21; part-3 21; part-4 21; part-5 21; part-6 21; part-7 21–22; part-8 22–23; part-9 23; part-10 23; part-11 23; part-12 23–24; part-13 24; part-14 24–25; part-15 25–26; part-16 26; part-17 26–27; as a place (Śāntiniketan) 5, 6, 117; talks 4, 7
Sanyasi, or the Ascetic 1, 10
Source Text (ST) 42, 43, 45, 46–47, 48–49
spiritual(ity) 6, 7, 8, 17, 27, 55, 72, 78–79, 86
s(S)port(s) (*līlā*) 3, 13, 14, 15, 16, 17, 30, 32, 35, 70, 73, 81, 87, 93, 98, 113; divine sport 73; particular sport 72; sport and atman 82; sport of joy; 97; sport and Supreme Atman 82; unique sport 72; wonderful sport 126
Śrīmad-Bhagavad-Gītā see Bhagavadgītā, The
Sri Ramakrishna 14–16

Tagore, Rabindranath: ailing physical condition 4; biographer 4; concept of joy 8, 12, 14; concept of love 9–17; language 43–47; life 2–4; philosophical interest 2; *see also* philosophy
Target Text (TT) 42, 43, 45, 46–47, 48–49

Upanishad(s), The: Aitareya 130n40, 130n43; Bṛhadāraṇyaka 8, 129n15, 130n31, 130n32, 130n33, 130n34, 130n35, 130n37, 130n39, 131n62, 133n98, 135n132, 137n165, 137n166, 138n185, 138n188; Chāndogya 106, 131n67, 137n161, 138n174; Īśa 129n12, 132n82, 132n83, 132n84, 136n154, 137n127, 138n170, 138n175, 138n176, 138n177, 140n213, 140n215, 140n225; Kaṭha 128n1, 131n71, 136n142, 136n147, 136n152, 138n170, 138n173; Mahānārāyaṇa 139n199; Māṇḍūkya 132n85, 132n86, 133n87, 133n89, 133n94, 133n95, 133n97, 135n125, 136n155, 138n172, 138n187, 140n226, 140n227, 140n233, 141n238; Muṇḍaka 129n13, 132n76, 134n106, 134n107, 134n108, 134n109, 134n112, 134n113, 134n114, 134n115, 134n122, 135n124, 135n130, 136n141, 137n164, 138n171, 138n181, 138n183, 139n202, 139n204; Śvetāśvatara 130n42, 130n45, 130n46, 131n70, 134n105, 134n118, 137n163, 140n219, 140n225; Taittirīya 131n65, 134n117, 134n119, 134n120, 136n151, 138n184, 139n198
upāsanā 6, 7, 36, 37, 58, 59, 71, 72, 88, 89, 95, 100, 101, 110, 111, 127

Vaiṣṇavism 8, 13
Vedanta 9
Veda(s), The: Ṛg 131n69, 132n72, 135n126, 135n138, 135n139, 136n140, 136n143, 136n144, 136n145, 136n146, 137n161, 137n162, 137n165, 137n166, 137n167, 137n169, 139n206; Sāma 137n161, 137n162; White [Śukla] Yajur (Saṁhitā)129n11, 129n16, 132n72, 132n79, 132n80, 132n81, 135n126, 136n143, 136n144, 136n145, 136n146, 137n167, 137n169, 139n191, 139n192, 139n193, 139n194, 139n196, 139n197
vijñāna 14–16, 17
vijñānī 14
Vivekananda, Swami. 13, 14, 16–17